MAX WEINBERG WITH ROBERT SANTELLI

THE BIG BEAT

BILLBOARD BOOKS
An imprint of Watson-Guptill Publications/New York

CONVERSATIONS WITH ROCK'S GREAT DRUMMERS

Dedication page photo and page 96 photo by Barry Goldenberg; page 4 photo by Robert Santelli; page 7 and 13 photos from the Johnny Bee collection; page 16, 21, 74, and 86 photos from the Michael Ochs Archives; page 33 photo from the Harold Kudlets collection; page 39 photo by Elliot Landy/Starfile; page 44 and 55 photos by Tommy Wright; page 60 and 71 photos by Jim Marshall; page 79 photo from the Hal Blaine collection; page 94 and 173 photos by Max Weinberg; page 101 photo by Randi St. Nicholas; page 108 photo from Jimmy Lee Velvet/Elvis Presley Museum; page 113 photo from the D.J. Fontana collection; page 123 and 176 photos from the James Karnbach collection; page 130, 137, 142, 154, 161, 187, and 189 photos by Dezo Hoffmann; page 149 photo by Bob Gruen/Starfile; page 168 photo from the Jim Keltner collection.

Cover design by Jay Anning

Copyright © 1984, 1991 by Max Weinberg

This edition published 1991 by Billboard Books, an imprint of Watson-Guptill Publications, a division of BPI Communications, Inc. 1515 Broadway, New York, NY 10036.

All rights reserved. No part of this publication may be reproduced, stored in a retrieval system, or transmitted, in any form or by any means — electronic, mechanical, photocopying, recording, or otherwise — without prior written permission of the publisher.

First published in 1984 by Contemporary Books, Inc.

Library of Congress Cataloging-in-Publication Data

Weinberg, Max.
    The big beat : conversations with rock's great drummers / Max Weinberg with Robert Santelli.
        p. cm.
    Reprint. Originally published: Chicago : Contemporary Books, c1984.
    Includes index.
    ISBN 0-8230-7571-0
    1. Rock music—History and criticism. 2. Rock musicians—Interviews. 3. Drummers (Musicians)—Interviews. I. Santelli, Robert. II. Title.
ML3534.W44   1991
786.9'166'0922—dc20   91-3981
                                                                     CIP
                                                                       MN

Manufactured in the United States of America

1 2 3 4 5 6 7 8 9/96 95 94 93 92 91

*For Becky
and for my parents*

Contents

	Foreword by Bruce Springsteen	vii
	Introduction	1
1	Johnny Bee	5
2	Dino Danelli	17
3	Levon Helm	27
4	Roger Hawkins	45
5	"Pretty" Purdie	61
6	Hal Blaine	75
7	Earl Palmer	87
8	Russ Kunkel	97
9	D.J. Fontana	109
10	Dave Clark	131
11	Kenney Jones	143
12	Charlie Watts	155
13	Jim Keltner	169
14	Ringo Starr	179
	Index	191

Foreword

Max has hit me up for a few words on what I think it takes to be a great drummer. Well, if you look at the musicians in this book you'll see that they all have one overwhelming characteristic in common. All of these guys have their own distinctive voice — that *sound* that from the very first backbeat you know it's them. It ranges from Charlie Watts' laconic two and four to Dave Clark's drum-corps formalism; from Bernard Purdie's soulful precision to Levon Helm's country slip and slide. All of these men are featured players in creating the *sound* of their bands. As much as Mick's voice and Keith's guitar, Charlie Watts' snare sound *is* the Rolling Stones. He's a great example of the kind of power and character a great drummer can bring to his band, deepening not only the physical force of the music, but also the depth of emotion and heart the songwriter gets out of his characters. When Mick sings, "It's only rock 'n' roll but I like it," Charlie's in back showing you why! All these players share this gift plus the incredible emotional flexibility to set up in the back of the bandstand — behind the egomaniacs and show-offs out front. But then I guess all these guys figured *that* one out.

So, Max, take it away, and in the words of the greatest band-leader of all time, James Brown, "Give the drummer some!"

BRUCE SPRINGSTEEN
Los Angeles, California
May 1991

Preface to the New Edition

The Big Beat was first published during the summer of 1984 as I traveled around the world on the "Born in the U.S.A" tour. That was a special time for Bruce Springsteen and the E Street Band. Playing concerts with our records at the top of the charts — it doesn't get any better than that. Of all the places I could have been in those stadiums we played, I had the best seat in the house! Every city, practically every show, was a drummer's dream come true. To Bruce and my colleagues in the E Street Band, thanks for the lift.

The Big Beat was another dream of mine. In my wildest imaginings, I never thought I'd one day be asking Ringo Starr every question I'd ever wanted to — and then some. Naturally, once I got into the mechanics of writing a book I knew I'd have to do more than simply dream to get it done. It took lots of work — nineteen months altogether. Today, seven years later, when I hold *The Big Beat* in my hands and reread the stories of these musicians, I feel good. I feel good that I started it, and that I finished it. I feel good that I was able to set these stories down as my contribution to the folklore of rock and roll.

Since 1984 I've enjoyed the comments of people I've met who have read *The Big Beat*. Yet, I've also run into many people who haven't been able to find it. So, for all of you who ever wanted *The Big Beat*, here is a new Billboard edition. Someone once suggested that I add a few new chapters on drummers who have come up since the first edition was published, musicians like Larry Mullen, Jr. of U2; Sheila E.; the great studio ace, Vinnie Colaiuta; and Neal Peart of Rush. They're all fantastic. But I decided to keep the book as it was. There is a different cover, but the stories inside remain the same. I suppose I'm in it, too, by way of the questions I asked. These were the things I was interested in knowing, and I guess that's what *makes* a book of this sort. For me, *The Big Beat* represents a time in my life when I had the bright idea of writing a volume on my favorite subject — and actually *did* it. My favorite post-publication comment came from Charlie Watts, who said, "You really *were* serious about writing a book...."

I asked Bruce to write the Foreword for this new edition because I knew he had definite ideas about what makes a great drummer. I've had many discussions about drummers with my friends and colleagues — Bruce, Little Steven, Bob Santelli, Jon Landau, and others. There was never any shortage of observations or opinions. Through these conversations we became more aware of the subtleties of great drumming. Bruce's comments are right on the mark when he talks about the importance of a drummer's characteristic sound. As you discover the drummers in this book through their words, you'll see their personalities emerge. But, of course, when you hear them drum, you don't need to discuss it. The big beat speaks for itself.

Acknowledgments

For making this book possible, I am grateful to those drummers who generously shared with me their time and thoughts. Their commitment to the music, I found, is upstaged only by their love for it, and for expressing those sentiments so honestly and openly, this book is theirs.

But many others shared the work in assembling this book, and I would like to thank them publicly here.

Bob Santelli is a professional whose help with the interviews, editorial input, and advocacy of what was often an opposing point of view gave the book an energy it would not have had otherwise. I thank him for the long hours he put in.

Sandra Choron's role was that of agent, but her input far exceeded those responsibilities. Her belief in the book and her confidence in me helped to focus my dream, and she did more than her share of editing, advising — and browbeating — without which this book could not have become a reality.

Rick Vittenson of Contemporary Books expressed an enthusiasm for this project long before a single word was ever written, and his ongoing interest in seeing the book through is greatly appreciated.

Thanks also to:

Garry Tallent, for sharing with me his rock and roll scholarship (and his records). He helped connect the history to the music.

Bruce Springsteen, for his encouragement and timely musical

and editorial ideas.

Jon Landau, for his advice, drum tips, and help in research throughout.

Dave Herman of WNEW in New York for his help in securing the Ringo Starr interview.

Bill Flanagan of *Musician* magazine for his consistently inspiring interview technique.

Steve and Maureen Van Zandt, for their enthusiasm on the subject.

Scott Fish, for his encyclopedic knowledge of drumming and for his help with the Russ Kunkel chapter.

Patty Romanowski, for her editorial assistance. Once again, those long hours are much appreciated.

Thanks to all those at Billboard Publications who made this second edition possible, including Tad Lathrop, Glenn Heffernan, Ken Schlager, Bob Benjamin, Irv Lichtman, and Thom Duffy.

Thanks, also, to those who helped along the way: Gene Thaler, my first drum teacher; Gary Chester, Pick Withers, and Andy Newmark; Gary Lazar of Gary Lazar Management in Detroit; Kathy Willhoite of Contemporary Books; Jay Bergen of Dolgenos, Bergen & Newman; Bruce and Madlyn Goldberg; Meg Butler for her excellent travel coordination; Jill Fermick; Julia Collins and Sharon Wheeler of CBS International in London; Roger Scott of Capitol Radio in London; Art Collins, Jane Rose, Colin Burn, and Sara Marks of Rolling Stone Records; Ian Stewart of Rolling Stones Management; "Colonel" Harold Kudlets; Diane Butler and Mitch McGee of Muscle Shoals Sound Studios; Jerry Zaro of Ansell Zaro Bennett & Kenney for his guidance; and especially to Joan Woodgate of Startling Productions in London.

For their help with the photographs, I thank Barry Goldenberg and Photo-Dynamics, Elliott Landy, James Karnbach, Ron Furmanek, Bob Alford, Virginia Lohle of Starfile, Peggy Allen, Michael Ochs, Jim Marshall, Tommy Wright, and Jimmy Lee Velvet of the Elvis Presley Museum. I'd especially like to thank Dezo Hoffman for his generosity, ideas, and, of course, his photographs.

A special drum roll goes to my parents, Ruth and Bert Weinberg, and to my sisters, Abby, Nancy, and Patty, for their patience during the years when I was finding my own big beat.

Finally, there is a chance to thank my wife, Becky, for her love of obscure sixties rock and roll bands, her editorial suggestions, her constant support, and her French toast — that's what really got me through.

Introduction

When the pulse of rock and roll grabs you and won't let go, it becomes the Big Beat. That's how it was when Earl Palmer laid into Little Richard's "Lucille," sounding as if he were using baseball bats and kicking a thirty-foot bass drum. Hal Blaine pounded his beat into nearly two hundred gold records for artists as diverse as Elvis Presley and the Fifth Dimension. And Ringo Starr used it to turn on the world.

But the Big Beat can best be defined as an approach. Johnny Badanjek, whose drumming with Mitch Ryder and the Detroit Wheels helped define the outer limits of white rock and soul music, described it this way: "When your left side aches because you pulled a muscle, you say to yourself, 'I'm going over the line tonight, but hell, let's keep going.'" He termed what happens in that moment the spirit of rock and roll. This book is about finding the rhythm that spirit embodies.

This is how the spirit captured me: The night that Elvis Presley first appeared on "The Ed Sullivan Show," my older sisters dressed me as Elvis, complete with mascaraed sideburns and a rubber-band-cardboard guitar. Amazement gripped us as Elvis and his band took over our living room. My sisters swooned when he sang "Love Me Tender" and we all lost our minds when they tore into "Hound Dog." But when D.J. Fontana's drum roll hit, I put down the "guitar." The lick came around again and I picked up that beat, banging on the floor. "Max — PLEASE!" my mother cried out. But it was too late. D.J.'s drumming rolled out across the airwaves, filled up my senses, and swept me away.

It is with this spirit that the stories of these fourteen drummers were received. Of course, these aren't the only drummers who have significantly contributed to rock's rich history. These are my own heroes and influences, the players whose records are most often found on the top shelf of my record collection. Some of them, such as D.J. Fontana and Ringo Starr, inspired me to become a drummer in the first place. Others, like Bernard Purdie, Jim Keltner, Levon Helm, and Russ Kunkel, have led me to become a *better* drummer.

There are others who could have — some might argue, should have — been here. Two, Keith Moon and Al Jackson, left behind a wealth of drumming genius, and their influence and style have been absorbed on virtually every level of rock and roll. They live on through their influence, and it pains me to think that I never got the chance to talk with them. Their styles define the poles of the rock and soul spectrum: Moon's playing was the height of wild abandon while Jackson plumbed the depths of a less-is-more approach.

And there are others — people like the original Motown drummers, Benny Benjamin and Pistol Allen; Chicago bluesman Fred Below, who worked with Muddy Waters and Chuck Berry; Earl Palmer's great New Orleans compatriots, drummers Charles "Hungry" Williams and John Boudreaux; Panama Francis and Gary Chester of New York; Buddy Harmon of Nashville; Led Zeppelin's John Bonham; Ginger Baker of Cream; Carmine Appice of the Vanilla Fudge; John Densmore of the Doors; and Mitch Mitchell of the Jimi Hendrix Experience. It's unfortunate that space and circumstance did not allow their inclusion in this book. Each of them, of course, remains an indispensable part of the story of the Big Beat.

But these fourteen drummers, some legendary, some obscure, are representative of a certain era of rock history. They aren't just superb drummers; they're historical figures, too. All of us who drum carry a part of their beat and are descended from the tradition they inspired. They developed a vocabulary that current rock drumming only expands upon.

This book is about them. It's drummers talking drums, but it's not just drum tips and shop talk (though you'll find some of that here). The real essence of *The Big Beat* is the stories and insights these musicians offer — many of them told here for the first time.

During the period of their greatest achievements, most of these men stayed in the background as accompanists, letting their music speak for them. *The Big Beat* is my way of shining the spotlight on them. It has been a pleasure to participate in putting their experiences into words.

Note

The selected discographies that appear at the end of each of the following conversations are only samples of the best work of each of these drummers. They are not intended as complete discographies; they're simply my favorites.—M.W.

Johnny Bee

1

"When they talk about Detroit rock & roll, they're talking about high-energy music, not something that's going to put you to sleep."

NINETEEN SIXTY-FIVE was a great year for rock & roll. The British Invasion was completely changing the face of pop music. Songs like the Rolling Stones' "Satisfaction" and "Get Off of My Cloud," the Beatles' "Ticket to Ride" and the Animals' "It's My Life" hit the charts. The press had a field day with this invasion, and the endless comparisons to the Revolutionary War raged on. When I was a freshman in high school, these groups were all my friends cared about. From the heartland, Mitch Ryder and the Detroit Wheels were among the first of teen-age America's musical militia, and Johnny "Bee" Badanjek was one of the most exciting drummers in rock.

In 1965, the Detroit Wheels were young and eager to make it. With Johnny in the driver's seat, they left behind Detroit's cars and bars, on their way to New York City. There, the Wheels cut "Jenny Take a Ride," and it became a monster hit. Johnny's beat kicked that record up the charts and, along with the great Motown records, put Detroit on the rock & roll map. "Jenny" became the first of a string of Wheels hits that every sixties garage-band rocker cut his teeth on. "Devil with a Blue Dress On"/"Good Golly Miss Molly," "Little Latin Lupe Lu," and "Sock It to Me—Baby" are the classics.

The Detroit Wheels were one of the best bands I'd ever seen. I remember seeing them in 1966 at Trude Heller's, a Greenwich

Village hot spot. Trude's was small, dark, steamy, and smoky—a great place. One night my entire band went over from Jersey to catch their set. The place was jammed, and the air was charged with anticipation.

Suddenly the lights cut out and the Wheels hit the bandstand. Back at the drums in his puffy-sleeved shirt and leather vest, a cigarette dangling from his lips, was Johnny. He looked kind of scary. At just the right moment, he hit a snare shot and Mitch dropped to his knees and ripped his shirt open. The joint went nuts. When they left the stage an hour and fifteen minutes later, *I* was exhausted.

Johnny inspired me that night, and since then I've always loved his straightforward style.

When the Wheels split up, he was eighteen and a seasoned professional. He hit the road as a drummer who could get the job done. From coast to coast he hauled his drums, and as his reputation grew, the gigs got better. After recording with Edgar Winter in 1973 (on "Free Ride") and playing a spell with Dr. John (Mac Rebennack), Johnny set out on his own. With Wheels lead guitarist Jim McCarty, he formed the Rockets, a hard-hitting, blue-collar rock & roll outfit. They're the kind of band you like to start your weekend dancing to.

Johnny and I met at one of our group's gigs in Detroit. It was a thrill having him there. We talked that night about the drummers we liked and the records we listened to. After the show, as he was leaving, I asked Johnny to get together with me some time and listen to some of those records.

On a cold winter day in 1983, we finally sat down, played some of those hits, and recalled the last time we had been together.

MAX: *The last time we saw each other was when our band played the Joe Louis Arena here in Detroit and Mitch [Ryder] came up to sing. During the sound check he said, "You guys play your 'Detroit' medley too slow. Now, when I get up there, play it as fast as you can." So he comes up and within the first three measures, turns around and says, "Faster, faster! It's not fast enough!" Now, how did you play those songs so fast?*

BEE: Well, when we recorded "Devil with a Blue Dress On," we were nervous because the Rolling Stones were in the studio, so I guess we just took off. They were there with Bob Crewe, who was our manager and who also distributed the Stones' records in the United States. When they came to New York, they'd hang around the studio and office. Mick, Keith, Andrew Loog Oldham, their manager, and Bill Wyman were there for "Devil with a Blue Dress On." The fact that the Stones were there was a big thrill for me.

JOHNNY BEE

From left to right: Johnny Bee, Jim McCarty, Earl Elliott, Mitch Ryder, Joe Kubert. Johnny was only sixteen when Mitch Ryder and the Detroit Wheels cut "Jenny Take a Ride."

How long had the Detroit Wheels been together then?

I was sixteen when we recorded "Jenny Take a Ride," and the band had been together in Detroit for two years before we went to New York. So, I guess the Wheels were together from 1963 to 1967, and we recorded from the end of '64 to the middle of '67.

I remember when we first arrived in New York we had to get five cabs to take us to Bob Crewe's office with all the stuff we brought with us on the train. We unloaded our boxes and things, hauled them into the elevator, and stacked everything up real neat. And then Bob walks out and says, "Oh, you guys are finally here. You should probably go to the hotel, check in, and then come back." So we take all the gear back down the elevator, back into another fleet of cabs, and over to the Coliseum House at Seventy-first Street and Broadway. I guess we stayed there for two or three years: the Coliseum House, room six-fourteen. It was a big suite with two bedrooms. Two guys in each room, and one guy had the studio couch each night in the living room. And I'll tell you, we had no stove, no refrigerator, and cockroaches like crazy. If you turned on the light and counted to ten, they'd all be dancing!

Bob Crewe was one of the legendary producers in the sixties. How did you get hooked up with him?

Well, some disc jockey from Detroit sent him a tape. Crewe dragged his feet for months, and finally the D.J. called him back and said we were going to sign with Motown. Crewe finally moved and sent us contracts, and we went to New York.

How would you work things out in the studio?

Crewe was right on top of it. He would sit there while the band was in this little rehearsal hall playing, and he'd tell you what to do. He'd say, "Play something like a Drifters' tune." He'd tell you what to play, sitting there with a pad and writing the words.

Today so much time is spent trying to achieve the right drum sound. Was there any concept of getting a particular "drum sound"?

Not really. I just sat down and played them. I might have tuned them a little bit here and there, but they were studio drums. I never used my own drums.

See, these studios would have these drums all set to go so you didn't have to do anything. You didn't have to spend hours getting the sound. It was like you're in at two and you're out at eight. You tune the guitar up and *bam!* You hit it. Later on, the band started branching out in terms of what we really wanted to play. We were actually a blues/rhythm & blues band. We thought a lot of the material Crewe was doing was too poppy or too commercial, except for some of the R&B copies—covers of James Brown and stuff like that. Eventually, we started hanging out with people in the Village like John Hammond Jr. and Barry Goldberg, and we met Mike Bloomfield and Paul Butterfield. These guys were really a big influence on us. We started using other session people. We'd start bringing in a harp player, and Barry Goldberg wound up playing keyboards on "Devil with a Blue Dress On." "Devil" was our first gold single. Then five or six months later, Mitch's management broke up the band. They thought the band was expendable.

At the time, Bernard "Pretty" Purdie was sort of the head honcho of New York studio drummers. Were you aware of him?

Oh, yeah. I used to see Bernard Purdie all the time. We'd see each other as one session was finishing and another was beginning. He was a big influence and a real nice guy. I used to talk with him all the time. He'd come into the studio, and I'd sit and watch him warm up. The thing with our band was that we never really experienced anything with anyone in New York City. We were kids from Detroit. We had our own little world—just the five of us. We played every night from nine to four A.M., and on the one night we had off, we stayed home and watched TV. Later on, when we were getting known and did our concert in Central Park, we met the Vagrants, the Rich Kids, the Young Rascals, Leslie West, and others. We'd go with them to the Rolling Stone or Ungano's, and clubs like Trude Heller's. We used to play there a lot; also her son's club, the Eighth Wonder, around the corner. Between those two clubs and the Metropole, that was about it.

What did you think of the music scene in New York at the time?

The first few years of the band—1964 and 1965—it was real quiet, real low-key. Then we met the people in Greenwich Village, like the Blues Project.

Did you ever meet Dylan back then?

We'd seen him a lot in the Village, but I was never aware of the folk scene. In fact, I didn't like him at all. Mitch used to play his records, though. He got into his *Highway 61* album, and I'd say, "Hey, the guy is singing flat!" That shows you how close-minded I was.

What were touring and doing shows like for you in the sixties?

Well, for one thing, we *never* had a road crew. That didn't exist back then. You had a road manager to watch the money, but we had to set up all our own equipment. A lot of times I'd use the drums of Paul Revere and the Raiders' drummer because we played with them a lot. Otherwise, I'd have to set up my own drums in front of fifteen thousand people. We had the number two record in the country—number two in *Billboard*—that was "Devil with a Blue Dress On." And I'm setting up my own drums!

When "Jenny Take a Ride" came out, we went to the West Coast and started doing all sorts of shows with the Yardbirds. It was real strange—we'd share dressing rooms with Simon and Garfunkel. There'd be fifteen acts—the Yardbirds, the Four Seasons, us, lots of others, and Simon and Garfunkel, who'd be the headliners. There'd be the Yardbirds with Jeff Beck playing B. B. King licks in the corridor backstage, and McCarty going, "Johnny, you gotta hear and watch this guy play guitar!" We were all young kids. Nobody was into drugs, nobody was into anything, it seemed, except the music. It was all music.

Kids today don't feel the excitement we felt when a rock & roll show started at eight o'clock and ended at ten, after seeing ten acts play three songs apiece. You'd go on stage and wouldn't even work up a sweat. From the audience's point of view, though, it never stopped. You'd see the Yardbirds with amps falling over and smoke all over the place, and after that here comes these two guys, Simon and Garfunkel, and no band. Eighteen thousand people or whatever and "Hello, darkness, my old friend. . . ." (Laughs.) You could hear a pin drop. It was great.

What was the setup of the gig?

Well, a lot of times, we were the backup band. We'd go to a show in Virginia Beach and have about two hours to work up five acts. Acts like the Orlons. We had to learn all the Orlons' music, then Johnny Tillotson and then Chuck Berry. Chuck never rehearsed; he just flew on in, grabbed McCarty's guitar, and said, "Boy, watch my foot!" He'd say, "See that foot? When the foot hits the floor, you break." That was it, you'd just launch right into it. And boy, he had a foot! Anyway, we'd be trying to do all these tunes. I mean, how could you remember all these songs in two hours? It was tough.

Tell me about those Caravan of Stars tours of Dick Clark.

It was more of the same kind of thing, with lots of groups. We were on with the Strangeloves, the original band that did "I Want Candy"; Lou "Lightnin' Strikes" Christie, who was the headliner; Keith Allison; the rest I forget. I remember Danny Thomas's son was on one tour—the Tony Thomas Group. Tony said, "Now look, I don't want to use my father, so don't mention him when you introduce the band." And the guy who would do the introducing says, "Okay, you got it." So

"He came to the Fox Theater when I was thirteen—James Brown and a big line-up. Me and McCarty went down to see the eight o'clock show. The movie—some vampire movie—cuts off, and all of a sudden, POW! You're hearing this incredible music. . . ."

the guy walks up to the microphone and says, "Now ladies and gentlemen, the next group is a special group you haven't heard too much from, but I'm sure you're going to enjoy them. So let's have a nice round of applause for Tony 'Make Room for Daddy' Thomas!" (Laughs.)

It seemed that Wheels picked up on the white R&B thing that was happening in the sixties pretty early on.

Oh, yeah, because none of us were writing songs in those days. Crewe wrote most everything, and to fill out the show, we did a lot of covers. There was this club in Detroit called the Village, where the inner-city blacks would go. There was a house band, and they'd do "Turn On Your Love Light"—and *these* guys could sing. Mitch was the only white guy in the place. It was a real strange place; the owner would never turn on the heat—he'd let the place heat up from all the bodies. During intermission gay dancers in leotards would come out and dance to a conga player, beatnik-style. And everybody would flick cigarettes on the stage because these guys were dancing barefoot. It was one of *those* places. The Temptations used to hang there. Everybody kind of started there, and Mitch was singing with black groups, so he really learned a lot.

Was there a separation between blacks and whites in Detroit at the time?

Yeah, it was real separated. In fact, I didn't even know who James Brown was until I went downtown. He came to the Fox Theater when I was thirteen—James Brown and a big lineup. Me and McCarty went down to see the eight o'clock show. The movie—some vampire movie—cuts off, and all of a sudden, POW! You're hearing this incredible music, but there's no band to be seen. There's no band on stage. Suddenly this twenty-piece band rises out of the floor with three drummers! Man, I'll tell ya—rollin' and smokin' all the way! From then on, I knew who James Brown was. Man, that's when I started learning a lot on the drums, watching those black R&B drummers. When James Brown hit the stage—forget it. There never has been, probably never will be, an act in this business to equal James Brown. What that guy did! We were spellbound.

How did all those R&B drummers change your drumming?

Well, I remember one guy, when I was fourteen years old, telling me, "Now the first thing you got to remember is those drums ain't gonna bite you. So HIT them damn things! When you hit those drums I want you to hit them HARD! Speak to me! Come on!" Our whole band was watching this guy inspire me. I'm a little kid behind these big drums, and he's yelling, "HIT those drums!" Those guys downtown—they taught me something.

Motown's great drummers must have been very influential.

I was aware of all the drummers at Motown, but not by name. You know, if you caught the Motown Revue—Marvin Gaye, Stevie Wonder, the Marvelettes, Supremes, the Miracles, and the Tempts—they changed their drummers, but you never knew who the drummers were. They never listed the names of the drummers on the early Motown records. I'd like to know, for instance, who the drummer was on the Miracles' "Mickey's Monkey." Now that guy had a *hot* beat.

On "Shakin' with Linda" from the Breakout *album, you sound like a Motown drummer.*

That's all the influences coming out of me. I'd see these guys at sessions or at clubs like the Twenty Grand. These black drummers would come and play with these little sets that you'd think they bought in a pawn shop, and you wondered, how did they get that sound? They were so soulful. Yeah, the influence for my style was the sound I heard from black drummers, but I listened to everybody. I watched every drummer I could. You know we played the NARAS [National Association of Recording Arts and Sciences] Convention in New York City, which presented all the R&B awards to black radio stations. Little Richard, Otis Redding, Sam and Dave, were on that show, and we were the only white group. This was around 1967, and for three days and nights in a theater in New York City, I sat around and watched. It was great. Everybody who ever inspired me was on that show.

I remember traveling to New York with my girlfriend from New Jersey in 1966 and 1967 to see the Murray the K shows. It was the first time I saw the Wheels.

Yeah, I remember Mitch did a song called "I Found a Love" where he would fall to his knees. Before that, we were in Pittsburgh one night playing with Wilson Pickett, and we asked Pickett if he was going to do "I Found a Love" in his show. He said no, so we did it. He came out and listened to our version and was so knocked out that he said it was one of the greatest versions he'd ever heard. That prompted him to ask Mitch to do a tour with him.

When you appeared with these black acts, what kind of audience would you play to?

White audiences, although some were split, depending on the city. Black artists—Joe Tex, Wilson Pickett, Sam and Dave—were coming into their own because their records were crossing over from the small R&B stations. We were appreciated by the blacks. Mitch was really a soulful singer. Later he got more away from it. But in the original days in New York City, boy, that kid was a singer's singer. Brian Wilson once told *Rolling Stone:* "I don't know what it is about Mitch Ryder, but he has one of the greatest voices in America." The blacks actually showed us all the way. I remember once we caught the five A.M. show with Ray Charles and his big band. We were the only white people in the place. It was in Cleveland, and it was one of the greatest shows I'd ever seen in my life. We got out of there seven o'clock in the morning. You know what Ray's ending to the show was? He walked off the stage and then came back and did another tune with the whole place up on their feet. And then a guy came up on the stage as Ray was thanking everyone. This guy then starts to pull Ray off the stage saying, "The show's over, the show's over." And Ray says, "What are you talking about—the show's over? These are my people!"

"I remember one guy telling me, 'Now the first thing you got to remember is those drums ain't gonna bite you. So hit them damn things! When you hit those drums, I want you to hit them HARD!'"

And the place went wild. Ray blew the roof off the joint. It was a great piece of show business.

I've always heard the term Detroit rock & roll applied to the Wheels, Bob Seger, Ted Nugent, and the Rockets, among others. What does that term mean to you?

When they talk about Detroit rock & roll, they're talking about high-energy music, not something that's going to put you to sleep. It's get-down rock & roll. You work in the car companies and on the assembly line all day, right? When you're through, you just want to get out and have a good time and get rid of all that boredom. "By days we make cars, at night we hit the bars," was a line from a song.

Along with Motown, the Wheels really put Detroit on the rock & roll map.

Yeah, even Seger will attest to that. He said that we were the first guys to come out of the city and make it as a group. It's just too bad that we had to break up when we did. See, the company thought Mitch was going to be the white James Brown. He was going to be real big, they figured. They wanted to get him a horn band and put him in motion pictures. Basically, it came down to money. It was a self-contained band, and we all split everything evenly. At this time the band really started making a lot of money. Mitch, they thought, was the real thing. They thought the band couldn't go any higher. But what they were so wrong about was that we had a great guitar player, McCarty, who was well respected by everybody. And this was when Hendrix and Cream and the Who were starting to break with the big guitar sound.

What did you do when Mitch split the band?

The band stayed together for a year after the split with Mitch. We continued to play R&B stuff and then made the switch and began playing psychedelic stuff too. We went on the road in the Midwest, where promoters were saying, "This psychedelic crap will never happen out here." The band dwindled on, but there was no center for creativity. No one was writing. So we broke up. I started doing sessions, but there wasn't too much work. I started playing some Las Vegas show gigs with big bands. It was stuff I didn't care to do—risqué jokes, cymbal shots, burlesque. I got out of that real fast, and started doing obscure sessions. Then I finally got back with Mitch a couple of years later. I was playing with his band called Detroit on the road and flying to play with Edgar Winter. You see, Edgar always had a big problem with drugs in his band, and his manager, Steve Paul, wanted to get a straight band together—people they could count on. So many promoters in the early seventies were sick of bands so high they couldn't show up. Edgar liked Chuck Ruff, the drummer, but I think he had a tempo problem. I think Edgar wanted someone with more experience, too, although Bobby Ramirez, White Trash's original drummer, was amazing. And that band was great. We did a lot of gigs together. I'd be on stage with the Detroit band playing, and behind the curtain Ramirez would be on his drums playing right

Johnny Bee, 1983

along. While White Trash was on stage, I'd do the same thing with Ramirez.

Then White Trash broke up, and Edgar asked if I'd be interested in playing with him. At that time the Detroit band was breaking up too. I said I was interested. But it meant living in New York again. I had a family here in Detroit, and I didn't know if I wanted to move them to New York. I stayed with Edgar two to three months. I think I was too crazy for them, though.

You played on Edgar's big hit "Free Ride," right?

Yeah. You know, Rick Derringer told me the true story of what happened with "Free Ride." I didn't know I was on the album when it first came out. I did the sessions, I came home, I was sitting at this bar called the Red Carpet, and a real good friend, Steve Gaines from Lynyrd Skynyrd, said to me, "You know, you're playing on the *They Only Come Out at Night* album. You're on the song 'Free Ride.'" I said, "No, I'm not." He said, "Yeah, I heard it. It's in the stores." So I went and got the album, and sure enough, he was right.

So when I met up with Rick later on he told me that after I left the band, Edgar got Chuck back in and went to another studio in Long Island and recut everything. But it just didn't happen, so Edgar put out the original version. It was fun working with Edgar, but there was something missing for me in terms of personal satisfaction. Like when the Rockets play, it's full-tilt, right to the floor. With anyone else, with the exception of the Detroit Wheels, I didn't get that kind of thrill. I had a little of it with Alice Cooper when I did sessions with him because Bob Ezrin, the producer, knew me and knew how to get it out of me. With Dr. John, the same thing; it was a really good experience.

How did you get hooked up with Dr. John?

Through Bob Ezrin. He was doing Alice Cooper and Lou Reed, and he called me up. "Look, I'm going to do this Dr. John album and I want you to play drums on it," he said. I went out to the Coast, worked with Doc, and he liked it so much, he wanted to take me on the road. So I worked with him for nine months on the road. That band that he had was a great little band. I learned a lot. And the black people were telling me, "Don't just go *boom,* when I say *boom, BOOM!* Drop down on it and we're there." And boy, I'll tell you, when you went *boom,* you went *BOOM!*

That's part of the spirit of playing rock & roll drums. That and when your left side aches because you pulled a muscle. You say to yourself, "I'm going over the line tonight, but hell, let's keep going." Sometimes it gets to you—traveling, you know. You get on the road and sometimes you want to come home and you can't. You get a fever or catch the flu and you just want to lay in bed, but you gotta play, because the show must go on. But when the band is locked in, and you have one of those nights where everybody's on—everybody's really *there*—then it's worth it. It's worth everything in the world.

SELECTED DISCOGRAPHY

Singles

WITH MITCH RYDER AND THE DETROIT WHEELS

"Jenny Take a Ride" ("Jenny Jenny"/"CC Ryder" medley) (January 1966, New Voice)
"Little Latin Lupe Lu" (April 1966, New Voice)
"Devil with a Blue Dress On"/"Good Golly Miss Molly" (medley) (November 1966, New Voice)
"Sock It to Me—Baby" (March 1967, New Voice)

WITH THE ROCKETS

"Oh Well" (July 1979, RSO)

WITH EDGAR WINTER

"Free Ride" (October 1973, Epic)

Albums

WITH MITCH RYDER AND THE DETROIT WHEELS

Take a Ride (1966, New Voice)
Breakout (1966, New Voice)

WITH THE ROCKETS

Rockets (1979, RSO)
Rocket Roll (1982, Elektra)
Live Rockets (1983, Capitol)

WITH ALICE COOPER

Welcome to My Nightmare (1975, Atco)

WITH DR. JOHN

Hollywood Be Thy Name (1975, United Artists)

Dino Danelli

2

"Felix and I used to go to a record store up in Harlem, and one day we came across 'Good Lovin','Mustang Sally,' and a few other records. We learned them and then changed them around so that they became our songs."

LIKE THE DETROIT WHEELS and the Righteous Brothers, the Young Rascals were raised on rhythm & blues, and during the sixties, they played out their influences as blue-eyed soul. The Rascals were the most successful of all these groups. Above everything else, they were known as hot musicians, and their drummer, Dino Danelli, was one of the best in popular music. In his native New Jersey, he was a legend. There he got his first taste of the rock & roll life. His home town, Jersey City, faces east, and any musician knows that to make it on the East Coast, you have to cross that river to New York City. The kind of joints Dino worked up and down the coast fired his determination, and he plotted the course. He was barely into his teens when he made that river crossing.

As a Rascal, Dino became a pop star and was a joy to watch. With his head switching from side to side, his sticks twirling off the backbeat, Dino used showmanship to add impact to the groove he laid down. Applying a jazzman's sense of discipline to a rock & roll spirit, he drummed the Rascals into rock history. "Good Lovin'," "I've Been Lonely Too Long," "People Got to Be Free," "You Better Run," and "Groovin' " are all songs that sound as fresh today as they did the first time I cranked them up on my radio, over fifteen years ago.

During the fall of 1981, Steve Van Zandt recorded his album, *Men without Women*. It was my pleasure to be a part of that project. In support of that album Steve put together a band, called them the Disciples of Soul, and began to tour. He had Dino on drums.

Around Christmas 1982, Little Steven and the Disciples of Soul played the Jersey shore. It was great to see and hear Dino once again. Backstage before the show I asked him if he still twirled his sticks. He told me he thought it was a corny thing to do; audiences were so much more sophisticated these days. "Nah," I said. "I think it would be great—it's part of you!" He smiled and shrugged his shoulders.

The Disciples played a smoking set. Near the end of their performance, Steve introduced each band member, saving Dino for last: "On drums, the legendary Dino Danelli!" Not missing a beat, Dino turned his head and suddenly sent those sticks twirling. The place went crazy.

MAX: *You once told me about how you used to lug your drums on the train fron New York to Jersey to play gigs when you were a kid. Let's start there.*

DINO: That's going back to when I first began playing drums. I was living at the Metropole [the famous jazz club on Seventh Avenue and Forty-eighth Street in New York City], where I first started to get a reputation as a drummer. But the *first* band I played with, even before my Metropole days, was King Curtis's band. I used to sit in with him and his band at a place in New Jersey called the Banker's Club. The Banker's Club was located in Union City, just across from lower Manhattan. The joint used to have an amateur night on Mondays and Tuesdays, and I used to go up there with just a pair of sticks and sit in with King Curtis. We'd play "Drum Boogie" and some other Gene Krupa songs. I got to go up there every week. It was great. It was my first introduction to being in a band. King was a real nice guy. He was always pulling for the guy who was trying to learn and make it.

So you hadn't been in a band before that?

No. I got a funny story that went down even before my Banker's Club days. I had a nightclub when I first started playing, around '58. Underneath our apartment house in Jersey City were these coal bins. Well, I cleaned out the bins, shingled the place up, and called it Dino's Casino. I built a little stage and set up a speaker, and I'd play my drums to a record on the hi-fi. Kids used to come from the neighborhood and sit and watch me play.

It started to get really popular. After a while kids would bring booze and girls, and it became a club. They'd call me up, and I'd tell them what time the first show was. There were two shows a night. I wouldn't charge anybody; people would just come and hang out. And musicians would show up: saxophone players and other horn players. It was really great. I was twelve years old and it even made the newspapers. The police raided and padlocked the place because there was liquor and everybody was under age. I got closed up. It was on the front page of the *Jersey Journal.* From Dino's I went to another place in Union City called the Transfer Station. It was the seediest place around. Nothing but truck drivers and slutty girls. That was great, you know. I met a hillbilly band just up from Tennessee whose leader was a guy by the name of Ronnie Speakes. That band was into playing or copying Elvis Presley-style rock & roll. What happened was, their drummer was leaving and Speakes asked me to join. I had never played rock & roll, but I joined them anyway. They brought me down to Tennessee with them. There I met one of the best drummers I ever heard in my life. He was a cripple, paralyzed from the waist down, so he had a special hook-up on his bass drum pedal so his leg would be higher than normal. He would play his highhats and would hit his elbow on his knee, and that would set off his bass drum. He'd leave out certain beats and just hit his bass drum, but always in the right spot. Bobby Coleman was his name. He showed me all these fantastic fills and a lot of rock & roll things that I never heard of before. Things like heavy backbeat, a very sparse bass drum, lots of syncopation. Bobby Coleman and Speakes introduced me to rock & roll roots.

When we came back to the New York area, we got a job at the Metropole. The Metropole was turning into a rock & roll place in the afternoon, but they still played jazz at night. Before this, I used to go to the Metropole and stand outside and listen to Gene Krupa play. He used to play there almost every month. I must have been eleven or twelve years old.

The Metropole used to leave its doors open to entice people to go inside. The front of the club was pretty much all glass, so I could stand outside and watch the whole show for free. When I got the gig with Ronnie Speakes and we began playing the Metropole, the people at the club remembered me. We'd play in the afternoon, and I'd stay around for the evening shows.

The people who ran the Metropole took a liking to me. I was like their adopted son, and they let me live upstairs in one of the dressing rooms. Being at the Metropole so much, my goals got bigger than just playing in Ronnie Speakes's band. And then one night I met Gene Krupa. We got to be friends, and he'd take me into his dressing room between shows. He'd always lie down between sets because he had heart trouble. But we'd talk, you know. He knew I really wanted to make it as a drummer. Just listening to him talk about the old days with Benny Goodman and the others was fantastic.

Did you ever get to sit in with Krupa's band?

Never sat in with Krupa's band, but I sat in with Lionel Hampton's band.

When the Young Rascals came out with "Good Lovin'," your publicity people made a big deal out of you playing with Hampton.

"Then one night I met Gene Krupa. . . ."

It made good copy, I guess, but I only played with Hampton's band for two nights. It was just a jam, but it was great playing with a twenty-piece band.

I think the real turning point in my life was when I went down to New Orleans. The music scene there is so alive and figured so heavily in the creation of rock & roll. I had never experienced that funky kind of music before. I never slept. I took in all that street knowledge, and it changed my musical outlook. I stayed in New Orleans about a year.

When I went back to New York, I put together a rhythm & blues band called the Showstoppers based on the things I'd heard down in New Orleans. We traveled around the Midwest. Nothing spectacular, just a real good show band. After that band broke up, I moved back to New York and the Metropole. This was about 1964 when the Twist was happening at the Peppermint Lounge. That was *the* club at the time. I used to go over and listen to Ronnie Hawkins and the Hawks with Levon Helm on the drums. That's when I met Felix Cavaliere.

Felix had heard about me, and I'd heard about him. He was supposed to be a happening organ player, and he'd heard that I was one of the best drummers around. At this time, a singer named Sandy Scott was in town looking to put together a band to take to Las Vegas. So Felix and me and a couple of other guys went with her to Vegas. When we were out there the Beatles hit with "I Want to Hold Your Hand." We didn't know what the hell to think of it. I knew something was happening that was going to be real big, but couldn't put my finger on it. Felix and I made a deal that he was going to go home and put together a band like the Beatles, and I'd continue playing with Sandy Scott until he called me to come home. The Beatles gave us the idea and the urge to strike out on our own.

Did you know any of the other Rascals then?

I'd met our singer Eddie Brigati when one of the bands I was in played the Choo Choo Club in Garfield, New Jersey. He used to live around the corner from the joint. He'd come up on the stage and sing a couple of songs with whatever band was playing. We struck up a good friendship and said maybe we'd put together a band some day. He had already known Felix. Eddie was the brother of David Brigati, who was in Joey Dee's band. Felix was in Joey Dee's band too. That's where the connection to Felix comes in. Gene Cornish was playing guitar with his band at the Peppermint Lounge, as was Joey Dee's band. He met Felix and Eddie and struck up a friendship with them.

I was still in Vegas, so one day Felix called me up and said, "I got these two guys and they're really good. You should split Vegas and come home now." So I went back and the four of us got together at Felix's house in Pelham, New York. We must have learned about twenty-five songs in one night, all the current Top Forty hits. We came up with the name Young Rascals at the Choo Choo Club. One night we were playing there and someone said, "You ought to call the band the Little Rascals." We said, "Rascals, yeah; well, why don't we dress up like rascals?"

I remember the first time I saw the group was on the sixties TV program, "Hullabaloo." You guys played "I Ain't Gonna Eat Out My

From left to right: Dino Danelli, Felix Cavaliere, Eddie Brigati, Gene Cornish

Heart Anymore" and you came out with knickers on. Did you ever feel weird wearing them?

Oh yeah. The first Brooklyn Fox Murray the K show we did was really weird. We came out on stage and got laughed at—*until* we started playing.

The Rascals were discovered at a club called the Barge in East Hampton, Long Island. How did you get that gig?

We were playing the Choo Choo, and these two guys who were opening this new club, the Barge, had heard about us. They liked us and hired us to play the Barge on Monday and Tuesday nights. Ahmet Ertegun, the head of Atlantic Records, as well as other record people who summered in the Hamptons, came in to hear us simply because the Barge was the happening local club. We signed with Ertegun and Atlantic because Ahmet had the best rap. He heard "Good Lovin'," and that was it.

"Good Lovin'" wasn't an original Rascals tune, though. How did you find that song?

Felix and I used to go to a record store up in Harlem, and one day we came across "Good Lovin'," "Mustang Sally," which Wilson Pickett cut, and a few other records. We learned them and then changed them around so that they became our songs. A lot of people think "Good Lovin'," which was originally done by the Olympics, was our first record. It wasn't. We had "I Ain't Gonna Eat Out My Heart Anymore" out first, but that tune only made it to around number fifty on the charts.

The cymbal part for "Good Lovin'" was a tricky bit of business.

Well, that was a combination of "What'd I Say" and some New Orleans riffs.

Were you being managed by Sid Bernstein at this time?

Yeah. Sid came out to the Barge, and heard us, and we signed with him. A week later we met Ahmet and signed with Atlantic.

Remember at the Beatles concert at Shea Stadium in August 1965, they flashed on the scoreboard THE YOUNG RASCALS ARE COMING?

(Laughs.) Yeah, that was Sid's idea. Sid, who promoted the show, told us all to be there because something was really going to surprise us. We were in the dugout. We had no idea what he was talking about. Then the scoreboard lit up with that line and fifty-five thousand people saw it. Then Brian Epstein, the Beatles' manager, came over to Sid and started choking him! (Laughs.) "Get that fucking thing off the board NOW! Get it OFF!" he was screaming.

What did you think of Ringo after you saw him perform?

I liked him. He had great style; I never saw anybody play the way he did. I liked his simplicity. That's why I like Charlie Watts, too.

Were the Rascals' arrangements spontaneous, or did you work things out?

Both. Felix and I always had a magical thing. There were times when I thought out in advance what I wanted to play, but most of the time, it just happened. One of the good things about the Rascals was that we had unlimited studio time; it was in our contract. Any time we wanted to rehearse or fool around, Atlantic would cancel whoever else was in the studio for us, so we could go in there and jam and come up with lots of material.

The songwriting started after "Good Lovin'." The first song I think Eddie and Felix wrote together was "You Better Run." I remember that the bass drum part I came up with for that record was really strange. It was a fast bass drum. And that was thought up in the studio just fooling around.

Rhythmically you were doing things that a lot of other bands at the time weren't, like you went from the straight four to a shuffle on that tune.

That was the jazz thing. Felix was into jazz too. He was very into Jimmy Smith. He also learned a lot from a guy named Carl Lattimore, but he had Jimmy Smith down pat. I got a lot of stuff from a guy named Willie Davis, who drummed for Joey Dee. Actually, I stole a lot of stuff from him. He'd play a solo and jump up on his seat. He had incredible showmanship.

When I say "Good Lovin'," what's the first thing that comes into your mind?

The Barge. Playing the Barge night after night with the kids going wild. "Good Lovin'" was the classic Barge song. That summer was the best summer of my life. We all lived across the street from the club. We had beautiful, rich girls all over the place. Max, it was like paradise! (Laughs.)

What about "People Got to Be Free"?

Jamaica. Me and Felix down in Jamaica. We were on vacation down there and Felix wrote it then. You know, we got a lot of heat because of that record. Atlantic said it was too political and that it went against the grain. They didn't want to release it but we stuck to our guns, and it turned out to be the biggest record we ever had. Basically, the song was a reaction to the bullshit things that were happening in the sixties.

On "It's Wonderful," you can hear that sixties psychedelic approach.

We were stretching out a bit, being influenced by what the Beatles were doing. To me, that stuff never came off right. I know I wasn't comfortable with it. It didn't come from us, and it wasn't the way we were used to making records. See, the whole era was changing. The guitarists were coming into the spotlight, and our music had always been organ-based. Probably that's one of the reasons why we did things like "It's Wonderful," with tapes and things to stay current. That's when each of us started looking different ways, anyhow. It was kind of the beginning of the end.

What was the last record the original Rascals made before the band broke up?

Search and Nearness was the last Rascals album we all made together. Felix and I went on with the Rascals after that, but Eddie had split. There were no hits on that record. It was over by that time. It started at the beginning of that album, and by the end, we had disintegrated totally. We were just showing up and doing our parts and going home. I wanted out at that point too. My ego was just as bad as theirs. I was adding fuel to the fire, I'm sure. It's sad, but we all were ready to go on to new musical things. It got to be such a formula. I know I got bored. So Felix and I said, "Let's do a couple of jazz albums." Columbia Records was interested. Atlantic was becoming disenchanted with us. So we went over to Columbia and made the *Peaceful World* album, a jazz-oriented record. We got all these great players, great jazz legends to play on the record. The album didn't really work.

Was this when you began getting into art?

I was always kind of into art, but not really until I could actually afford it. I was making steel sculptures, twenty feet high. I had a duplex apartment with a big airy garden, and I was doing all my work there. It was a very expensive type of art. At that point I was looking forward to quitting the Rascals and becoming a full-time artist.

You were often involved with the illustration of the Rascals' album covers.

The *Once upon a Dream* album was the best album cover. For that record I did sculptures that represented the dreams of each guy in the band. It even won a graphics award.

That's what made me think I could go into art and make it without any problems, not knowing that to make it in art is a lot harder than making it in music. A rude awakening for me! When the Rascals split up, I went over to Germany and was just going to get into being an artist and not play music ever again. I stayed in an art colony for five months, but I missed music too much. I couldn't stop my hands and

"That summer was the best summer of my life. We all lived across the street from the club. We had beautiful, rich girls all over the place. It was like paradise!"

THE BIG BEAT

Dino Danelli, circa 1967

What was playing the Woodstock Festival like?

That was a pretty good one, a pretty good gig. It was a little bit long, because by the time we got to play, it was a Sunday night, and they'd been going like that for, well, a long time. Some of the people had been there at the site for four nights or more. And it'd been raining. I don't know what people thought was going to happen—probably that there'd be a riot and everyone would break out and eat their way back to New York City, eating every cow and pig and barbecuing everything in sight. But inside there was a bunch of people having a pretty good time. With the times being what they were, there was what looked to be a lot of drugs, judging by people's behavior. It was just like some of them looked to be real tired and a little unhealthy.

Backstage was like it usually is for us: We would go in, shake hands, eat, play our gig, and split. There was never anything social. We never hung around.

Now, jumping ahead four years to Watkins Glen; that was even more interesting because the people's frame of mind was really right on. Everybody looked healthy; traffic would jam up, and people would get out of their cars and toss Frisbees and play guitars and relax. At Watkins Glen the people were on close to eighty or ninety acres with roads and sidewalks and flags. It looked like little towns out there. The authorities tried to shut it down, right? But the townspeople wanted to have it because it meant a lot of income for the town. They were having the festival at the racetrack, and in the last days they made the promoters buy several hundred thousand dollars' worth of crushed gravel and put down all those damn sidewalks and roadways. And then after that, they made them get another five hundred of those port-a-john toilets. One day before the music got started they made them buy another sixty-grand worth of storm fencing. The townspeople were going for it, but they had the county health department to worry about. There were about five violations that could shut the festival down. But they'd get on the phone and call in a hundred fifty thousand dollars' worth of whatever was needed. Drop it right in front of you.

Do you remember what you felt like right before you went on, looking out there and seeing all those people?

It was shocking. I had things that made me more nervous, but that was really a good one for "Let me get it!" A funny thing had happened there. We played for about half an hour, maybe forty-five minutes, and it started raining. Rick and Robbie took their hands off their instruments and ran to the side of the stage. And about this time a friend of mine, Jack Wingate, from London, Ontario, Garth's hometown, shows up and pulls out a bottle of that Glen Fidich Scotch. So we have a couple of social pulls on it; Garth has a couple of pulls too. All of a sudden Garth wants to play. And he goes back out and it was great. Garth started playing just beautiful stuff. You couldn't put your finger on it, but it stopped raining! All of a sudden it just dried up.

"We would start working on a tune, and the song would dictate who would sing it and who would play the supporting roles. And luckily, nobody had such a big head that you couldn't get a tub over it."

Your longtime on-off association with Bob Dylan has always been subject to close scrutiny. What effect did he have on the Band?

Well, I know he always had fun playing with us. We always felt like we were making music together. And he really opened up the door for us. Up until that time, we were just a backing band.

There are many stories about how Dylan picked up the group. Is it true that when you and Robbie went with Bob to do the Forest Hills gig, you'd joined up without Bob ever hearing you play?

Yeah, I believe that's true. Unless he heard a tape that somebody had played for him. But we didn't really know one another. After we played that show—this was after he'd made his "electrical debut"—he was talking about doing a long tour and taking us along. The Forest Hills date was like finishing up a commitment for him. Robbie and I finished that with him; then we got the whole group together and played all over the country.

You were still playing with them?

Yeah.

Then you left. Why?

We'd been together during that period for a couple of years. We toured Texas and California and a lot of the United States. Then the tour went to Australia and Europe, but I passed on that part. You see, Dylan would play Fort Worth, Texas, and it would be like any other Saturday night—great fun. People would be dancing and clapping along. But then we'd play Boston or the wrong part of the country, and we'd get an audience of folk purists who didn't believe in electricity or those who used the stuff. Bob would go out and play for an hour or so with his guitar and a couple of harmonicas. Then he'd come off, take a breath, and we'd all go out with him. We'd bring a couple of electric guitars, electric piano, organ, and a set of drums. Man, you'd think that Adolf Hitler had had the nerve to show his ugly head!

The crowd would boo. You'd finish a number and they would boo. Now that's a hell of a feeling. It didn't take me long to get a bellyful of that. I was starting to get a little hot under the collar. I could take it here—this is my country. But I couldn't see taking it in Europe. For the first time I couldn't stick to my policy, which was to whistle while I worked. I just said to everybody that I was going to take a pass when we finished the U.S. commitment, and that they should start to think of somebody to replace me. They got a fella by the name of Mickey Jones. I wished them good luck—there was no problem. It was just something I had to do.

Did you ever think that move could end your association with the group?

Well, yeah; I looked at it both ways. I felt that it might be a temporary thing. I knew that everybody else eventually wanted a recording contract of their own and to do something other than to play with Bob. But at the time it wasn't hard to imagine that it might not go that way for me. Maybe I'd have to play with some other people. But that would be all right. I went back to Arkansas and played with the Cate

LEVON HELM

The Band, circa 1969

Brothers a bit. They're a good outfit, and I ended up playing music just the same.

Those must have been some wild gigs with Dylan.

Well, the fellas still laugh about some of the stories. One chick attacked Bob and was going to punch him out. A couple of people in a couple of places really took it as far as they could. These people were flat out against us. But as far as I was concerned, there was never any falling out with us.

How did Dylan deal with it?

Well, I guess Bob figured it was his row to hoe. Maybe he thought he had to hoe every one of them to get to the point where he would be accepted. I went along. I helped him hoe quite a bit. I was on all those long rows, you might say. But then, I just decided that when we got to the short rows, I'd just let him kinda do it himself. Some of those gigs weren't anything to jump up and down about and celebrate. It was just another shitty day in paradise. But then, it could have been completely different—and it was. If we were in Fort Worth, it'd be wonderful. The people would dance, clap their hands, and have a good time. They'd talk to you, invite you to have a drink with them. You know, that's why we were playing music—to get to meet people and enjoy that fellowship. It won't work if you both don't show up. But the next night you'd be in Boston or somewhere where there would be a lot of folk purists. The minute thay saw that electric guitar—they'd go wild. I figured I'd go home, play some dances, and wait for the times to catch up. Eventually, when everybody got back from the tour and was back at Woodstock, we started getting a few nibbles as far as recording and releasing an album on our own without Bob. Once that started happening, I headed north, and we began what was later released as *The Basement Tapes*.

Did you really all live in that big pink house?

There were about three of us who stayed there at the house: There were also a few other places. We had three or four houses between us all. We weren't on top of one another but there was a certain type of clubhouse atmosphere. Everybody showed up, ate breakfast, and went into the studio to rehearse.

Working with Bob must have had quite an effect on the three main songwriters, especially Robbie.

Well, Bob certainly made everybody more aware of how to write. We used to have a great time sitting around and remembering old tunes. He and Richard Manuel would start notes to each other in a typewriter. One would go by and type up a verse, then the other would happen by and type a verse. There was a lot of fun to be had on that level.

Was there ever a time before Big Pink *and* John Wesley Harding *where a follow-up album to that '66 tour might have been a Dylan-Band collaboration?*

We never did think of it like that. We were just documenting songs and having fun and thinking we would come back and redo a lot of those tunes—take them into the studio under the right conditions and really give them a full chance. We didn't do that with most of the songs, but Garth had the equipment and turned on the machines, and sure enough, we had the whole thing on tape—whatever was going on.

What's your favorite Band album?

The most fun might have been the live album with Allen Toussaint, the *Rock of Ages* album. That was a whole lot of fun, having him come up from New Orleans, and having that horn section play with us. Man, that's first-class accommodations.

That version of "Don't Do It" is one of my favorites. Didn't you do a studio version of that?

Yeah, we cut it two or three different times. But the live album was the only time we put it out. It was always fun to play, and people always enjoyed it in our show. But we never could get it to fly right in the studio.

I'd like to talk some more about the Band's approach to recording and your method of getting that funky drum sound.

Again, that goes back to that Memphis sound. After J. M. Van Eaton and D. J. Fontana came through, there was Al Jackson with Stax—his snare's got that all-American thud that the early Sun records had. You know, one of our first records—it was a single and I forgot which one it was—but it came on the jukebox, and it must have been twice as low in volume as anything else; it snapped me and the rest of us awake. We realized that when we went in and mixed, we tried to make everything so bottom-heavy. We were always so concerned about getting the right amount of presence around the bass pattern, so it would stick up there like a big pillar. And by the time we got the wood on the backbeat cuttin' through just right, we had to start redoing our stuff and mixing with more highs and letting a lot of that sound come through on its own.

Levon, I'm curious about the photograph that's on The Band *record, where you're in a big room, set up very informally. Is that how you recorded?*

Not exactly. There was a little bit more technique in the recording and miking end of it. Actually, a lot of that stuff was cut upstairs at A&R Studios on Seventh Avenue in New York City. We would usually use the big room up there on the seventh floor. That studio was so big, they used to do a lot of those live dance party records there. When we played there, I would set up in the middle of the room. They had a sound booth over against the wall, and Garth would put a couple of his speakers into that sound booth so he could distort them, or whatever. The piano would be in a standard sort of place, and we'd pull a couple of chairs up for Robbie and Rick, and they'd pull up their amps beside them. We'd have a couple of barriers around the drums to keep them from leaking. We'd have the mikes on the amps. The bass would usually go direct, and we'd have live vocals.

For that second album, we'd go in and start around seven or eight o'clock at night. We'd get food sent in and have a good time until everybody started to get a little tired. It was fairly professional. We used *The Basement Tapes* as a reference point, a way to keep track.

Did it ever get down to where you had something on a rehearsal tape and went to record it, and it didn't come out as well?

Well, not really. We could usually manage to get a better sound. But every now and then you'd run across one that wouldn't want to happen right. Like "Cripple Creek," which took awhile. But after you get it, it's like, "Well, how can it go any other way?"

How many members of the Band still live in Woodstock?

Just Rick and myself. Garth has a place here and comes back and forth. But he's fairly involved with his studio in California. Robbie is mostly into the movie people out there. He always wanted to do that. Richard says he's gonna move back to Woodstock.

Is he out on the West Coast?

Yeah. Of course, Richard is one of those key guys. Rick too, because he helps Richard write so good. So I'm kind of lookin' forward to seeing them get back together. Richard can write good songs when he wants to. And Rick knows how to get them out of him. Rick is like a damn musical sponge. You can drop just one bit of music out there and, boy, he can soak it up and squeeze out a cupful. He's one of the best guys to play catch with. If you got some musical balls to bounce around, he's the guy to play catch with.

How do you feel about getting the opportunity to act in movies like Coal Miner's Daughter?

From where I sit, I scored big in that department. Doin' *Coal Miner's Daughter*, why, that was a lot of fun. They were all great people to work with. I didn't expect to get drafted, much less get to play. What a team! All you had to do was show up. To be a part of the

"The most fun might have been the live album with Allen Toussaint, the Rock of Ages album. That was a whole lot of fun, having him come up from New Orleans, and having that horn section play with us. Man, that's first class accommodations."

team in that film, you couldn't miss. You have Michael Apted, the director, tellin' you, "That's fine. Now do the same thing, only say it slower this time. Take your time and really mean it." So you do it again a couple of times, and you get it pretty close. And then they turn the camera around to Sissy Spacek, and now we're cookin'. While I'm saying one of those things to her, they catch her just where it looks so pitiful you almost cry. Put that in there and it makes you look a lot better.

As a swan song and as a rock movie, The Last Waltz *was bittersweet. After all those years spent together, how did you feel about ending it that way?*

I was probably the least in favor of doing it that way, without being in any kind of intractable position. I was always one of the ones who enjoyed it less, as far as the Band going out of business. I thought people could do their own things within the framework of the group. I was glad that some of the people were able to get involved with what they wanted to have happen. Working with a group can make it hard for a lot of things to come your way. You don't get considered for some projects because you work under that kind of banner. I was glad to see that change. All of a sudden everybody was really on his own and doing the things he wanted to do. I could certainly see people not wanting to travel anymore. People had families, and we'd been doing it quite a while. I'm the one that don't mind traveling. The hotel manager don't bring me down. I'll sit there and jaw with him all day. I don't give a damn. But as far as seeing the Band fold up, I didn't take great joy in that part of it.

It's been seven years since the Band's last gig. What's the feeling like?

It's not been too bad because I've been real busy. Out of all them years, I played a lot of those nights. If I'd sat around and thought about it, it might have gotten to me, but I took advantage of who I knew and the musicians I was able to meet, and I got to play with quite a few of them. It's in my plans to play with the rest.

We began our talk earlier this afternoon with your memory of you and your sister playing and singing popular songs around your home town. Last week I saw you and Rick Danko at a small bar singing and playing what were probably some of the same songs.

Yeah, I've come all the way back to playing guitar and mandolin and harmonicas. But it *is* really all the same. The main thing that juices me up is to get over there the night of a job, wherever it is, and the man that's runnin' the joint knows I'm comin', and he invites me in and helps me get my stuff set up. And I play and he pays me. That's the only way I've ever really wanted it.

SELECTED DISCOGRAPHY

Albums

WITH THE BAND

Music from Big Pink (1968, Capitol Records)
The Band (1969, Capitol Records)
Stage Fright (1970, Capitol Records)
Rock of Ages (1972, Capitol Records)
Moondog Matinee (1973, Capitol Records)
The Last Waltz (1978, Warner Bros.)

WITH BOB DYLAN

The Basement Tapes (1975, Columbia)

SOLO

Levon Helm and the RCO All-Stars (1977, ABC)
Levon Helm (1978, Capitol)

WITH RONNIE HAWKINS

Mr. Dynamo (1960, Roulette)

Roger Hawkins

4

"Lay back—and burn!"

ROGER HAWKINS'S drumming on *The Best of Percy Sledge* should be required listening for all drummers attempting to learn the art of soulful drumming. On cuts such as "When a Man Loves a Woman," "Dark End of the Street," and "Take Time to Know Her," Roger demonstrates the necessity and value of playing with a relaxed intensity. The control and understatement of his style underline the emotions of the songs and the singer. That record is an important volume in the history of soul music and I became a student of it. Long before I wore out my first copy I came to love Roger's drumming.

Since 1964, Roger Hawkins has been the heartbeat of the Muscle Shoals Rhythm Section (MSRS) and has consistently maintained his position as one of rock's greatest and most respected drummers. Subsequently, the MSRS emerged as one of the tightest studio ensembles in rock, and the power of the music they created was their calling card.

Moving effortlessly from artist to artist, the MSRS—Jimmy Johnson (guitar), David Hood (bass), Barry Beckett (keyboards), and Roger—have supported a large and impressive roster of performers for over twenty years. Gaining their initial success backing two of the greatest soul singers of the sixties, Aretha Franklin and Wilson Pickett, they extended their range to include such artists as Paul Simon, Bob Seger, and Rod Stewart, each of whom has a very distinct style. Maintaining the highest levels of musicianship, the MSRS has a remarkable ability to adapt to any musical approach.

Roger Hawkins grew up in Florence, Alabama, Muscle Shoals's sister city. Situated in the northwest corner of the state, the town lies just three hours south of both Memphis and Nashville. The musical influences of those two cities on Roger's style and the Muscle Shoals sound is apparent. A mixture of urban blues from Memphis and the take-your-time approach of Nashville's country music, Muscle Shoals's style is something akin to what Roger calls "rhythm & blues with a laid-back feeling." By any name, it feels good.

The success of Roger's career paralleled the rise of Muscle Shoals as an important recording center. With three studios in town—Fame (the most successful), Quinn-Ivey Studios, and the Bevis Recording Studio—there existed a small but booming local music scene.

It is important to note that the *original* house band at Fame Studios, apart from MSRS guitarist Jimmy Johnson, included drummer Jerry Carrigan, bassist Norbert Putnam, and piano player David Briggs. Except for Johnson, these players, who worked on Fame's big 1962 hit, Arthur Alexander's "You Better Move On," became disenchanted and left for Memphis where they did, indeed, become more successful, working with Elvis Presley and others.

The success of "You Better Move On" focused some attention on Muscle Shoals and the musicians who filled the vacancies at Fame—Roger, David Hood, and piano player Spooner Oldham. With some years of experience under their belts, the three eventually worked all three studios. It was at Quinn-Ivey, as Roger told me, that "When a Man Loves a Woman" was cut. By May of 1966, the record went to Number One. At the age of twenty, Roger Hawkins had played on his first hit.

"When a Man Loves a Woman" had tremendous impact, and word spread through the industry about this group. Jerry Wexler, a co-owner of Atlantic Records and a top producer at the time, was so impressed that, in 1966, he brought Wilson Pickett down to Muscle Shoals to record. By then Barry Beckett had replaced Spooner Oldham. Wexler brought quite a bit of his work to Fame Studios, and the results included hits such as Pickett's "Mustang Sally" and "Land of 1,000 Dances," two bar-band staples of my youth that bear the unmistakable touch of the MSRS—excitement made more thrilling by the dynamic control of the players.

Jerry Wexler has called Roger "the greatest drummer in the world." Drumming for Aretha, Roger's performances demonstrate that, though controlled intellectually, the most commanding drumming is inspired by the heart. "Respect," "I Never Loved a Man (the Way I Love You)" "Chain of Fools," "Baby I Love You," "(Sweet Sweet Baby) Since You've Been Gone"—to each Roger brought the critical elements of soulful drumming: emotion, subtlety, and restraint.

Roger's talents have enabled him to hold up more than his share in maintaining the MSRS's importance as both a musical and a production group. As he explains in our conversation, the fact that it was *their* sound that brought the outside world to Muscle Shoals to record led the boys to strike out on their own in 1969, when they formed the Muscle Shoals Sound Studios, diversifying into music publishing, record production, *and* the operation of a twenty-four-hour recording studio. It all works due to the long-standing cooperation and understanding among the four musicians whose vision that studio was. As Roger tells it, "We work as a team."

Life in Muscle Shoals, Alabama, seems to flow in much the same way as the music of the Muscle Shoals Rhythm Section: sure and steady. People take their time. It was a very hot summer day in 1983 when I met Roger Hawkins for the first time. He picked me up at my motel, and we headed down Main Street toward his studio. On the way I saw a sign: WELCOME TO THE CITY OF MUSCLE SHOALS—HIT RECORDING CAPITAL OF THE WORLD.

As we drove through the center of Muscle Shoals, Roger looked to his left, past a liquor store. "If you'd been here last week," he said, "you'd have seen them tear down the shack where we recorded 'When a Man Loves a Woman.'" He pointed to a twenty-foot-wide space between two parked cars.

We continued on to the studio, a huge building no more than one hundred feet from the Tennessee River. It was once a Naval Reserve complex. Roger told me it was particularly fitting that they'd ended up there; long ago they had played dances in the gym that now houses studios A and B.

We went inside, down a hallway, past walls lined with gold records. Music rang through the walls. As we sat down to talk, Roger put his feet up, clasped his hands behind his neck, and settled back.

MAX: *Memphis, Nashville, and Muscle Shoals, Alabama, were all important centers for the blues, country, and rockabilly—the roots of rock & roll. How did living in this area affect your growth as a musician?*

ROGER: Well, when I first became conscious that there was such a thing as a recording studio player, my dream was to go to Nashville to play. But later on, I realized the best country music in the world was being made one hundred and fifty miles away. 'Bout that time, it was Booker T. and the MGs going on in Memphis, and we seemed to be more influenced by that style of music because the best had already been done in country, it seemed. So we drifted toward the blues-soul thing.

But going back to your question about rock & roll, I can tell you the first beat I played. It was back when rock & roll wasn't played with all straight eights on the cymbal or hi-hat. It was like a *da-da-DA*, a one and two, but it wasn't a real shuffle but kind of in between. Some of the guys were playing shuffles, and some weren't. You've probably heard it where the drummer might be playing a shuffle, but you hear a straight rhythm from the piano or guitar. I remember watching my friend Mike Sheppard play, and I went home and tried it. And I got this thing goin' and it was great, a great feeling was what it was.

I can tell by your grin that it was a real good time.

Oh sure, it's why you start. Well, maybe that's not exactly the reason you start. It's more when you later play with other musicians and you have a meeting of the minds and everybody looks at each other and says, "YEAH! Somethin's goin' on here. I like it!"

How old were you when you started?

I was thirteen years old when I joined my first band. It had drums, piano, and guitar. No bass, but we didn't really care. I saw these guys play at a talent show at a recreation center in Florence, Alabama, where I grew up. One guy had his hair slicked back like Elvis and all, and when they finished, I said to the piano player, "Hey, you guys need a drummer?" He didn't know if the other guys wanted one or not, but he said he'd ask them. He did and they called me a couple of days later. The piano player, by the way, was Spooner Oldham.

Was Elvis an early influence?

Well, when Elvis and Sun Records was really happening, I was about eleven or twelve years old, so I was kind of oblivious to it all. I didn't buy those records or study them. I didn't care one way or the other about any of the artists. I just cared about playing. I liked records with drums on them—"Teen Beat" by Sandy Nelson and Cozy Cole's "Topsy." Really, I was influenced by any records that had drums on them. I bought "Drumsville" by Earl Palmer. I was also into Joe Morello on "Take Five" and Buddy Rich and anybody else who played good drums.

What kind of material did your band play?

We were doing "Matchbox" by Carl Perkins, "Hound Dog"—rockabilly things. In fact, I can remember sitting in my bedroom with my record player and a bass drum, snare, and a twelve-inch cymbal trying to learn the opening riff for "Hound Dog." I sat there for days trying to figure that out. I did the same with Motown records. That's how I learned to play—by listening to records. That's how I learned to play in the studio, too. I would pick out the drums and try to emulate what was happening on my drum set.

When did you get your first drum set?

When I was about twelve or thirteen. It was a little simple Slingerland set. I played it all the time because I was real fat, ugly, and none of the girls liked me. I reckon I'd been playing three months or so. I was just getting into it. We were all terrible, but to us the band was sounding great.

What kept you at it?

I enjoyed it. It being a small town, there weren't a lot of musicians or bands around. No clubs to sneak into. So I was pretty much confined to a bedroom and record collection. There were no drummers to go watch.

Did any of the big national acts come through or near Florence?

Lloyd Price and his band came through once. Man, they were so far into what they were into, I could not believe it. I mean, I was amazed. I learned a good lick from the guy who played drums with Price. They did some kind of cha-cha—"Tea for Two"-type thing—and on all the breaks, he would put his elbow on the snare, press down, and raise the pitch of the drum. It was a real nice effect, and I still use that today.

When you were sixteen or seventeen, the British Invasion hit America. How did that affect your music scene?

Well, the music was on the radio all the time, but we were completely closed to it because at the time we were doing mostly black, R&B music. So the English didn't have an effect on us. If the Beatles wanted to do what they wanted to do, why, that was just fine with me. I never tried to imitate them, never. As a matter of fact, I wasn't much impressed when they first came to America. I thought our style was a much tighter style than what they were doing. My mind just wasn't open at all. To me it was a sloppy sound. By this time I had progressed to the point where I wanted to hear things tight. Anything loose turned me off.

How did you get involved in studio work?

Well, my parents got divorced when I was fourteen, so that gave me a freedom, so to speak. When I was fifteen, I was playing up and down the East Coast with a country act. I left school and played. I played nightclubs in Atlanta, Georgia, and Orlando, Florida—all kinds of places. One night I was in Macon, Georgia. I was eighteen and had a vision of myself at forty years old playing in a nightclub. Well, I didn't like what I saw. I knew that Rick Hall had a studio back in Florence called Fame Recording Studio. I felt that if I could just get back there and hang out, maybe I could learn what to do in the studio. So I quit the band and moved back to Florence and hung out at the studio. I played on demos for free and did anything I had to do—run errands, whatever. Then Jerry Carrigan, Norbert Putnam, and David Briggs moved to Nashville, and I guess because I showed some dedication, I was the logical successor.

Around that time I was, technically speaking, the best that I've ever been. But I didn't know what to do with it. I didn't know anything about the studio. I was taught about the studio by Rick Hall. He used

"I can remember sitting in my bedroom with my record player and a bass drum, snare, and a twelve-inch cymbal trying to learn the opening riff for 'Hound Dog'! . . . that's how I learned to play—by listening to records."

to say, "Even if I ask you to go out in the middle of the studio and play a paper bag, if that's what I want, then that's what you do." He really gave me some wisdom about the recording studio and how players should aim to please the producer. The producer is always right; if he tells you to play on the snare side to get a crisper sound, you do it. I really got past the "he's trying to tell me how to play" routine real quick.

Who was playing bass at the studio back then?

A fella by the name of Junior Lowe. Junior was probably the first bass player I ever played with. I remember being at Spooner's house and we heard the roar of a car comin' down an old gravel road. Then this '52 Oldsmobile with pipes and pinstripes pulls up, bass strapped to the roof, and Junior Lowe gets out. He played a stand-up, and I couldn't believe what it added. He'd play the style where you pop the strings. So Junior played bass, a fella named Terry Thompson played guitar. Thompson didn't make it; he really liked speed and alcohol. He went to Lexington, Kentucky, to dry out, and he died there. He was twenty-four years old, a great guitar player. Spooner, of course, was on keyboards.

Beyond its musical greatness, as a historical event, Percy Sledge's "When a Man Loves a Woman" was very important. What's your recollection of recording that song?

Well, Rick Hall was making R&B records at Fame, you see, and there was a local disc jockey named Quinn Ivey, who still lives in Florence. And there was a guitar player, Marlin Green, who also worked at Fame. Well, Quinn wanted to have his own studio; he put in this little mono studio, as was Fame at the time. It was funky and friendlier than Fame. Rick Hall had a habit of coming down hard on you at the wrong time. He'd do *subtle* things like hit the talkback button and say, "Roger, your drums sound like shit." That would embarrass me to high heaven. I would want to crawl under the drums rather than play them. The atmosphere at Quinn Ivey's studio wasn't fancy, but you were appreciated more. We had more fun and more freedom.

Quinn had this dream of discovering a big artist. Rick had already found someone named Arthur Alexander and made a record called "You Better Move On" a few years before that; it was a hit record. So the thing to do was find a black artist and make a record and get rich! Quinn Ivey decided he would do this, so he found Percy Sledge. Rick had passed up Percy. So Quinn signed him up and recorded him. I played the drums, Junior played bass, Spooner played Farfisa organ, there were some local horn players, and Jimmy Johnson ran the board.

Some guys in Percy's band had the song "When a Man Loves a Woman" and Marlin Green got with those guys and changed the song around to what he thought the song should be. We cut two or three things that day, and that song was one of them. At the time, I didn't really think anything of it; I don't think anybody did. When I first thought it might be something was after they had taken the tape and mastered it with the horns on it. The horns weren't done live; they went and put the horns on later. Anyway, when I heard it, it gave me chill bumps.

You mentioned that Quinn Ivey's studio had a more laid-back atmosphere, and that comes through on the record. Was the session really as relaxed as we might think?

Well, to tell you the truth, I don't ever remember being relaxed on *any* session. I know the red light's going to come on in five seconds and I gotta count the song off. I mean, it may sound like I'm playing relaxed, but what's going on in my mind is something entirely different.

What is going on in your mind in a situation like that?

If I'm doin' what I'm supposed to be doin', nothin'. I'm just playing the drums.

Did you like the way you sounded on that record?

At the time I loved it, but now I hate it because it sounds so loose. When I listen to it, it sounds like the drums are just oblivious to what's going on in the song. I mean, we didn't even have headphones. But I hear the innocence in it.

A lot of Percy's songs—"Dark End of the Street," "Take Time to Know Her," "Out of Left Field"—contain drumming that sounds like you're full of energy.

The intensity in those days was much lighter, whereas now, in terms of dynamics, you have to play really hard. Back then, you played real soft.

What brought about that change?

Closer miking techniques, I would think. At first it was one mike over the drums and a mike on the bass drum. Now they put a mike on everything. You can't hardly start out from a whisper and go very loud. The drums just don't speak that way when they're miked really close.

It seems to me that what the engineers like to hear is balls-out playing, and they only turn the mikes on a little bit. A lot of times, an engineer or producer will hear records and it sounds like the drummer is beating the shit out of his kit when really the guy is just playing. So they tell other drummers, "Okay, now hit 'em HARD!" And you really can't argue with them, because they're paying you to do what you do, so make them happy. And the only time I'll say something is when I play so hard that the drum has lost all its tone, and the producer says to play louder. I say, "I'm sorry, but I can't play any harder." I think that aside from some hip engineers, only a drummer would know that point.

As a producer, this must help you work with drummers more effectively.

It sure does, and it helps me work with other musicians as well. A lot of times everyone will tend to play too hard. And sometimes the nice textures are in soft or medium execution. Dynamically, at least you've got somewhere to go.

"... I don't ever remember being relaxed on *any* session."

Much of today's drumming sounds as if everything is played at one volume.

Yeah, and a lot of the hits today are hits because the overall record is a sound and not so much a song. Hits today are created by sounds and illusions. But a good song will play itself. There's nothing to do on a good song except stay out of the way and keep it going. A lot of times there's stops in songs where you're just dying to put in a wonderful drum fill. But that fill would cover up the singer's reentrance into the song. That's the reason I hit those two shots in "When a Man Loves a Woman," where Percy comes back in—not to cloud his entrance. You've got to keep it simple.

Wilson Pickett is one of the greatest R&B singers and many of his sixties hits were done at Fame.

Yes, but not all of them. Some of the better Wilson Pickett songs—"Midnight Hour," "634-5789"—were done in Memphis. Of course, "Mustang Sally" and "Land of 1,000 Dances" were good. But damn, how could you beat "Midnight Hour" with Al Jackson?

Can you tell me about Al Jackson?

Al was a sensitive guy. He wasn't boisterous at all. In no way did he ever try to shove his weight around. He was real friendly, and of course we all know about his playing. He was a big influence on me. I was always interested in the kind of music they were doing at Stax, so naturally, I listened to Stax records. I loved Al Jackson's backbeat. Although now that I think of it, it might not be that his backbeat was so laid back. It could be that the musicians he played with were rushing. Working with the Linn drum machine, I'm finding more and more that musicians will say to a drummer, "Man, you're dragging," when a lot of times the drummer is right on it. *They're* ahead of the drummer. The Linn forces the musician to play right in time, and now they don't have the ol' drummer to kick around anymore. With the Linn, what can they say? Many times I've watched musicians overdub to the Linn drum, but when they would get to the chorus they leave the Linn behind and go right on. At first they want to look at the drummer, but there's no drummer there. Then they look at each other and say, "Oops. I guess we're rushing" (laughs). *Caught!*

Al Jackson was the master of that simple, soulful backbeat. I've heard that he could count off a take, go out, play a round of golf, and come back and hit the same tempo?

He could do that. I mean *he had it!*

What was working with Wilson Pickett like?

We just worked it out in the studio. He had a lot of input. On "Land of 1,000 Dances" he gave me the pulse that he wanted me to play by walking up to me and saying, "Hey man, play THIS." And he clapped it out and gave me the lick.

Jerry Wexler produced those sessions. I heard that Jerry originally came down to Stax and worked with the MGs. But something happened there.

It was a disagreement between Jim Stewart and Jerry Wexler

concerning Stax's distribution deal with Atlantic, which prompted Jerry to come to Muscle Shoals. "Land of 1,000 Dances" was the first recording I did with him, and boy, was I scared. He had a pretty heavy reputation.

I've heard that Jerry Wexler thought you were really a soulful drummer. How would you describe the term "soulful drumming"?

For me, it goes back to complementing the song and the feeling you get for the artist. I can't really define what soul drumming is, but I can define what *great* soul drumming is—Bernard Purdie.

Both you and Purdie were extremely important in Aretha Franklin's career. After you worked with Wilson Pickett, Jerry Wexler and Tom Dowd brought Aretha down to Muscle Shoals. And you played on "Respect," "Think," and "Sweet Sweet Baby (Since You've Been Gone)."

"Say a Little Prayer," a whole lot of things. They all were recorded by a mixture of players from Memphis and Muscle Shoals. Tommy Cogbill on bass, Jimmy Johnson on guitar, Spooner on organ, Chips Moman on guitar, Bobby Womack sometimes.

Those records were her biggest hits and established her as the greatest female soul singer of her time. What do you think was so special about those sessions?

Aretha's emotion made everything work; I played to her voice. On her sessions it was like the drums were playing themselves. I mean, you've got Aretha Franklin doin' what she does plus playing piano at the same time. There wasn't any effort at all because of her.

I hear that stuff today and it just destroys me. I say to myself, "My God, what a record!" At the time, we were scared; all we wanted to do was continue to play on the dates. That was the secret concern of everybody. The first time we went to New York was to play on some King Curtis stuff. And on the plane coming back, it was just Jimmy Johnson and I, and we said, "Well, at least we got to do this once in our lives." We didn't know they liked us as much as they did. We were just glad to be there. You know, there were only two Aretha Franklin songs recorded in Muscle Shoals—"Never Loved a Man" and I can't remember the other one. But they were the only two. The rest were recorded in New York.

What was Wexler's production approach?

Well, he wouldn't waste any time. And when it was time to record, he'd keep us going even if someone made a mistake. He did what he was supposed to do. He kept us at ease.

Did his New York kind of energy ever seem too fast to the Southern musicians?

Not at all, because he was seeing something that he was not used to seeing. He'd been used to being tied down with an arranger when they used to go in and, say, make the old Coasters records. He once made the comment that he liked it at Muscle Shoals because he wasn't tied down; before, he would have to go in with an arranger and be at the arranger's mercy. You paid for the arranger and it took too much time to change anything—it cost too much—so you were stuck with it.

> "I can't really define what soul drumming is, but I can define what great *soul drumming is*— Bernard Purdie."

With the Southern musicians, it was all head sessions; you could mix, match, add, delete. He loved working that way. And there was a lot of input from musicians.

That input is most evident on "Respect." What a track that is! Roger, if you had to direct a player to hit that kind of groove, what would you tell him?

Brother, lay back—and burn!

When did you and other members of the rhythm section decide to start your own studio?

The reason we got our own studio was that Rick Hall was making a deal with Capitol Records to distribute his Fame label. At that time I was playing a little club gig in Tennessee and at 3614 Jackson Highway [the original Muscle Shoals Sound Studio] before we bought it. I'd go over there and play on country demos. I'd play at Quinn Ivey's studio and at Fame too. There would be some days when I would leave the house with my drums in the car, go play in one studio for a few hours, take the drums down, and go to another studio for a few hours, set the drums up, play, break them down, and drive to Tennessee and play four sets that night. I'd go home, go to sleep, get up the next day, and start all over again. It was called hustlin'. Wherever *it* was, I was.

So Rick was making this deal with Capitol, and he offered us a yearly salary to play for him and no one but him. The salary he offered us, though, was lower than what we were making just freelancing. In the meantime, Fred Bevis, the owner of the 3614 Jackson Highway studio—Bevis Recording Studio—wasn't doing too well. He said to me and the guys, "You know, you guys should buy this studio." We didn't want to get into that just yet, but years and years before, Jimmy Johnson's uncle had known someone in Memphis at the studio where Al Green used to record; this was way before Al Green's time. We'd gone to record there once, and it sounded great to us. Because we didn't have any money, the owner of the place let us sleep in the studio that night. So while everyone was asleep, I woke up and looked in the control room. There was Jimmy Johnson looking at all the dials. We talked and decided that night that one day we'd get a recording studio. Then Fred Bevis suggested we buy his studio. I knew we had a good account with Atlantic Records, but I wondered, "If we bought the studio, would that account go to Rick Hall or would Atlantic stay with us?" Well, I figured they would go with us. But the studio needed some updating. It was a four-track, and Atlantic was making all their stuff on eight-track. We didn't really have any money, but I called Jimmy Johnson anyway and said, "Let's buy Fred's recording studio." He said, "You're crazy." We stayed on the phone for eight hours. At the end of the eight hours, we had it all figured out. We went to talk with Fred and worked out a deal. At the time it was Jimmy Johnson, Barry Beckett, David Hood, and me. Well, Rick had given us an office over at his studio. We couldn't even decide on where to hang a picture on the wall! So Jimmy and I bought the studio

ROGER HAWKINS

Roger Hawkins at Muscle Shoals Sound Studio, early 1970s

without telling David and Barry because, right or wrong, we didn't want any input—we just wanted to do it. But, before we bought the studio we went to Jerry Wexler and asked him if he would go with us if we made this move. Jerry said he'd give us his support providing Barry and David were involved. So they came in for a twenty-thousand-dollar-a-year guarantee. We borrowed twenty thousand from Atlantic Records to get an eight-track machine in there.

How did you arrange financing? You guys were so young, twenty-one years old or so.

Fred Bevis believed in us so much that he signed the note with us. There was about fourteen or fifteen thousand dollars owed on what he had. So Jimmy and I gave him our life savings, which was three or four thousand dollars apiece, and he went on the note with us. We made the arrangement with Barry and David, then made the arrangement with Jerry Wexler and we were in business.

Did making that move change your life?

No, it didn't, because what we would do—and still do, as a matter of fact—is only take money from the sessions that we make. We would never have gotten state-of-the-art equipment if we had taken salaries from the studio time. We always turned it back in and updated the equipment and tried to keep the studio competitive with others in the area. The money that we made was in production or playing, nothing from our business.

What are the individual responsibilities of the four of you?

It's pretty loose. Jimmy takes care of the engineering pretty much. David books the studio. Barry has been busy with his productions. When Barry started producing, the rhythm section didn't play together as much, and it still doesn't play together as much. But his success only helps us. When Barry records, where do you think he records?

You know, talking with studio drummers, I've noticed that today they'll be into one thing, and six months later, they're into something else. Different artists with different styles demand versatility from a drummer. Do you think the key to success in the studio is an ability to adapt?

I do, but it's not like it's engraved in granite. You can't be conscious of that, otherwise it will make you nervous. At least it does for me. I never walk into a studio and make a mental note that I'm gonna adapt to whatever is going on. I just kind of let that come naturally. I don't have any rules whatsoever. I just naturally adapt to it.

Some of your best work was with the Staple Singers. "Heavy Makes You Happy," "Respect Yourself," and "I'll Take You There" are a few songs. You got into a style of playing the side stick snare. You were playing conga parts, clave parts, and you'd play the bell of the cymbal. How did this develop?

I think it developed in 1971 or 1972. Right around '69 and '70 we had already attained recognition; we had played on hit records, and people were coming up and saying, "Oh man, you're the greatest!" Well, by that time, and I'll speak for myself, I had become a "hip" studio player. At that point I don't think I was even sweating anymore. So Chris Blackwell, president of Island Records, comes down and we do "Sitting in Limbo," by Jimmy Cliff. We did "The Harder They Come" too. Then we went on the road with Stevie Winwood and Traffic in 1972. We went on a U.S. and European tour, and I guess just being with those guys and being exposed to the reggae thing had a big influence on me. So we came back and recorded with the Staple Singers. On tracks like "I'll Take You There," you really couldn't use the bass on two and four like real reggae, but I found you could put a lot of its little statements in and keep the bass drum on one and three. I think Americans move their asses to one and three. But we started emulating some reggae licks. That, plus the tour with Traffic, got me out of the "cool session player" head and back into being a musician. Even though a lot of the stuff we did wasn't great and wasn't right, it was loose and it sure was a helluva lot of fun. I don't think I've ever forgotten that. It reintroduced me to the *vibe*, if you know what I mean. I don't ever want *that* to leave me again. That's what the Staple Singers' record had—a good vibe. "I'll Take You There" is probably my most favorite track that I've ever played on.

With a new song, how would you pick out a basic beat?

I don't really look for anything at first. I imagine that the song is finished already and I imagine that I'm hearing the finished product on a small car speaker. And then what should be played somehow comes to mind. Many years ago I thought of just the drums, but I try to look at things overall now. Jerry Wexler once said to me, "You know what you do? You *produce* the drum part." I said, "Yeah, well, I guess that's it." I'm just really drumming off memories of drum parts, memories of other records. When Hal Blaine was really doing it with all of his tom-toms, you know, and the song that I was recording lent itself to a Hal Blaine style, I would actually imagine that I was Hal Blaine sitting there.

Tell me how you came to work with Paul Simon on "Kodachrome."

He had heard the Staple Singers' stuff, and I heard that he called Al Bell, president of Stax Records, to see if he could use those same musicians. He didn't know we were completely disengaged from Stax. Al put him in touch with us, and he came down and recorded. The first day, we did three or four songs within eight hours. It just amazed Paul, because he was used to working six or eight days on one song.

What was Paul's approach?

He let *us* pick the tunes that we wanted to play on. It was a smart thing to do. I mean, if you go to record with players you really don't know, you just start running some songs down and see what they like.

There's a very interesting drum part in that song. It's a very fast, galloping kind of figure. I can't tell if it's a hi-hat that you use or not.

It's a tape box—an overdubbed tape box. It's just a box that tape comes in. I played it with drumsticks. Paul had a lot to do with that. We experimented with a few boxes to find the right one, one that sounded the way he wanted to hear it.

There's a story that Paul gave you a tape of just guitar and voices for "Loves Me Like a Rock" and he said, "See what you can come up with for this one."

That's right. He wanted us to put instruments on the tape, so we did. David and I overdubbed on the tape. I think it was the second time through that we got it. Now, if you listen to the record, it really drags terribly toward the fade. The tempo goes down drastically.

Most people wouldn't notice that. But being the drummer—

I noticed it. And the reason I noticed it was because I didn't want anyone to think that I was the drummer who made the tempo go down the stairsteps.

You hit these bass drum bumps—I guess you know what I'm referring to.

Yeah, when Paul sings "Loves me like a rock..." there's a hole there to do something, and I thought, "Well, shit, maybe the bass drum would sound like a rock." A lot of times the lyrics of the song just dictate what you should play.

I'm curious about your tuning.

I don't tune for the drums much anymore because of the sophisticated equipment that's around today. I tune for the tape pretty much. Lots of times I've had my drums sounding great, but they just didn't sound good on tape. So I started adjusting to what sounds good on tape even though the drums get looser and looser and harder to play. But they sound full on the tape, and that's where it really counts.

You must have other studio work where once you get the drum track, that's it, the pressure's over. Then they spend the next month figuring out what the guitar part should be.

Yeah, they spend all that time making "great sounds." Then you hear the record back whenever the thing comes out and you hear all of these "note-playing fellows" sounding "just great." And you're stuck back in the past there on what you did that day, just to give them the pulse. To me, that's sickening. That's not music anymore. It's not a meeting of the minds. It's business.

In addition to being a drummer, you own a studio, you produce records, and you're part of the Muscle Shoals Rhythm Section. Lately the Section has been playing together. It must give you a good feeling.

It's the same feeling that it's always been. Whenever we sit down and play, that feeling is always there, and it always turns out good. I don't care if it's been six months since we played together. Playing with the same guys for so long, well, it's just really hard to impress Barry, David, or Jimmy because they've heard me do it before. And it's the same with them. I mean, if Barry plays a hot lick, I don't congratulate him; he's *supposed* to do that.

There was one point when everyone was getting busy individually, and I wondered if we had the magic anymore. But we do. It still happens every time we play. I don't know what it is, but when the four of us sit down to play, it's almost like a burden's been lifted from our shoulders. It's like, "Hey, we're home."

SELECTED DISCOGRAPHY

Singles

WITH WILSON PICKETT

"Land of 1,000 Dances" (September 1966, Atlantic)
"Mustang Sally" (December 1966, Atlantic)

WITH PERCY SLEDGE

"When a Man Loves a Woman" (May 1966, Atlantic)

WITH ARETHA FRANKLIN

"Respect" (January 1967, Atlantic)
"(Sweet Sweet Baby) Since You've Been Gone" (May 1969, Atlantic)

WITH THE STAPLE SINGERS

"Heavy Makes You Happy (Sha-Na-Boom Boom)" (April 1971, Stax)
"Respect Yourself" (December 1971, Stax)
"I'll Take You There" (May 1972, Stax)

WITH PAUL SIMON

"Kodachrome" (July 1973, Columbia)
"Loves Me Like a Rock" (September 1973, Columbia)

WITH ROD STEWART

"Sailing" (November 1975, Warner Bros.)

WITH BOB SEGER

"Night Moves" (March 1977, Capitol)

Albums

WITH PERCY SLEDGE

The Best of Percy Sledge (1969, Atlantic)

WITH BOB SEGER

Stranger in Town (1978, Capitol)
Against the Wind (1980, Capitol)

WITH BOZ SCAGGS

Boz Scaggs (1969, Atlantic)

"Pretty" Purdie

5

". . . With Aretha? I was there. Oh man, it was nice; the air was light; I was floating in seventh heaven."

ONE OF MY FAVORITE "Pretty" Purdie stories is told by my friend Shelly Yakus. Shelly is the recording engineer responsible for the big drum sound of Jimmy Iovine's productions and was an assistant engineer back in the sixties. He recalls a session for which Purdie was booked. His drums were set up before his arrival, and just as the date was ready to roll, Purdie swaggered in and surveyed the studio. He had a briefcase with him, and from it he took out and unfolded a large sign. Without saying a word, he walked over to his drum kit and hung the sign on the wall behind it. The sign boasted something like, IF YOU WANT HITS, CALL PURDIE.

Some of the other musicians on the date got a load of the sign and said, "What's this shit?" It follows that one cat went over to the sign while Purdie was out of the room and turned it around. FUCK YOU, it said on the other side.

Purdie's sign told the truth. When Bernard Purdie sat down to play, he came up with the grooves. From his first million-seller in 1962, Les Cooper's "Wiggle Wobble," to today, Purdie's drumming has always been direct, heartfelt, and funky. As Roger Hawkins said, "Purdie's soul drumming is great soul drumming."

Although he has played with such stylistically diverse leaders as

Dizzy Gillespie, Gato Barbieri, Steely Dan, and Jeff Beck, Pretty Purdie made his mark supporting such important R&B artists as James Brown, Aretha Franklin, and the great soul saxophonist King Curtis. For all these artists Purdie provided the stability of the studio sideman while still injecting a generous portion of his own distinct personality.

Purdie knows how and when to make his move. Listen to "Memphis Soul Stew" from King Curtis's album *Live at the Fillmore West*. Jerry Jemmott, the bass player, pumps the bottom as the King calls out the recipe: "Gimme some of those fatback drums!" Purdie's on it before the end of his introduction, rolling off and strutting his stuff.

That show was notable because it featured not only King Curtis and his backup band, the Kingpins, but also Aretha Franklin as headliner. Aretha performed brilliantly that night [her performance can be found on her *Live at the Fillmore West*]. Her cuts are classics: "Respect," "Spirit in the Dark" (with guest Ray Charles), and her stirring rendition of "Bridge over Troubled Water." Aretha's voice soars, and it's easy to imagine Purdie himself rising along with the music.

Purdie always loved playing behind Aretha and he thinks he's done some of his best work with her. The proof is on her 1971 hit single "Rock Steady," one of my all-time favorite songs. "Let's call this song exactly what it is!" Aretha wails. And in the song Purdie introduced a lick that was copied and expanded upon by drummers all over the world.

It's become known as the hi-hat "bark." You know it when you hear it: three short "barks"—*psst, psst, psst*—on the hi-hat. In "Rock Steady" it occurs at the end of the stop time breaks toward the end of the song. This is Purdie's moment, and he strikes a four-bar solo that hits right on the money. You can hear how he turns the beat around for two beats in the fourth bar and then cuts loose with his "bark" and then, ever so coolly, he's back to the beat for the fade.

Purdie drummed on James Brown's biggest and baddest hits: "Papa's Got a Brand New Bag—Part 1" (1965); "I Got You (I Feel Good)" (1966); and "Cold Sweat—Part 1" (1967). On that last one, right before the final fadeout, you'll hear Purdie pull off a quick offbeat lick that cuts perfectly. As they say, "tain't no big thang"; just Purdie being pretty.

Purdie and I discussed a variety of subjects, not all of them musical. His recollections of working with Motown Records are enlightening, for they not only indicate how extensive and varied that work was, but also explain some of the mysteries about those sessions. Some of what Purdie has to say is controversial, to say the least. And the value of Purdie's surprising account of events involving certain English groups is left for the reader to judge.

I first met Bernard Purdie and became his student at a time in my life when I had no money, no car, and had moved back to my parents' home. My bright adolescent dream of making it big was turning to a darker reality. But Purdie's teaching went beyond drumming and eased my transition into adulthood. He helped me to understand the importance of taking and accepting responsibility. "This is hard work, boy," he'd say, and he made me work to find my own way. He taught me about the role of the drummer, about how to help my fellow players achieve *their* best. He showed me how to listen, not only with my ears but with my heart.

Young drummers are always told that it is *very* important to maintain a positive attitude. You know, keep smiling when the engineer's on your case or when the tempo's moving around and "you've got to keep it in the pocket." Well, it's all true, and for me, Purdie has the last word on the subject: "An ugly drummer makes ugly music." With a perspective like that, it's no wonder he's called "Pretty" Purdie.

MAX: *When we met I was at a point where I had no direction. My dream of the big break was slowly vanishing, and I didn't have the experience to get better gigs.*

PURDIE: That's saying it like it was!

But I met a singer, Dolores Hall, who had been working on Broadway and recording her first album. She told me to come to a session and meet this drummer she'd been working with. I asked her who it was and she said, Purdie. "Pretty Purdie?" I asked. She nodded; I was in awe. So she brought me to the session. I was sitting in the back; you didn't even know I was there. I was amazed at what I saw. I had just turned twenty-one, and the confidence you exuded completely impressed me. It was the first time I'd ever seen a drummer take control like you did.

It was my band!

No doubt about it! I went up to you after the session and said, "Hey, how are you doing?" And you said, "Pretty." I asked you if you gave lessons and you said you sure did. So you gave me the particulars and told me to come on down. It was a real important meeting for me. Your method of teaching was like finding yourself through drumming. I came to you like a lump of clay—"Mold me, do something with me."

But do you also remember this—that when I met you, I didn't say anything and I let you talk. You told me what was on your mind. You ran down everything you knew, what you were all about. You also ran down your technical experience, how you were able to read music and how long you'd been playing. So it didn't make sense to me to go into technical things with you because you had already done it for ten years. You could read, but you couldn't interpret. Your biggest problem was that you didn't understand what you were doing or where you were going. You needed direction.

You said my problem was attitude. And I didn't know what you were talking about.

Of course you didn't. You thought you knew it all. You told me about how much you had learned and knew about music. So I asked you, "Why are you here?" And you said, "Well, I've watched you play. I like your playing and I like your command of the instrument." Then I said to you, "Sure, you like it. That's what I was trained for." You see, my attitude was in the right place. But you had a very negative attitude and music style. I wasn't interested in your personal problems, but apparently you had them too. I got into everybody's personal problems before it was all over because we had to create this thing between us. The first thing you started talking to me about was your girlfriend. It happens with everybody, every student I had. It took me ten to fifteen minutes to get past the girlfriend to get down to what we had to do. But it was cool. I went through it before you did and I knew what it was like. A teacher can't just turn off that stuff.

As far as I was concerned, you had the ability to be a big-name drummer, a sustaining drummer. You had all the qualifications of being a studio drummer too. You had the training, but you had to learn how to put it to use. You had to get rid of the thing where you told your teacher you knew more than he did.

That's what I did? (Laughs.)

Ummhmm.

I learned from you that the basics were most important, and that I had to become a group player.

That's right.

We all have a person who helped us learn the things we needed to learn. I recall you mentioning a Mr. Haywood. Was he one of your early influences and teachers?

Leonard Haywood was my music teacher in Maryland, where I grew up. He was also the drummer for a Big Band. It was a dance band—the Clive Bessicks Orchestra. What I used to do was get Mr. Haywood drunk on the nights he had to play. I had the gin and he'd drink it, and by the time midnight rolled around he was wasted. So I would end up playing and finishing the gig. He knew what was up. But he let me play my little game. If he didn't drink, he was the baddest drummer in the whole world.

What was it about him that made him great?

He was a timekeeper. He used to teach, and every Thursday I would be there at his house all day. I had no money to pay for any lessons, so I would sit on the steps of his house while he was giving lessons inside. This started when I was seven or eight years old. When I was ten, one of the students he had was playing, and he wanted me to show this kid how to play something. Now, he's only had this boy but a year. What Mr. Haywood did for that boy inside a year would choke a mule. Mr. Haywood told me to leave after that. He said, "When you come back here next week, if you don't play better than this boy, don't ever come back!" I went home and practiced every day with whatever I could practice on. I didn't have drums of my own. I practiced beating my hands on tin cans, whatever I could find, all day long. I came back the next week, and I was every bit ready. I wanted to show Mr. Haywood I was better than that student of his. Well, Mr. Haywood let me play for three minutes and then told me to go and sit down. He didn't waste any time. He knew I had practiced.

I remember after I had been studying with you for a while it began to sink in. I'd come in, and you'd make me play to see if I was practicing. I was playing a lot back then, but I wasn't into practicing.

You played your ass off. You always could. But I would say, "You didn't do your damn homework." And you'd look at me as if to say, "How the hell did he know that?" It was all over your face.

I remember I did something to you one day. I told you I could play rings around you. And you were so upset with me that you went home and you practiced. You came back the following week and played your butt off. So I said, "Oh, you've been practicing?" I was so frustrated with you, I could have killed you! I must have told you ten times to leave and don't come back, remember? I'd say, "Get out! I don't want to see you here no more!" I'd be so mad at you because in you I saw me. I too was arrogant. I too was Mr. Know-It-All.

I remember bringing a tape to you that I had made with a band in 1972. I thought I played great. You cut it to shreds. I mean, I set myself up for it.

You sure did! (Laughs.) When I finished with you I went downstairs and told Iris, my secretary, "Well, I guess Max won't be back anymore. I think I finally got through to him." She said, "What did you do to him?" Well, I told her. I said, "I told it to him like it was. He thought his do-do didn't stink."

That tape was really bad.

It was horrible! You missed the fills. You never completed two of them. You never completed the fills!

(Laughs.) Boy, you're really giving it to me! But let's talk about your drum style.

What I play is melody drums. I play the song. Playing the notes that are in the song on the different drums so people can understand what you're doing. It's not just a lot of bing-bang, bing-bang. I actually play and accent—breathe with the drums. And I play for my audience.

You've always been successful playing behind sax players.

A saxophone, to me, is a lead voice. I play best with lead instruments, mostly vocals. My next best playing is behind a horn player, mostly sax.

You were in King Curtis's band, the Kingpins. What was working with Curtis like?

It was wonderful. There was always space, always room to do your thing. Curtis gave me the opportunity to play a twelve-bar or sixteen-bar solo, which was long enough for me to get into something sweet, and short enough not to get boring. That's all I ever wanted.

Curtis bridged the gap between jazz and pop for a lot of musicians. You had players like Jerry Jemmott, the bass player, and Cornell Dupree—

Richard Tee played piano. We had Billy Preston on organ, Donny Hathaway, Paul Griffin on piano too.

That rhythm section of you, Jerry, and Richard Tee was incredibly hot.

Every rhythm section Curtis ever had was incredibly hot.

Another successful gig for you was with James Brown in the sixties.

Yeah, but we went through some changes.

What do you mean?

Oh, he fired me because of my arrogance. You see, I got accused of making a mistake onstage, so I got fined. But it wasn't me that made the mistake. I told him I'd pay the money this time, but it was not me who made the mistake. And I refused to tell him who did it. As far as I was concerned, it was his job to find out. You see, you didn't make mistakes when you played with James Brown. You'd make a mistake while he was singing, and he'd turn around and say, "Ten dollars." I was mad, so I said to Brown, "I'll do your records, but I ain't going on the road with you because you were wrong for what you did."

We didn't speak for a year. He respected me, but he wouldn't tell me that. So what happened, two years later, his hit records stopped coming. One day Sammy Lowe, an arranger, called me and wanted me to do a session. I said sure. But he didn't tell me it was a James Brown session. So I get there at the session and Brown doesn't show up. It's seven o'clock and we were ready to hit. I had a twenty-three piece band—ten rhythm and thirteen horns. All the music was written out. So we went over a couple of the songs, but nobody really got into it. Finally James comes in at eight o'clock and says, "Let's go." And he walks over to me and says, "Okay, Purdie, here's your chance." I said, "Now, James, why'd you say that?" I went up to Sammy Lowe and said, "Mr. Lowe, I want you to forgive me tonight because I'm gonna show my ass." He said, "Purdie, you do whatever you got to do, but just play the music." As soon as Sammy went to make the two-bar countoff, just when he got to one of the next bar, I was into it. That particular song was "Kansas City." That night we recorded six songs that all became million sellers. I mean James came back to me and apologized. He even asked me that night about going out on the road. So I told him, "Yeah, I'll go out with you, but I want a thousand dollars a week, all expenses paid, first-class tickets, and I need ten thousand in advance to cover my debts and pay my bills. And you also got to sign a five-year contract."

He screamed, "But I'm James Brown!" And I said, "And I'm Pretty Purdie, and you asked *me*." So that was how we became the best of friends.

"Cold Sweat" and "Papa's Got a Brand New Bag" were two of James Brown's greatest records.

Yeah, and we're all a little prejudiced for that time because those are the records that all the new guys are learning from; that's what everyone goes back to.

Those records crossed over where white kids picked up on them. I believe you were the first to play those sst-sst *hi-hat "barks."*

I did that with demos like "High Heel Sneakers" ["Out of Sight" by James Brown].

Demos that became masters?

Yeah. I did it on "He's So Fine," the song some other drummer took credit for. This guy started naming all the songs that he had done with all the different groups; half of the songs that he did in the sixties I had to fix up—go in and overdub. It was just a job for me.

What did you do? I don't quite understand. Would they wipe out the drums entirely?

Whenever they could, they would, otherwise you'd go right over it.

There seems to be a lot of confusion over who played what.

That's all right. But a lot of it *is* known because of the payment of money. There's a record of it in the union files. That's how I discovered that I've been on over three thousand albums. Now, I didn't say three thousand sessions; it could have been fifteen or twenty thousand. I don't know how many sessions. But I can go back and find out because it's been documented. I can go to the union and find out how much money was paid to me for all these different records, take a few weeks and compile it all together, and I'd know how many sessions I'd played on from 1960.

Being the premier black session drummer in the sixties—

Watch it, watch it (laughs). But I wasn't there first. Panama Francis was number one. He was at Atlantic in the fifties.

My question is if you would know whether all *the Motown records were recorded in Detroit?*

Of course I would.

Did you play on any of that stuff?

I played on five hundred tracks. Right in New York at A-1 Studios.

Why would Motown record at A-1 Studios in New York?

Money. They paid demo wage here in New York. All that belonged to Jobete Music [the music publishing division of Motown]. All of those tracks. All the stuff that was done in New York was sent out to Detroit. All they were doing was fixing up the tracks. The drummer that died—

Benny Benjamin.

Yeah. There's no way he could have done two or three thousand tracks.

You know, when you listen to those records, there's such a consistency of style. For example, that intro pick-up. I've heard conflicting stories: One was that they tried to get drummers to play Benny Benjamin's particular style because he was Motown's first drummer. They needed

"You see, you didn't make mistakes when you played with James Brown. You'd make a mistake when he was singing, and he'd turn around and say, 'Ten dollars.'"

other drummers because, from what I've been told, Benny was a very sick guy.

He was a junkie. But that didn't stop him from being a fabulous drummer.

Naturally he's got the reputation for playing on all those great Motown records.

That's cool with me.

Were the songs you played on finished songs?

They were demos, but they were finished songs.

Do you mean they used these demos for masters?

Of course they used them for masters. That was the way it was in the sixties. "Mercy, Mercy" by Don Covay was a demo.

So what you're saying is that the demos were released as master recordings.

That's right. The demos that we were doing at that time we got paid ten dollars apiece for. Doris Troy's "Just One Look" —ten dollars.

Finished records, and they were paying you demo wage. If the Motown sound was Detroit, why did they cut so many of the records in New York?

They couldn't find anybody to play the way we did and as good as we did, so they used the demos. You get a record that's happening and you can't duplicate it, so you have to go and use the original.

Why didn't Motown fly you out to Detroit to cut a master of a song that originally you did a demo of back in New York?

Why should they bother? We'd cut it once. They knew they wouldn't get anything better than the demo. And we made the demos in New York, not Detroit, because Jobete was at 1619 Broadway.

I see. You were making publisher *demos.*

Right. And we were doing this every day from about 1962 to 1965.

In New York, there was a change from the singing groups, who would need back-up musicians, to self-contained groups that could play their own instruments, write their own songs, even produce themselves. How did this shift cut into the studio scene in the sixties?

It didn't, not until the seventies. Many of the sixties groups had studio bands doing their recording for them. We'd imitate their sound. But we'd play it better than they ever could.

Take a band like the Rolling Stones or the Beatles, English bands that were extremely successful. Now, they wouldn't have studio musicians—

Yes, they did. Because in the beginning, their *music* was wrong.

What do you mean "wrong"?

The drums, the time—it was way off. That's why I played on their songs.

You played on Beatles' tracks?

Twenty-one of them.

Do you remember which ones?

Ummhmm.

Which ones?

That's information I don't disclose.

Why won't you name the tracks?

Because if I need that information to get me some money, then I'll have what's necessary. I also played on songs by the Animals, the Monkees—

Everyone knows the Monkees was a fabricated band. But the Beatles—

Ringo never played on anything.

Ringo never played on anything?

Not the early Beatles stuff.

If what you're saying is true, tell me how you got involved with the Beatles.

I just worked on tracks that came to the United States from England. All I did was just straighten them up.

You can't say who brought the tapes of the Beatles songs over to America?

The guy that's dead.

Brian Epstein, the Beatles' manager?

Yeah, Epstein. But nobody knew what was going on. There were no names on anything. The only person who knew what was what was the engineer.

Who was the engineer?

Well, we don't want to get into that.

But it's an important part of your story.

Of course it is, but that's the only legs I have to make any money out of anything, because eventually it's gonna be brought out. One of these years I'm gonna make me some big money.

So the Beatles would bring—

The Beatles had nothing to do with it. They weren't here in New York. This is Epstein I'm talking about. Epstein was the one who brought the stuff here with the engineer.

If no one said to you that the songs were from the Beatles, how did you find out it was them?

I got paid twice. I got paid to keep my mouth shut the second time. They paid me for my month's work, for working on the tracks. Two or three weeks later, Epstein called and said, "Listen, I don't want this business getting out on the street." And I said, "What are you talking about?" He said he wanted reassurance that I'd keep my mouth shut. He said, "And I think this will reassure it." He handed me a check. . . ."

"I got paid twice. I got paid to keep my mouth shut the second time."

So your story is that the drums had to be redone on those early Beatles records. Ringo didn't play on all those incredibly exciting tracks. But since you won't disclose what tracks they are, let me ask you this: Did you do this with any other bands in the sixties?

I did it with the Monkees and the Animals, like I already said, and one or two things with the Rolling Stones.

Bernard, that is an incredible story. Let's leave this and continue with something we touched on before.

Fine by me.

When you look back to the days you played with James Brown and the other soul greats, do you still see them as the highlights in your career?

Oh, definitely. They were some of the greatest times I've had. I don't think I'll ever have it like that again. I was doing everything I ever wanted to do.

You played with Aretha Franklin too. I know that you thought the world of her. But just when things were going great with her, you and Aretha parted ways. Did you have a falling-out with her?

That's the reason I split—so we wouldn't have a falling-out. I didn't want money to ruin our relationship. I said, "I'll love ya to death, but I'm not gonna let money get between us, so I'll leave." I cried many nights because I loved that woman. When that woman sang—it was heaven to me. Every time she sang, it was like she was singing to *me*. That's how I felt. Nobody ever did that for me. And all the singers I work with know. I tell them that if they can reach where Aretha went, I tell them to go right ahead. Because if they do, I'm gonna let them know. I'm still lookin' for somebody else who could do it for me like Aretha, but I've never been able to reach that same high. I was *there*. Oh man, it was nice; the air was light; I was floating in seventh heaven.

You played with Aretha, King Curtis, and Ray Charles at the Fillmore West in San Francisco, the night they recorded those classic live albums. Would you tell me about that night?

The first night we played, we all showed off, the whole rhythm section. Saturday night we got a little better. Then came Sunday night. Well, Sunday night we had a press party. Now at this press party Ray Charles shows up. He wanted to meet Aretha Franklin, since he had never met her before. He said, "I want to *see* her for myself." I used to laugh when he said things like that.

Well, after the press party, it was time for the show. Eight o'clock and we do King Curtis with his Kingpins. We were supposed to play forty-five minutes, but we got carried away and played for an hour and twenty minutes. That made up his album, *Live at the Fillmore West*.

After his set we were supposed to take a five-minute break and bring on Aretha. But Aretha was so upset that we had no break.

What was she upset about?

We played too long. She wanted to sing and get out there on stage.

"PRETTY" PURDIE

Pretty Purdie with Aretha and King Curtis at the Fillmore West, 1971

So we got no break. Her show was normally an hour, but she got happy. She goes off while we're doing "Spirit in the Dark," but then she comes back onstage. Ray Charles was in the wings. The whole place is screaming "Aretha, Aretha!" and the next thing you know, you hear a "Whoa!" Aretha yells, "I found Ray Charles, y'all!" And the Fillmore West went wild. You could feel the place moving. The sound was deafening. Deafening! I'm saying to myself, "What is happening?" I thought the place would crumble from all the noise any second.

Well, Aretha comes out and starts singing, and Ray Charles comes up to the microphone and starts singing with Aretha. All of a sudden he turns around and yells, "Purdie! Bring it down. Bring it down to half time, Purdie." So "whap, whap"—two shots: I cut it, you know. By this time Curtis, he's coming back. He starts playing a little more saxophone. And while they're making this transition, Ray goes around and sits at the piano, and Aretha sits down next to him. And they get into this thing, "The Spirit in the Dark." Curtis was out playing his little thing, and Ray Charles yells, "I got it, Curtis." I said to myself, "Oh man, this is going to be a long one." I had to readjust myself, get the groove. But I had to psych myself. After two and a half hours, I was a tired motorcycle.

Those songs you played with Aretha are really classics. Has there ever been a time in the last twenty years that you haven't played?

Sure. I went through a change where I was producing records. It turned me around. It was bad for me. It was good for me to get it out of my system while I still had enough time to get back into playing. But it was bad that I had stopped playing for a couple of years. Now I know what playing does for me. I know where it takes me and how it makes me feel. My goals now are the complete opposite of what they were twenty years ago. I'm looking for peace of mind these days. I went through a lot of changes that I didn't have to go through; all I really had to do was be cool. But I've grown up too, Max. Just like you did. I know my responsibilities now and I don't mind taking them.

Purdie, there's one last thing I wanted to ask you: What ever happened to the sign you used to hang up behind you whenever you did a session?

Oh, I still have it.

What exactly does it say?

"Pretty Purdie: If you need me, call me—the little old hitmaker."

SELECTED DISCOGRAPHY

Singles

WITH LES COOPER

"Wiggle Wobble" (December 1962, Everlast)

WITH DON COVAY

"Mercy, Mercy" (October 1964, Rosemart)

WITH JAMES BROWN

"Out of Sight" (September 1964, Smash)
"Papa's Got a Brand New Bag—Part 1" (September 1965, King)
"I Got You (I Feel Good)" (December 1965, King)
"Cold Sweat—Part 1" (August 1967, King)

WITH ARETHA FRANKLIN

"Rock Steady" (November 1971, Atlantic)
"Day Dreaming" (August 1972, Atlantic)
"Until You Come Back to Me—That's What I'm Gonna Do" (December 1973, Atlantic)

WITH STEELY DAN

"Kid Charlemagne" (July 1976, ABC)
"Deacon Blues" (June 1978, ABC)

Albums

WITH ARETHA FRANKLIN

Live at Fillmore West (1971, Atlantic)

WITH KING CURTIS

Live at Fillmore West (1971, Atco)

WITH GATO BARBIERI

Yesterdays (1974, Flying Dutchman)

WITH STEELY DAN

Aja (1977, ABC)

WITH DIZZY GILLESPIE

Dizzy Gillespie at Montreux (1980, Pablo)

Hal Blaine

6

"My attitude was that I never went into a session that I didn't want a hit. . . . I got hungry for gold records."

IF HAL BLAINE had played drums only on the Ronettes' "Be My Baby," his name would still be forever uttered with reverence and respect for the power of his big beat.

But "Be My Baby," however stirring, is but one of literally hundreds of hits Hal Blaine appears on. During the sixties, Hal was, undoubtedly, the busiest, most recorded, and most successful studio drummer on the West Coast. His sound and style captured the imagination of the recording industry, particularly the producers, songwriters, and musicians. Drummers all over L.A. aspired to the standards Hal established, and these drummers emulated his approach. Jim Keltner, himself a legend, explained this phenomenon: "If you wanted to work in L.A. at that time, you had to sound like Hal Blaine."

Someone once said that there are probably fewer people for whom Hal hasn't drummed than those for whom he has. His list of credits is both long and impressive. The discography of his work that appears at the end of this chapter shows just how prodigious and varied his work has been.

The classic Hal Blaine sound is the one he produced in the course of his work with the Mamas and the Papas, the Fifth Dimension, and the various rock and folk rock groups with whom he recorded in the sixties. His popping snare, glittering cymbals, and tasteful fills and accents propelled the Byrds' "Mr. Tambourine Man" (1965), the Mamas and the Papas' "California Dreamin' " (1966), and the Fifth Dimension's "Up, Up and Away" (1967), to name a few. Arguably, Hal has placed more hits at the top of the *Billboard* charts than any other session drummer before or after he began recording.

In 1962 Hal was booked on a session that began one of the most successful and important musical relationships of his career. Hired to play on the Crystals' "He's a Rebel," he began a long-lasting association with the tune's twenty-two-year-old producer, Phil Spector.

Spector was breaking new ground with his style of rock & roll production. Inspired by the symphonies of Wagner and the straight-rocking of Chuck Berry, Spector's "Wall of Sound" and tight arrangements gave Hal the opportunity to achieve the most in big-beat power. This was really Hal's first experience creating his own sound. Unlike most studio drummers, who tuned their drums tight, as a jazz drummer would, Hal lowered his tunings so his drums sounded like cannons.

The atmosphere in Spector's studio proved a great training ground for the musicians he employed. Dubbed the Wrecking Crew, this studio group included Hal, Steve Douglas on sax; Carole Kaye, Ray Pohlman, and Joe Osborne on bass; Al Delory, Leon Russell, and Don Randi on keyboards; Barney Kessel, Tommy Tedesco, and Glen Campbell on guitars; Sonny Bono on percussion; and arranger Jack Nitzsche. Spector had a sound in his head and these musicians translated it into hits—"He's a Rebel" (1962), "Da Doo Ron Ron" (1963), "Then He Kissed Me" (1963) by the Crystals, and the phenomenal "Be My Baby" (1963), "Walking in the Rain" (1964) and "Baby I Love You" (1964) by the Ronettes. The excitement never waned.

As a young drummer, one of my favorite groups was the Beach Boys. I used to spend hours playing to their records. The beats were simple and the grooves were steady. I'd seen them in concert and always thought that the late Dennis Wilson was an exciting drummer. I didn't know back then that Hal played on most of those Beach Boys records.

Shortly after the success of their first record, "Surfin' Safari," the Beach Boys, with Brian Wilson in charge, decided to use the same band on their records that Phil Spector used. Brian was greatly influenced by Phil's approach, and adding his own shimmering layers of harmonies and surf-inspired sound, he produced his own pop masterpieces.

The Beach Boys' signature sound has always featured sweet, multipart harmony vocals over dense, wavelike rhythms. Hal was a great interpreter of Brian's ideas, and on songs such as "Surfin' U.S.A." (1963), "Fun, Fun, Fun," "I Get Around," "Dance, Dance, Dance" (all 1964), and the classic "Good Vibrations" (1966), he always seemed able to conjure up the one lick, fill, or effect that perfected the sound. Some of his best work is found on those records.

There's little else to say about Hal Blaine that the music itself doesn't communicate. I recall in 1970 reading an impressive magazine article on the business of rock & roll recording. There was a piece on Hal. It spoke of his two and three "traveling" drum sets, his passion for collecting antique Rolls-Royces, and his lofty six-figure income.

But I'll tell you something that impressed me even more. Eleven years later, our band played Wembley Arena, near London. After the show, while we were all relaxing backstage, Bruce asked me to come into his dressing room. I went in, he pointed to the wall and said, "Look at that." I looked at the wall but didn't see anything except peeling wallpaper. "Look closer," he said. Finally, I got right down to the spot he was pointing to, and right there, in a crack in the paper, rubber-stamped on the wall, it said HAL BLAINE STRIKES AGAIN.

MAX: *How did that stamp come about?*

HAL: I always stamp my charts. And there is a reason why I started that; it wasn't all ego. It did become that years later because drummers from all over the world would say, "Hey, man, I played that part where you recorded with Sinatra," or whatever. I'd get a lot of show drummers writing me or calling me from various places—Vegas, Atlantic City—that they had just played a Paul Anka show or some recording sessions and saw my stamp. When I first ventured into Twentieth Century-Fox, I did a session. We went there and did something, I forget what it was, but I had a callback to overdub some stuff a couple of days later. When I walked in, there must have been five hundred pieces of music in a pile and the problem was, "Hal, find your original parts. We need to add something to them." It took forever to go through that music to find my original drum parts. So from that day on I started signing my parts in heavy black in the upper left-hand corner. I would just sign my name as a reference so that if it ever happened to me again, I could sit there and fan through the music, and the minute I saw my name I could pull that sheet. And it did happen.

Eventually I had a rubber stamp made up, and from that day on I've always stamped every piece of music I play, whether it's a demo or something I play at a friend's house. And that's how the stamp started.

I know much of your work today consists of movie and TV soundtrack sessions. The place I want to start is back when you did some of your first movie dates—with Elvis Presley.

I was just getting into recording then. I'd been playing with a band

and we went to Hollywood. It was there that I joined Tommy Sands, who, back in 1957 and 1958, was right under Elvis. He was King Number Two, a teen-age idol who married Nancy Sinatra. He was a superstar. So, I went on the road with him. From there I joined up with Patti Page, who was a Number One nightclub act, a wonderful lady. I love her to death. Well, working with Patti was a big break in my career because Patti's husband, Charles O'Curran, was Elvis's choreographer at Paramount. It was because of my relationship with Patti that her husband automatically called me to do Elvis's movies when the time came.

What were those sessions like?

To me, they were just more sessions. I didn't realize history was being made. It wasn't too long before Elvis's death that Joe Esposito told me Elvis's favorite record was "It's Now or Never," and I would imagine it was because of the operatic connotation—"O Sole Mio." I think Elvis, in his own way, felt a little inferior in the music business. I think he had an inferiority complex about his singing because of the rock & roll connotation of junk, garbage, unschooled music, and I think that "It's Now or Never"—"O Sole Mio," in effect—made him feel like he was doing something musically valid. And he was singing his butt off then.

Did he ever give the impression that he thought he was inferior?

No. He was confident. I just think that maybe he felt inferior down deep because of a lot of the bad publicity he'd gotten. You know, it's a strange thing. I remember being on the road with Simon and Garfunkel, doing concerts to standing room only. They'd come off the stage sweating, having done a wonderful show. The people are screaming and applauding. They want to tear their clothes off. They love them. And you get some schmuck in the corner who's mopping or sweeping, who had to work that Sunday night, and as you're running by this guy, he says, "What's all that crap about? You call that music?" And that puts the whammy on the whole night. All Paul or Artie would hear is that old geezer who hated what just went down, never mind that he's sixty years old, not in tune with what's going on, and had to work on a Sunday and couldn't be home drinking beer. They don't hear the thirty thousand they just entertained the shit out of. The point I'm making—the correlation between Elvis and that type of thing—is that deep down, when Elvis heard of some critic who said, "Well, he might be the King of Rock & Roll, but he still can't sing"—those are the reviews that stick, not the ones that say thirty thousand people were heavily entertained.

How did Elvis's sessions go down?

The sessions were simple. The first session I ever did with Elvis—it was a Hawaiian film. I was told to have a lot of Hawaiian stuff. I went to the drum shop and ordered everything that looked native to me. I didn't care if it was from India or Bali or Pakistan or wherever. They all became Hawaiian instruments, as far as anyone at Paramount was concerned. And when I came in with this array of stuff—I became the Hawaiian technical director.

The Wrecking Crew:
(1) Jay Migliori, sax;
(2) Lou Blackburn, trombone;
(3) Steve Douglas, sax;
(4) Roy Caton, trumpet;
(5) Al Delory, piano;
(6) Don Randi, piano;
(7) Phil Spector;
(8) unidentified;
(9) Hal Blaine;
(10) Jack Nitzsche, arranger;
(11) Ray Pohlman, bass;
(12) Lyle Ritz, bass;
(13) Sonny Bono, percussion

How did you actually get to appear onscreen in the Elvis movies?

I did a lot of those at various times. It was really a matter of being in the right place at the right time. Elvis was working with Charlie O'Curran, who I mentioned before. Charlie said something about putting a band together for some scenes in the movie using the band I had at the time: Jack Nitzsche was playing with me; Steve Douglas played saxophone. It was terrific fun.

These guys were part of the Wrecking Crew, the band on all the Spector stuff. When Spector came out here, he had this coterie of musicians, and he had this unique sound in his head. No one else ever produced records like that. What was working with Phil Spector like?

With Phil, you were putty in his hands. And that was part of it. One of the tricks that Phil used to do—still does—he used to hold me back. All of those sessions had one drummer—me. But there might be eleven guys playing percussion. I used to give Sonny Bono a cowbell to play. Anyone who came around the studio was handed something to play. Everybody had fun on Phil's dates. There was a sign that read, "Closed Session. Do Not Enter." But anyone that passed, Phil used to grab and drag him in the booth—put 'im to work. Every producer in town used to hang out the minute they heard there was a Friday-night Phil Spector session going on. That was part of Phil's philosophy—he got these guys who were tired, who worked all week. You were exhausted, but somehow you came in on a Friday night and you just busted your head for Phil. You just had to have a hit. It had to be solid gold. First of all, he was the first guy who came along who used more than one guitar. It always used to be one guitar, piano, bass, and drums. Phil was the first guy to use two, three, four guitars, two basses in unison, four piano players. Leon Russell would be sitting there, Al Delory, Don Randi. These guys were great piano players, and they'd all be on the same gig. Those Friday night sessions were parties and yet Phil didn't let you take a break, ever. Finally, you'd have to say, "Come on, Phil! I have to go to the toilet!"

Phil is the greatest director in the world. He had a way of holding you. He treated the musicians like race horses: "Don't play yet. Don't play yet." He would rehearse the guitar player for an hour. He would rehearse the bass fiddles. He'd rehearse the band. "Everybody play, but Hal, don't play. I'm getting a sound here." Then he would say. "Hal, play now!" In the booth it was like charades. He would say, "Watch me," and you'd read his lips. He would give you an "easy, easy," and then he would give you a "Go crazy!"

Like on those fades—

He said he was going to put out an album of fades some day. And I wish he would.

On "Be My Baby"—that fade is great. You build the tension through the whole song; and the release comes at just the right moment.

That's such a classic because of that beat—boom—ba—boom—CRACK! From that day forward it became a standard lick. And I can't really put my finger on how it happened. It probably was Phil who said, "I wanna hear the fourth beat EXPLODE!" And I accidentally did the quarter-note triplets on the end—*boom boom boom boom boom boom.* I somehow did the quarter-note triplets and Phil loved them. That became part of his tag. He couldn't fade the record until that quarter-note triplet happened. You'll hear that on every record. It was like Hitchcock being in a scene in each of his movies.

But they really were classic licks. To this day, when I'm doing a session, I will still see, once in a while, an arranger write "Spector," and I know what he's talking about. A lot of drummers I talk with will say, "I did a thing this afternoon and at letter F it said 'Hal Blaine's sound.' " It's a compliment. I recently got my 189th gold record. I'm hoping to hit two hundred.

Did Carole Kaye play bass on a lot of those tracks?

Yeah, Carole Kaye and also Joe Osborne, who was also such an incredible bass player. He still is, too. Joe is one of those guys that I have found through the years who knows how to sit back on something. I mean, you're looking down the railroad track, which is the tempo, but you can go a little faster to one side of the track or a little slower to the other side. That's the same train that's going down that track. Most drummers play on top of that track, which can make it very uncomfortable. It's the same tempo, but it's on top. Holding back on it was the thing that used to happen so well with Joe and I, especially when we played with Simon and Garfunkel. We all had that thing about laying just to the left of that track, keeping the right tempo, but still it was just a hair back that gave it that nice feel. We didn't have to think about it; just did it automatically. And when I work with various bands today, but not all bands, you have to *think* a lot about "let's lay back a little bit," 'cause you'll hear the producer say, "Guys, it's kind of on top. We wanna relax it a little bit." That's the key word—relax. It's a thing you *feel*.

Who were your early drum influences?

Who were my heroes? Gene Krupa. I grew up in that era—Krupa, Buddy Rich, Tiny Kahn. I was listening to all of the Big Bands. So naturally, I loved every drummer in every Big Band. I remember as a kid in Hartford, Connecticut, I got hold of a wind-up record player and I had old 78s from somewhere. You could really hear drum licks when the record would wind down and get slower. That probably influenced me, and I didn't realize it until just now, talking about it.

You've worked on both coasts. How does the work here in L.A. differ from New York?

Well, California musicians came into the studio out of the sunshine. They came to make a record and have fun. They were making money and having a ball doing it. The New York guys had nothing but shit trying to park, fighting with cabbies, dragging drums up nine flights to a studio. Just the whole feeling of California is reflected on the records. We had been on buses, in clubs, and on the road. All of a sudden we were released in a diamond mine here in California. But not only were we making the bucks, it was attitude. There was a phrase I coined some years ago: "If you smile, you stay around awhile. If you pop, you're out."

What sorts of changes have you seen over the years?

One of the things that's so funny today is you get young engineers who only know one form of drumming—LOUD. So when I come in on a session and I listen to a song, there are dynamics—it's paced out and beautiful, and I play it that way. The singer is talking about picking flowers for his girlfriend. Why would I be exploding my drums? It seems that every drummer who goes in today plays explosions. That's all these young engineers know—be it ballad or Beethoven. I'll never forget, I used to go to RCA when I was working with H. B. Barnum, who was a very fine arranger. H. B. liked me, liked my work, and gave me my first real recording sessions. I was doing Sam Cooke, some great people. I remember the engineer at RCA saying to me, "Listen man, what the hell are you doing? You're busting our needles in there, you're playing so goddamn loud. You see those mikes, sweetheart? We got microphones here. All you have to do is tap it very lightly. We'll get the loudness in there, don't worry about it." Now H. B. would say, "Uh-uh, baby. This guy's here because he plays the way we want him to play." This engineer used to refer to eggshells all the time. "Think of eggshells, man. We want you on eggshells out here." And I used to say, "Well, how in the hell can you play relaxed when you're thinking of eggshells? How can you walk on eggshells and be comfortable and relaxed? I know when to play soft. I play soft in the soft parts and loud in the loud parts." And H. B. used to say, "You better start listening to this drummer, because this is what's happening." It was H. B. who really stuck up for me in the early days

"Well, California musicians came into the studio out of the sunshine. They came to make a record and have fun. . . . The New York guys had nothing but shit trying to park, fighting with cabbies, dragging drums up nine flights to a studio."

when guys were saying, "Hey man, you're bending needles on us."

There's another reason why those records seem to be such great hits. Everybody and everything in the studio was tuned in to the record we were doing—the artist, the time of day and the time of year, the sunshine—everybody was in a very happy frame of mind. *That's how the California sound came to be.*

It was a teen sound made by adults.

We were all like kids and every one of us was over twenty-five. Except the Beach Boys—they were kids. But they were in awe of us because we were making the hits. The perfect example is the Tijuana Brass and "Taste of Honey," where the bass drum part was a fluke. The thing where we went *boom boom boom boom* was supposed to be an open break. But the band kept coming in wrong. On one of the takes I just slugged the bass drum all the way through, just kept the beat going as a gag and then brought in the brushes and *bang*, that was it. They said, "Wow, that's beautiful, leave it."

After the Beach Boys cut their first national hit single, "Surfin' Safari," they hired you and other studio players for their records. Why was it important to them to have you play drums and Steve Douglas, for instance, play sax?

Well, maybe because all we were interested in was making hit records. My attitude was that I never went into a session that I didn't want a hit because I got hungry for gold records. Terry Melcher with the Byrds spoiled me when I jokingly said, "Boy, I'd love a gold record." This is when we were cutting "Mr. Tambourine Man." He said, "You got it. If we have a hit, you guys will get a gold record." Of course, from then on I got greedy. If I was doing a session, I'd say, "Man, this smells like a hit. If we have a hit, can we get gold records?" They'd say, "Damn right."

You specialized in rhythmically interpreting the songs of musicians like Brian Wilson and Paul Simon in New York. How did working with Simon and Garfunkel compare to some of your other session work?

One of the most gratifying experiences was working with them both here in California and in New York. Anything you wanted to do for Paul and Artie and Roy Halee, you did it. You had carte blanche. And they always recorded it.

There's a great story about them sticking you in an elevator shaft for "The Boxer."

It wasn't *in* the shaft; it was in the hall right in front of the elevator. Have you ever heard the story about the elevator and the policeman? Well, I'm wearing the headsets and I'm sitting at my drums in front of the elevator. It's a Saturday or Sunday afternoon, and the building is closed. I'm playing the drums, and at one point, all in perfect syncopation, as my hands hit the drums—just prior to the elevator door opening—there was a seventy-year-old rent-a-cop and it was *la de da-POW!* He hears this *pow* and thinks it's a gun. He thought that he was shot or something. I mean, it was like the door opens, the explosion of the drum, a look of disbelief, the door closes, and we never see him again! (Laughs.) The poor old man could have died right there.

Hal Blaine Strikes Again! Hal, what makes Roy Halee such a good producer?

I think the fact that he's not afraid to try anything, and he listens to everything. There was never, "Save it for your own record, sweetheart," that kind of crap. I've always maintained that one guy doesn't make a record. Phil Spector alone never made a great record. He made great records with all these people. Brother Julius, the little black man who used to clean up, he was part of that recording scene. Brother Julius must have been sixty-five or seventy years old, and he'd sweep up the studio at Gold Star. Brother J. We'd give him money all the time. He used to come in and make suggestions like, "Hey, Mr. Spector, you sure is doing it." "Hey, Hal, git those drums bigger!"

Can you tell me about Jack Nitzsche, the piano player?

Jack was very interesting because he was so far ahead of his time. Jack, I think, was another of those guys who suffered from an inferiority complex. A brilliant guy, real studied and learned in music. He was the first guy in Hollywood to have long hair. He was a very close friend of the Rolling Stones. He brought them to my house.

What did you think of the Stones when you first met them?

I thought they were terrific. Charlie Watts's big thing was playing with the garage door opener at my house. He had never seen anything like it. They couldn't figure out how the door opened. So Mr. Jokester, Hal Blaine, says, "Oh, this garage knows my car whenever I pull up." They didn't know I had a button on my dashboard. They had their first big concert here in L.A., and we whisked them away, being chased by a thousand screaming fans. We went right up the hill to my house, and as I approached the garage, I pushed the button. Well, it was open and I pushed the button again and it closed behind us. They couldn't figure it out.

How did the advent of the self-contained group affect what you were asked to play in the studio?

The only effect it had was that people would come in and play a Beatles record and say, "We want this sound." To me, copying Ringo was the easiest thing in the world because it was strictly backbeat, just about four on the floor or two on the floor.

I was strictly on Ringo's side, as far as him being a big star and making a lot of money. I thought it was great. I wished it could have happened to me. He fit into that group perfectly. I've always said that if Pete Best stayed on with them—who knows—maybe the group would never have happened. But I never put Ringo down.

You're acknowledged as being the first studio drummer to use a multi-tommed drum set. How did that come about?

I wanted to play more elaborate fills. I wanted to play more syncopated offbeats. I only had two tom-toms to think about—a small tom and a floor tom, which was the standard set, and in addition I had a set of metal timbales that I tuned mid-rangy. They had a great decay, like the doppler effect, and you couldn't really do that with your tom-toms. I liked that effect. So I took these two metal timbales, put a tom-tom holder on one of them, the smaller one, and added a set of legs, so it would stand on the floor. We were doing some records for Terry Melcher, and he just collapsed when he heard the sound of these two drums. Then I said, "Geez, if I had a whole set of those, the single-headed timbales, then I could tune each one to the perfect decay I need." I also did every radio station ID in town—you know, with those fast sixteenth note tom runs from high to low.

What do you typify as the best Hal Blaine record?

Gosh, I don't know. That's so hard. They're all part of me. They were different moods and different modes, different studios and different eras, different artists and different times. You got certain lyrics and key phrases that turn on certain juices. I was talking with Tommy Tedesco, and he was questioning some of the Presley stuff. We had done a record with Elvis when he had done his first special on television in 1968. It was a song called "Memories." Tommy called me and said, "You know, I've been listening to this record; it's making me crazy. It sounds so much like me." I said, "Of course, you were there when we did it. Bones [Howe] was the engineer." Tommy said, "I knew there was something." Well, a lot of those things we don't remember. Anyway, I said, "I remember that." I remembered because I was going through a lot of emotional marital problems then. Whenever I hear that song, it makes me cry like a baby. "You know," Tommy says, "that's exactly what happened to me. I'm driving down the freeway and I'm crying like a baby."

You must have a real rewarding sense of accomplishment.

I was very lucky to find my niche in life—being an accompanist. I remember singers coming up to me and saying, "I love the way you play for me; you never seem to step on my lines." Well, I was never a solo artist. I wasn't a Buddy Rich. I'll tell you a story. Milt Holland, the percussionist, and I were working years ago at World Pacific Jazz Records. I got a call for a Kathy Rich session, Buddy Rich's daughter. I said, "Wow!" Buddy produced it and he was real sweet. I was getting into my car after the last session when Milt Holland comes running up to me and says, "Listen, Hal, Buddy would never say this to you, but I want you to know what he said." Milt went up to Buddy before that and said, "Hey Buddy, how come you're not playing drums on your kid's album?" Buddy turned around and said, "I wanted the best."

SELECTED DISCOGRAPHY

Singles

WITH ELVIS PRESLEY

"Blue Hawaii" from *Blue Hawaii* (1961, RCA)
"If I Can Dream" from *Elvis TV Special* (January 1969, RCA)
"Trouble" from *Elvis TV Special* (January 1969, RCA)

WITH THE RONETTES

"Be My Baby" (October 1963, Philles)
"Walking in the Rain" (December 1964, Philles)

WITH THE CRYSTALS

"Uptown" (May 1962, Philles)
"He's a Rebel" (November 1962, Philles)
"Da Doo Ron Ron" (June 1964, Philles)

WITH THE BEACH BOYS

"Surfin' U.S.A." (May 1963, Capitol)
"Fun, Fun, Fun" (March 1964, Capitol)
"Dance, Dance, Dance" (December 1964, Capitol)
"Help Me, Rhonda" (May 1965, Capitol)
"Wouldn't It Be Nice" (September 1966, Capitol)
"Good Vibrations" (December 1966, Capitol)

WITH THE MAMAS AND THE PAPAS

"California Dreamin' " (March 1966, Dunhill)
"Monday, Monday" (May 1966, Dunhill)
"I Saw Her Again" (July 1966, Dunhill)
"Creeque Alley" (May 1967, Dunhill)

WITH THE FIFTH DIMENSION

"Up, Up and Away" (July, 1967, Soul City)
"Stone Soul Picnic" (June 1968, Soul City)
"Aquarius/Let the Sunshine In" (April 1969, Soul City)
"Wedding Bell Blues" (November 1969, Soul City)

WITH THE TIJUANA BRASS

"Taste of Honey" (November 1965, A&M)

WITH SONNY AND CHER

"I Got You Babe" (August 1965, Atco)
"The Beat Goes On" (February 1967, Atco)

WITH THE BYRDS

"Mr. Tambourine Man" (June 1965, Columbia)

WITH JOHNNY RIVERS

"Memphis" (July 1964, Imperial)
"Secret Agent Man" (April 1966, Imperial)
"Poor Side of Town" (November 1966, Imperial)

WITH PAUL REVERE AND THE RAIDERS

"Kicks" (May 1966, Columbia)
"Hungry" (July 1966, Columbia)
"Good Thing" (January 1967, Columbia)

WITH THE GRASS ROOTS

"Midnight Confessions" (October 1968, Dunhill)

WITH THE ASSOCIATION

"Windy" (July 1967, Warner Bros.)

Earl Palmer

7

"In those days when I was coming up, you could always tell a New Orleans drummer the minute you heard him play his bass drum. . . ."

Go TO NEW ORLEANS if you want to hear hot drumming. Like the gunslingers of the Old West, the Gulfport drummers are legendary. Men like "Baby" Dodds, Dixieland's early stylist; Zutty Singleton, who was Gene Krupa's favorite; and Charles "Hungry" Williams, who broke his right foot and was good enough to play his bass drum with his left.

And for his drumming on such classic hits as Fats Domino's "The Fat Man," "I'm Walkin'," and "Blueberry Hill," Lloyd Price's "Lawdy Miss Clawdy," and Little Richard's "Lucille," "Good Golly Miss Molly," and "Rip It Up," Earl Palmer is remembered as one of the greatest drummers in the history of New Orleans rock & roll.

Earl grew up near the French Quarter but spent much of his childhood on the road, dancing in a vaudeville act with his mother. As a kid, he loved to bang the drums around, and by the time he could reach his bass drum pedal, he'd found his calling. When he left the army in 1945, he'd already spent many of his twenty years behind the drums.

The turning point in his career came shortly after World War II when he joined the band of local trumpeter Dave Bartholomew. Theirs was the swingingest group in New Orleans and they began to see a lot of action in Cosimo Matassa's J&M recording Studios. After they backed Fats in 1949 on his hit "The Fat Man," word hit the street that this band was hot and the drummer made it smoke.

Earl's time is solid, his syncopation subtle, and his drumming emotional. One of his most soulful performances is on Fats's "Walkin' to New Orleans." Earl's beat is simple, dignified, and reinforces the song's sentiments, "I got no time for talkin'/I got to keep a-walkin'."

Parading is a way of life in New Orleans, and the rhythm of the people in the street was captured on those early records. Nurtured by that heritage, Earl's rock & roll drumming contains all the vitality and drive of a handful of street musicians who inspired the second-line march. As Hal Blaine related to the West Coast style of the sixties, so Earl Palmer did to the development and success of the fifties New Orleans sound.

The musicians on these New Orleans classics—Earl, Salvador Doucette on piano, Lee Allen and "Red" Tyler on saxes, Frank Fields on bass, Ernest McLean and Justin Adams on guitars, and Dave Bartholomew on trumpet—were among the first generation of rockers, and they charted a course for all of us to follow.

In 1957, Earl left New Orleans and moved to Los Angeles. He quickly established himself in Hollywood, where he later played on records by Frank Sinatra, Diana Ross, Bonnie Raitt, Randy Newman, the Temptations, and the Righteous Brothers. On the Righteous Brothers' sessions, Earl worked for Phil Spector and won acclaim as the drummer on "You've Lost That Lovin' Feeling," as well as Ike and Tina Turner's "River Deep, Mountain High."

In 1982, he was elected secretary-treasurer of Local 47 of the American Federation of Musicians. Handling a variety of financial responsibilities, he is prohibited from playing for money; his drumming is limited to an occasional benefit or impromptu jam session. Viewing his executive work as a challenge, Earl is as committed to his union title as he was in laying down all those great tracks.

Does he miss playing? "Well, a little," he admitted. "But not as much as I thought I would. After all, I played a lot of years. . . ."

It was those years I had come to talk about. The union hall was deserted as Earl began to talk about his life in the South. As the memories drew into focus, his eyes lit up, and it seemed as if he'd never left.

EARL: New Orleans is a fascinating place for me, especially since I've been away for so long. I go back to visit; I enjoy it, of course, a lot more than most tourists, because I'm from there. I know the town; I know the city. I know the people and everything.

MAX: *What part of New Orleans are you from?*

I'm from the section called the Tremé, which is north of Canal Street and west of the French Quarter. Six or eight blocks from the French Quarter.

What was it like growing up there?

Well, it was a lot of fun. I was dancing, you know, before I started playing any drums. Yeah, I was a tap dancer in vaudeville shows with my mother from the time I was four years old. I did that continually on and off until I went in the service at seventeen. But I fooled around with the drums since I was five or six years old. When I was seven years old, my grandfather bought me a set. Oh man, it was a miniature set of those old-time sets they used to have with the waterfalls and the nude ladies on the bass. A bass drum wasn't a bass drum unless it had a picture on it in those days.

I played in the school there when I was a little bitty kid. Played snare drum. I didn't play it very well, but I was the littlest kid in the band, so they used to throw money.

You always hear about the influence of marching bands on New Orleans drummers. I've always thought that the connection between white European music and the black African style was an interesting aspect to that type of playing.

Well, there is a great connection between the French Creole atmosphere and black New Orleans. This is where the music is distinct, because it's a mixture of the Dixieland, yet there's a lot of an Afro involvement too. It came from the slaves who were brought here from Brazil. That's where our Mardi Gras in New Orleans comes from, though I understand that all the slaves who were brought here were not from Africa. Many were from the islands and down in Brazil and places like that. So this is where that Mardi Gras tradition came from in New Orleans.

In those days when I was coming up, you could always tell a New Orleans drummer the minute you heard him play his bass drum because he'd have that parade beat connotation. The newer drummers don't because many of them don't have the old New Orleans music ingrained in them. But there was a time some years ago when you could tell where a guy was from the minute he played the bass drum.

I remember the time when I was supposed to be the best drummer in New Orleans. What I always wanted to do, but was never allowed to do, was play a funeral parade. That kind of thing was always saved for the older guys. Now you have very young guys who play good and today play in funeral parades, street marching bands, and everything. But in the days when I was coming up, they wouldn't let us young guys play those. We'd be the best players in town, playing the clubs and all. But the old guys played the funeral parades in the Dixieland bands.

I always wanted to play the bass drum because being from New Orleans, the bass drum was the basic pattern for that kind of music. Anybody could beat on the ground with two sticks, but not everybody could play that bass drum.

How did you develop your bass drum technique?

That may have come from me being a tap dancer in my youth. I couldn't run very fast, but my foot was fast. I guess I always had an advantage over the drummer who wasn't a dancer because if he didn't have it built in him, he had to learn time and rhythm which, since I was a dancer, I already knew about.

When we played Zurich on our last tour, we went to see Fats Domino one night. He had no sound monitors, so we asked him what he listened to on stage. He said, "All I need to hear is the bass drum."

Fats's music is totally New Orleans, rhythm & blues. This is the background he had as a kid. I remember one of the first jobs he played, I recommended him for this club. All he played was boogie-woogie and "When the Saints Go Marchin' In" and things like that. And nothing that he did has changed except that he's gotten to be a better musician. But I mean his style, his feel, everything is still the same. Same roots, same basic feel.

The funeral celebration is a fascinating part of New Orleans culture. How did that come about?

Well, there used to be clubs in New Orleans like the Elks and so forth. And it was a fad that when you had a club and a member died, that you would honor him by having a funeral procession. They played the funeral dirges with the hearse and the cars all the way to the cemetery. The funeral would be over, the body "planted" as they say, and the "second line" would be people who followed the funeral procession and the band. They followed it to the cemetery and danced all the way back.

I'll tell you about a planting I remember maybe four years ago when I was in New Orleans with Peggy Lee and playing at the Fairmount Hotel. It was the funeral of Professor Longhair. I was going to go and see him the night before he died. So when the funeral came up, I took Tom Garvin, who was Peggy's conductor at the time and a good friend of mine. I showed him something he'd never seen before. And Dave Bartholomew, whose orchestra I worked in before I moved from California and who did all those Fats records and all the records in New Orleans, came by to go to the funeral. Tom was just flabbergasted. He'd never seen anything like that before in his life. They had three bands and about five hundred or six hundred people in the second line. He couldn't believe it. He said, "I heard of this, Earl, but I just don't believe it." I said, "We're not going to stand here all day. We got to leave, 'cause this will go on for the rest of the evening."

How many musicians play in something like that?

Oh, they had three bands—the Olympic Brass Band and two other bands. I don't remember which ones they were, but they were spaced, you know, in between. But so many people wanted to follow the procession. There were motorcycle cops, the whole thing. It was really fantastic. It was one of the biggest funeral parades I've ever seen.

Professor Longhair has been called the original rock & roll pianist from New Orleans.

Right. I played on some of his early stuff: "Tipitina," "Ball the Wall." Everybody knew Fess. His funeral originated uptown, but when I knew him he lived in my neighborhood, the Tremé, so everybody from that part of town knew him. Plus, as he became popular, everybody uptown knew him because this was where he began to make a name for himself. So people from all over town turned out for the funeral. It was quite a thing.

I listened to Fats's first record, "The Fat Man" from 1949. It seems that the rhythms and the drumming, just the music in general, became much more intense after the Second World War.

My whole explanation for it is that after the war was when the rhythm & blues advent started. That backbeat became a little more pronounced. Before that they were either playing bebop or they were playing Dixieland. And in Dixieland there wasn't a very strong afterbeat [backbeat] throughout a tune. When they go on the shout chorus [the last chorus], they used to play a strong afterbeat and get on a big trash-can cymbal and this is when they really heard it. But as opposed to rhythm & blues, there was an afterbeat throughout the whole piece, like now. So this is my feeling why it may have sounded more intense.

Did you naturally move toward playing rhythm & blues?

Oh, I didn't really get interested in rhythm & blues until we started making those records in New Orleans with Dave Bartholomew's band. Fats Domino, Little Richard, Smiley Lewis, Sam Cooke, and Professor Longhair's first records, Lloyd Price and all of those artists. You see, we were working in clubs in the French Quarter and on the highway. We were playing bebop on the job, and we'd play rhythm & blues on the record dates. But hardly ever on the job. We all had those kinds of roots.

Any particular reason you stayed away from rhythm & blues?

No, it just happened because we were in a group that wanted to play jazz, that wanted to play bebop. We used to do Four Freshmen and Hi-Lo's vocals and stuff like that and play bebop and jazz. We also played contemporary. We played some things that were popular hits and so forth. But the guy in my group, for example, Earl Williams sang and played bass, but he wasn't a blues singer. On the job we primarily played jazz.

If you listen to the original rhythm & blues and rock & roll records of the late forties and early fifties, you hear New Orleans musicians who come from a swing tradition suddenly playing rock & roll and hitting the heavy backbeat. You had straight eighth notes, but you guys put a swing to it.

Kind of open eighths, almost not quite a shuffle, kind of a quasi shuffle, a little in between straight eighths and a shuffle. One thing that made it a little easier for the drummers like myself and Hungry—Charles "Hungry" Williams, a fantastic drummer who never became well known—was that the rest of the guys weren't fighting you. It was a lot easier for us to effect that in-between shuffle and straight-eighths feeling. Nowadays if you try and play in between

"It had a New Orleans flavor to it, you know, more basic than what we were playing on the job. You couldn't call it bebop and you couldn't call it jazz. It was sort of a new approach to rhythm music."

that way, you're gonna have part of the guys playing straight eighths; the other guys will be playing a shuffle and maybe one or two guys who understand that feeling or concept will be playing in between with you. That rhythm all stemmed from that regional New Orleans thing. It wasn't hard straight eighths and it wasn't a Louis Jordan shuffle. It had a New Orleans flavor to it, you know, more basic than what we were playing on the job. You couldn't call it bebop, and you couldn't call it jazz. It was sort of a new approach to rhythm music.

Thirty years ago, did you ever think you were breaking new ground?

No, we didn't. We really didn't. We thought of breaking new ground in the sense of new songs, and Dave Bartholomew was writing most of those. We just thought that we were doing something that would bring an artist to New Orleans to record. We didn't really have the idea that it was something totally new.

With all the hundreds of sessions you've done, what do you remember when you look back to those sessions with Fats and Richard?

They were fun because when, for example, after Fats began making some money, well, he and Richard both were guys that would come in and play and leave their diamond rings all over the piano and get up and walk out and leave. I was always the one collecting their rings so no one would walk off with them. Jesus Christ, if I would have kept them all I would have been a rich man! But I mean they were funny guys. Fats was the kind of guy that would listen to Dave, but he never wanted him to know that he was listening. Like Dave would say, "Fats, why don't you do such and such?" And Fats would say, "That's what I'm doing!" Dave would say, "okay." And it absolutely wasn't what he was doing. But then he'd do it. (Laughs.)

Now, Little Richard was also a fun cat to work for. For example, Richard always carried his bread with him. If he played a dance at Labor Union Hall and we'd have to record the next day in the studio, he'd be sitting at the piano doing the date and have his briefcase sitting beside. It was chock full of money, but he always carried it with him because he didn't trust *nobody*.

Lee Allen, the saxophone player, was constantly sticking his hands down there, and Richard would say, "Get out of here and leave my money alone." Lee Allen was constantly reaching his hand in there. "Gimme some of that money!" They were funny days, man.

What was recording with Richard and Fats like in those days?

We recorded at Cosimo Matassa's first studio behind J&M Music Shop on Dumaine and Rampart. It was a little room, maybe ten by twelve. That's where we did "Detroit City" and "Fat Man Blues," those first Little Richard songs, and things like that. Lloyd Price's "Lawdy Miss Clawdy." We only used three mikes; we didn't have but three electrical outlets.

Any mikes on the drums?

No, no mikes on the drums. That was all leakage. Something about leakage in those days. It didn't sound like leakage. If I remember correctly, one of the mikes used to be in the piano, and Lee Allen and Tyler on saxophones would be blowing into the other side of that piano mike. The other mike would be for the bass and the guitar and one mike for the singer. The drummer didn't have any mike.

How would you tune for that sound?

Well, for Fats and Little Richard sessions I used to have my bass drum tuned almost like a parade drum—loose and flappy. I don't mean really boomy like a big parade drum, but I had it kind of open with two heads on. Coming up in New Orleans, playing drums, everything you did was an assimilation of what you heard around you. And what I heard around me in those days were the Dixieland bands and the parade bands.

What was working with Dave Bartholomew's group like?

Those were great times. I played in Dave's band, and, as a matter of fact, it was one of the finest bands that I played with for all-around entertainment because we played all kinds of music. He was commercial as a leader went, but when he had an audience that would allow us to play some jazz—bebop—he'd go with it. He was a good trumpet player himself. But he was a businessman first. He had a lot of young guys in the band; some old guys too. But he'd keep everybody happy by letting us play a little—with bebop and jazz arrangements. It was an organized group rather than just playing spontaneous bebop and jamming like we would do after a gig or something at the Dew Drop or one of those clubs. It gave us a very professional feeling by doing all kinds of music. Musicianship is what Dave taught me in those early days.

"For Fats and Little Richard sessions I used to have my bass drum tuned like a parade drum—loose and flappy."

Earl, you and Hal Blaine were two of Phil Spector's favorite drummers. Can you tell me about working with him?

Well, I think the first date I did with Phil was "Lovin' Feeling." He said he wanted a heavy backbeat but a deeper sound than a normal snare. So I said, "Why don't I play it on the snare to get the impact, and at the same time, hit in the middle of the tom-tom to get the depth?" And we stuck the echo on it; that's what created that heavy backbeat. It's laid way back on the beat, too. Strange thing about that "Lovin' Feeling" date—Phil would not compromise. If it wasn't right, he didn't care how long it took him. He took three days to get that one tune because of that syncopated breakdown after the first verse, where the drums lay out. He wanted that to lay way back, but not out of meter. He didn't want the drums in there even though they would have made it come out right. He would never do anything in pieces like nowadays. Each time we'd take it from the beginning because he wanted the continuity.

After the bridge hits—"baby, baby—I'd get down on my knees...."—you start to fill like crazy, almost a solo. Was that stuff ad-libbed?

Oh, yeah, those kinds of things were.

Did Phil give you visual cues from the booth?

No, not really. He'd stop me when he had an idea. He would say, "Now that you got the idea I want, do it the way you want to do it," which I thought was good producing; he gave you the concept and let

THE BIG BEAT

you come up with your own interpretation. He'd let you try anything as long as you didn't get a chip on your shoulder.

What were some of the other records you did with Phil?

Damn near everything he did after that until he went to the Tina Turner thing, "River Deep, Mountain High." That record broke his heart; he really put his heart and soul into it. After that, I think he went to England to work with the Beatles.

At the time, bands were in and singers seemed to be out. How did you view that change toward self-contained groups in the sixties?

The self-contained group is what got the record industry in the situation it is in now as far as musicians are concerned. Before that, there had been groups that used studio musicians. Later on, the record companies started to let their groups take more time. We used to do those things and do them fast because that was our thing. Then the groups learned them and performed them on the road. But during that time, the record companies didn't want to take time with the guys who were playing in the groups then because most of them could not read, and they would cost the record companies too much in studio time.

We'd do an album in six hours. Three hours in the morning and three hours in the evening because all the music was written, and we'd read it and be finished. But then later on they let the self-contained groups do their own thing and take more time. I think that came about because they were young groups and they were not concerned with how much money they spent.

Did you ever play on Beach Boys records?

Yeah, I did some things, but Hal did most of them. Don't ask me which ones I played on. I should have done like Hal. Hal used to get gold records for all the things he played on. I never did that, you know. I would like to have had a room with all those things in them. It would have been nice—show my grandchildren when they grow up so they wouldn't say, "Oh shut up, old man, and sit down." I could just say, "Look, I don't have to tell you nothing. There it is."

What you do have to show them is a recorded history of remarkable performances—"Long Tall Sally," "I'm Walkin'," "Lucille." When you look back on those early days, it is with much affection.

Oh, very much so, Max, very much so. Those were the days when you were younger and you had good times and bad times, but they were all learning times. You were around people who were at the same stage that you were and the same learning process. And being in New Orleans was also an advantage. Because there's a oneness that you don't find anywhere else. There's a musical understanding.

Yeah, there's something about New Orleans that you won't find anywhere else. I think there is more music in someone born in New Orleans than anywhere else. You know, if I had to be from anywhere else, it would be from right *outside* of New Orleans—so I could get down into that city each day!

SELECTED DISCOGRAPHY

Singles

WITH LLOYD PRICE

"Lawdy Miss Clawdy" (1952, Specialty)

WITH LITTLE RICHARD

"Tutti-Frutti" (February 1956, Specialty)
"Long Tall Sally" (May 1956, Specialty)
"Slippin' and Slidin' " (June 1956, Specialty)
"Lucille" (April 1957, Specialty)

WITH FATS DOMINO

"Ain't That a Shame" (August 1955, Imperial)
"I'm Walkin' " (April 1957, Imperial)
"Walkin' to New Orleans" (August 1960, Imperial)

WITH THE RIGHTEOUS BROTHERS

"You've Lost That Lovin' Feelin' " (February 1965, Philles)
"Just Once in My Life" (May 1965, Philles)

IKE AND TINA TURNER

"River Deep, Mountain High" (June 1966, Philles)

Tracks from Albums

WITH PROFESSOR LONGHAIR

"Ball the Wall" from *New Orleans Piano* (recorded 1953, released 1972, Atlantic)
"Tipitina" from *New Orleans Piano* (recorded 1953, released 1972, Atlantic)

Russ Kunkel

8

"The only thing I wanted them to hear from me was the sound of the drums the way they wanted to hear them."

IT'S ALMOST IMPOSSIBLE to talk about contemporary West Coast or California rock without mentioning Russ Kunkel. Beginning in the early seventies, his contribution to the growth of that style has been enormous. Russ is the quintessential Californian—relaxed and confident—and his drumming reflects these qualities. He is one of rock's most pursued session drummers. Jackson Browne, Linda Ronstadt, Stevie Nicks, and James Taylor, just to name a few, are among the many artists who regularly request Russ's talents, both in the studio and on the road.

Russ is Mr. Cool. His playing is always tasteful and controlled. Following Al Jackson's advice, he never gets in the way of the singer or the song. He always supports; his groove is understated, and he never resorts to theatrics. Russ also has a very distinctive backbeat. His snare drum seems to float through the music. His touch is delicate yet commanding, and he is very selective about where he places the beat.

Early in his career, Russ learned that if he was going to make it in music he would have to do it on his own. Therefore, unlike many other successful drummers, Russ decided against the security of a permanent band and struck out to make his mark as a session drummer. His breakthrough came when he played on James Taylor's "Fire and Rain" from *Sweet Baby James*. Russ's innovative use of brushes instead of sticks—a technique virtually unheard of in rock drumming before 1970—helped make that classic tune a huge hit. Next came Carole King's *Tapestry*, one of the biggest-selling albums in recording history.

Because he had to be responsible at an early age, Russ took control of himself and his life. I believe this is one of the reasons for his success. With that approach, it's no wonder he leaves behind him a trail of hit records.

MAX: You do most of your work on the West Coast, but you're not originally from California, are you?

RUSS: No, I was born in Pittsburgh and lived there until I was about nine and then moved to Long Beach, California, around 1959 or '60. I've lived in Southern California ever since. A lot of people were moving out to the West Coast at that time. What happened with my family was that my sister was getting married in California, and we went out for the wedding, really liked it, and decided to stay.

Did you play drums as a kid?

Well, when I was growing up I always lived in an atmosphere of band rehearsals because my brother, who is also a drummer, had a band and the band was always rehearsing at the house, so I was kind of brought into that idea pretty early on. I was always bugging him to let me play and was always getting kicked out of the rehearsals for being a little brat. I can remember when I was no older than about six, my brother gave me this snare drum. "Okay, now here's your snare drum. Play this for a while," he said. So I started banging on it.

I guess that was my first real interest in drums. But I didn't seriously start pursuing drums until I was in elementary school. I joined the school orchestra in the sixth grade. That worked real well until I learned some licks. They had me playing snare drum in the orchestra, reading real simple stuff. I'd memorize it and wouldn't read it anymore. All during the orchestra rehearsals, every chance I had, I'd show off my licks. I'd do it because there were cute girls in the choir and I got kicked out of the orchestra for it.

Did you take drum lessons?

When you joined the orchestra you took lessons. Part of the deal was a musical lesson in piano theory. You learned tunes to play at the assemblies twice a year. That was the extent of it, and that only lasted for about a year.

What made you continue to play drums then?

I met some people in junior high school at the height of the surf music era. I was already involved in surfing, and I knew I was going to play drums of some kind. So when a couple of kids put together a band and needed a drummer, I said, "Well, I'll play drums for you," even though all I owned was a practice pad and a pair of sticks. Eventually I got a snare drum and stand, and we played a few assemblies in school. That band led to a lot of other surf bands. A lot of musicians looked up to the Surfaris and the Astronauts and other surf instrumental bands. I think surf music played an important part in attracting a lot of people who would not normally have been musicians but who decided to get into surf music because it was easy to play.

Right around that same time my father died. That was another reason why we moved to California. My mom—and I guess I did too—we just wanted to move away. So it was my mom and I living together. I felt this real responsibility to take care of her. In the back of my mind there was always the thought of "I don't have a lot of time to screw around." But I also wanted to enjoy my youth. I had these other interests, and I was good enough in swimming and water polo that my coaches were trying to encourage me to train for the Olympics. My times were good enough that they thought shooting for the Olympics was something I might want to do. That was one of the first big decisions I had to make: not to go that way, but into music instead.

My first year of high school we had a pretty good band, the Barons. We worked pretty regularly. I think at our best we were making like five to seven hundred bucks a night, which was a lot of money at that time. We weren't that great a band, but we knew just about all of the Top Forty tunes and we did funny things onstage. So when I was walking home on the weekend, maybe with two or three hundred dollars in my pocket, I felt real good about music, and I decided that it all clicked with my responsibilities.

My mom was totally supportive of it. She was sort of the den mother of all the bands I was ever in. We used to store all the band gear in the living room of the apartment we had. We couldn't leave the equipment in the van because people were ripping off vans all the time. Nobody had a garage or anything. So it ended up in my mom's living room. You'd walk into the room to the back door and there would be one path around the Dual Showman amps. Everyone else's parents hated the idea that they were playing music and growing their hair long. But my mom was great. We'd come home after a gig and my mom would have a big pot of coffee ready and ask, "How did it go?"

Did you ever have to work a job outside music?

I did once during that time, which also helped me make my decision about music. I worked in a gas station for three weeks in the first part of summer. This was before the Barons really got rolling. And all I could see were my friends going off to the beach, surfboards on their cars, and I was in my Texaco uniform standing on the corner. I thought to myself, "I can't do this." This was in 1963.

When did you get your first set of drums?

For the longest time I didn't have any drums, and I was actually in bands without drums. A friend of mine, Michael Stowe—his father was a drummer, but he never played. I remember Michael telling me one day, "Well, my father's got this set of drums that he never uses. I'll ask him if you can borrow it." I said, "Yeah, I'd really like to, you know." I borrowed this man's drums for about two or three months. I'd go get them at his house, play them at the gig, make sure nothing happened to them, and return them. It was an old Ludwig kit, just three drums: bass drum, a fourteen-inch floor tom, and a twelve-inch

"I think surf music played an important part in attracting a lot of people who would not normally have been musicians but who decided to get into surf music because it was easy to play."

rack tom. I practiced in the apartment or outside on our patio. I recall the set had one cymbal and I had to rent a hi-hat from the music store.

I borrowed his drums for a while and then my conscience started to get the best of me. We started making a little bit of money and I think I actually saved some bucks, and my mom took out a loan so I could buy a set of Gretsch drums through another friend. They were a great color: gray sparkle. I'd never seen that color. It was really gray, not silver; it was like dark gray metalflake. I got those and used them until I saw Sonor drums for the first time. My mom bought me my Sonor drums.

The Sonor set was an early, early set, and I kept it for years. There was a music store in Lakewood, California. All the drums were up on a big, high shelf. When you walked in, that's all you could see. That's the first time I can remember fantasizing about drums. I walked into that music store and there was this set of drums. You remember those crazy little pins that were popular back then, when you looked at them, it was like an eye that opened and closed? Well, the set was made out of the same stuff. And as you walked around it the color and design changed. I thought that was the wildest thing I'd ever seen. I said, "That's the set. Who makes those drums?" I knew about Ludwig and all the regular drum manufacturers. The guy in the store said, "These people in Germany called Sonor." I said, "Wow, it looks really neat." So, I finally got those drums. That's all I played. All I did was buy more drums of the same kind. When I moved to Hollywood, I started to case the Wallach's Music City that was on Sunset and Vine. It's not there anymore, but they had a set in there: a twenty-inch bass drum, a twelve-inch tom-tom, and a sixteen-inch floor tom. And then I bought another twenty-inch bass drum because I was playing two bass drums and another tom, so it was like two toms, two bass drums, a snare, and a floor tom-tom. I bought the same kit again when I had some money, just to add to it. At some point along the way I took that finish off and put Contact paper on that looked like wood because the other finish was out of style. The psychedelic thing was over. But I loved the drums so much that I refinished the insides with white Verathane. They had a real hard surface on the inside. The set looked just like wood-grain drums. And that's the drum kit I played on "Fire and Rain."

I noticed that on your set now you have a cut-out on the front of your bass drum.

Yeah, Yamaha apparently did some kind of calculation on hole sizes for bass drum heads. It has something to do with the volume of air moving inside the drum. They came out with the size of a hole for a front bass drum head that's the proper size for each particular drum size. If you take the front head off a bass drum, the sound just goes right out and there's no air pressure built up there. I found out that the air moving inside there gets contained and helps make that chesty kind of sound. So, if the hole is there, but not quite as big, it lets the air go out, but it still retains some of that pressure. I think it's eight inches for a twenty-two-inch drum. Sometimes I use a little blanket in the bass, but I found something that works even better than that: Get one piece of foam that's about four to six inches thick that you just barely wedge between the front and back heads, so it's just touching. Not loosely fitting, just touching and just about three inches high. You can't see it, and it works just like a pad on a snare drum. It's just on a little part of the head, and sitting on the front head is what keeps it in there so it doesn't move around. With a blanket or a pillow or something, well, different pillows make different sounds. A down pillow is really good sometimes, you see. It's so loose that it's constantly changing. The piece of foam doesn't change, it's always there.

You mentioned "Fire and Rain" before. What led up to that session?

Of all those bands that I was talking about, hopping from one to another, playing all those gigs, one band got together that seemed to be the end of that era for me. It was called Things to Come. We were very influenced by the Yardbirds and the Stones and Van Morrison. We also had a couple of people in the band who were writing songs, so to further our career, we moved to Los Angeles. There we met a guy who was then the manager of the Byrds, Peter Fonda, and some other people. He put us in this place called the Sunset-Doheny Apartments right on the Strip and one block up from the Whisky-A-Go-Go. One of the things he made us do was kick our lead singer out of the band because he was a little crazy. He was great, but he was just a little off. So the band got cut down to just four people.

We lived in those apartments for about eleven or twelve weeks and played at the Whisky, opening shows for everybody you could imagine—the Byrds, Gene Clark, Cream, the Electric Flag, Traffic. We became the house band at that time. We even ate at the Whisky. Mario, the guy that still runs the Roxy, he was like our father. He'd say, "You guys be in here at five o'clock and eat before you play." He calls me Kunks. I'd come in and he'd say, "Go eat, Kunks!" He really took good care of us.

During that period we started doing a few more gigs here and there in San Bernardino—different concerts with different bands. We moved to a couple of different houses. It got to be a real chore, and the responsibility of the band, a good portion of it, started to fall on me. I was the leader, the organizer, trying to get everything going. The opportunities were all there, but the band wasn't going anywhere. It had reached its point. It wasn't going to get any better. It was obvious to me. Finally, I actually started to openly talk about it.

I had to. I had just gotten married and my wife was pregnant. All of a sudden there was another responsibility on the horizon. I saw the band wasn't going anywhere. There were a lot of pretty good opportunities around and people were starting to tell me, "Hey man, you ought to come over here and do this session and get to know these people." I had a good idea then that the band wasn't going to work, and nine months away was going to be a big responsibility that I had never dealt with before.

I had to make a move, and I didn't have much time to do it. I'd made a decision that I was going to be a session drummer because I knew that there was some stability in that in L.A. I started working for Joel Sill, who was running a publishing company called Trousdale Music for ABC/Dunhill Records. Leah, my wife at that time, was writing songs for that publishing company, and I started doing publishing demos for fifteen dollars a tune. We'd do five or six songs in a day. My whole mental concept was, "Okay, this is it. This is as serious as anything I've done. I'm going to go in and play this demo the best I can and maybe someone will hear it and want to know who the drummer was." All I wanted to get was one real session, because that would have meant eighty-five bucks. Eventually some real sessions came along instead of just publishing demos, and I did them and tried to have the same mental attitude about them. I'd see people around me making a lot of demands. I wanted to do it exactly the opposite. The only thing that I wanted them to hear from me was the sound of the drums the way they wanted to hear them.

What was the first real session you did?

Some stuff for Joel Sill. I think one of the writers who was writing for the publishing company at that time got a record deal for a single. His name was Dan Walsh. I'm on one of his tunes. Then I met John Stewart, and through John I met a guy who was playing with him named Chris Darrow. He played fiddle and was a friend of Peter Asher, the producer. Peter had come out to Los Angeles with James Taylor, who had just left London, where he was living and had done his Apple album. They were looking for a drummer. Actually, they were looking for a whole band to do James's next album. Chris had been working with me and with John, and he said to Peter, "Why don't you come to a rehearsal and listen to this guy play drums. He'd probably be great for James." Peter came and listened to some of the songs and he liked my drumming. He called me, and I went over to his house.

At this time Peter had maybe six hundred bucks, a big house with no furniture in it, and he was at the bottom too. He *had* to do it then. It was his big move. He said, "Yeah, I would like to use you." That was the beginning of the whole thing right there. Through that set of people and introductions, I started working with James on "Fire and Rain."

That was a great decision to use brushes on that song. You know, that was the beginning of the singer-songwriter era. Had you rocked that and played harder, that whole genre of music in the early seventies, I think, would have taken a different direction.

You know, speaking of singer-songwriters, some of James's best songs were on his first album, but it just was recorded so badly. It just didn't have the right sound to it. In James's band at that time was Carole King, Lee Sklar on bass, myself, and Danny Kortchmar [Kooch] on guitar. So whatever the sound was between Lee and me, whatever kind of sympatico was going on, started then. Lee was in a lot of other bands around Los Angeles. He was in a band called Wolfgang when I was in the Things to Come. We always wanted to get together because we always liked each other. There was just something that we had in common. The Taylor thing was really the first chance that we got to play together, and it worked. Then you had Carole, who was a fantastic songwriter on her own, playing keyboards. Her piano style was a big part of those records. Danny Kortchmar, who was James's best friend, added his whole R&B influence. The chemicals were all there for that to happen. "Fire and Rain" was a real magical record.

And I remember why I used brushes. We rehearsed the songs in Peter's living room, and I couldn't play loud because the neighbors would complain. So on the songs we rehearsed there I used brushes, but played them like sticks.

You also played some unique fills on that record, rather than merely keeping a very straight beat.

I think the reason for those fills was that no one encouraged me *not* to do them. As soon as I started to play them, Peter and James really liked them too. For the first time in his life James didn't have to carry the ball all the way down the field. There was something moving along with him so that he could kind of sit back into it a little bit. Also, the song had these gaping holes in it and no one was playing anything.

Were you strictly into rock or were you influenced by jazz?

I would say just rock & roll. The whole topic of jazz drumming was a very dark area to me at that point. I wasn't schooled in it and knew nothing about it. But I think virtually every drummer would say that one of their secret desires is to be a great jazz drummer, you know, "Let me be Tony Williams for a day."

Danny Kooch has been a big influence on me musically. He turned me on to a lot of R&B stuff, as well as jazz. While Danny was playing

"We rehearsed the songs in Peter Asher's living room, and I couldn't play loud because the neighbors would complain. So on the songs we rehearsed there I used brushes, but played them like sticks."

with James, he also had his own band called Jo Mama. Joel O'Brian was the drummer in that band and he was strictly a jazz buff. Jazz was all he wanted to play. It was interesting, because Kooch was always trying to get him to play more rock & roll. As for me, I would listen to Joel and say to myself, "God, I wish I could play like that." He would sit down at the drums by himself and get that smooth, swinging lilt going. I could never do that. Maybe I'd do it alone, but I'd never do it in front of anyone.

People always refer to your relaxed "feel." Do you think you always played like that?

I think it comes out of the fact that one of the things I hate most about playing is when I'm put in a position where I can't play with any certainty. You have to decide then, is this uncertainty coming from me or is it coming from what everybody else is playing? That's the only thing about playing that ever annoys me. When it's not right, you've got to try to decide if it's not right because of the time and groove. A drummer is responsible for both of those things. But you're also influenced by what else is being played, particularly by the bass player.

What do you do when it's not happening on that end?

I get very annoyed. I say to myself: "I'll be right. Let it start here." If I'm wrong, then we'll stop and figure out where to start all over again. But when in doubt, I'll just play harder and more assertive. Like, "Okay, the backbeat's *here.*"

What do you do when you get in a situation where the other guys in the studio aren't feeling where you feel the song should be?

If you're with people who you know, then you just talk about it: "What should we do about this?" Most of my dialogue takes place with the bass player. Like with Lee Sklar, we'll talk about what we should do to make whatever we're playing neater and a bit more special. There's a certain protocol that you have to go through sometimes. The producer will be wanting to get things going and get the song finished, and you have to say, "Wait a minute. Let's play this thing a couple of times and try out a couple of ideas to see if we can make this transition work right."

In Jackson Browne's music, for instance, one of the things that makes the dynamics work in his songs is that on almost every tune of his there's a part where there is just a hi-hat and a bass drum. That's just the way he writes. It's just there in the songs where all of a sudden you've got to spill out into nothing, but it has to have some kind of time. Over the years with him I've tried to find different ways to create that same thing. It's either a backbeat on the hi-hat or a backbeat on the bass drum. Or it's just quarter notes on the snare drum just clicking time away. If he keeps writing the same way, I'll be in a bit of trouble, because I've almost used up all my ideas on how to play his songs right.

If you had stayed in Pittsburgh, do you think your style would have been drastically different?

I think my playing was dictated by the people I was playing with—

James Taylor, Jackson Browne, and Carole King, who are very lyrical writers. I think if I grew up in Detroit playing with Bob Seger, I wouldn't play the way I do, or if I grew up playing with Mitch Ryder, I'd be totally different. My attitude was that I wanted to adapt to my environment. If my environment was going to be playing with these people, then in my innermost thoughts my feeling was to play perfectly for them. I didn't know what "perfectly" meant, actually. I don't think I could've ever said, "Boy, I'm going to play 'Fire and Rain' and this is the *perfect* thing for the song." I was scared shitless when the time came to play. If you can always manage to be in the present, taking in all that information around you, then you will do the right thing for that moment in that particular song. We drummers only get in trouble when we slip out of present time.

Is there a particular way you tune your drums to get that big fat sound?

I found this book called *Analytical Drum Tuning*. It's a fantastic book. It's like a little encyclopedia of drum tuning. It takes you about twenty minutes to read it. Every drum roadie in the world should get this book and read it. Joe Vitale found it and gave me a copy. It tells you every aspect about the whole thing: why a drum is tunable; when it's not sounding good; what could possibly be wrong with it. It's all the ABCs.

Let's talk about drum setups. How big is the set you use now?

Presently I'm using a small setup. It just makes more sense for everything. Without the security of all those tom-toms to play with, when you just have two drums to play, you just play more like an animal, and you get down to the real basics of it. It's like forcing yourself to do it right instead of relying on easy things that are there. It's a lot easier to just go around the drums to fill up a bar than it is to try to do it with your snare, hi-hat, bass drum, and maybe one tom-tom. If you place it in right, it's going to mean more.

As for cymbals, I don't want to have a lot of them, but I want them all to have a unique quality about them. One I want to hit and have it immediately explode and go right away. Another I want to have a real slow rise and have it just go off, but not get lost. I start forgetting about the sound of tom-toms that are there. It's a thirteen-inch and a sixteen-inch, the perfect gradation. Nice and full-sounding. I can use either one with the backbeat.

How were you able to avoid going crazy with the pressures of the music business?

One of the most comfortable places in the world for me is sitting behind my drums. I don't care how many people are out there in the audience. Of my waking hours, I think I spend more time on a drum stool than anywhere else. When I played at the Rose Bowl a while ago it was really exciting because I realized that I was just another tool in the big machinery of humanity. There were a hundred thousand people sitting out in front of me. I just happened to be the person playing the drums that day; that was my part. I only seldom get nervous. I only get nervous, feel strange, or wonder about success

"My playing was dictated by the people I was playing with—James Taylor, Jackson Browne, and Carole King, who are very lyrical writers. I think if I grew up in Detroit playing with Bob Seger, I wouldn't play the way I do, or if I grew up playing with Mitch Ryder, I'd be totally different."

when there's something else on my mind that has nothing to do with that at all. I can remember way back when I realized I had responsibilities ahead that I had to take care of. I think my biggest fear is not being able to handle those.

How do you prepare for that?

I guess just by saying to myself all the time, "I can handle it." I'll always try to do the right thing. I've always wanted to be successful, for no other reason, I guess, than that it's the American way. I think I realized that at an early age because of my father dying and me getting married when I was young and having to deal with those responsibilities. You learn that you have only two choices: You either do it or you don't do it. And nobody's going to do it for you. A lot of people are fortunate enough to come from wealthy families where they have something to fall back on. The only thing I had to fall back on was my ass.

SELECTED DISCOGRAPHY

Singles

WITH JAMES TAYLOR

"Fire and Rain" (September 1970, Warner Bros.)

WITH CAROLE KING

"So Far Away" (May 1971, Ode)
"Where You Lead" (May 1971, Ode)

WITH JACKSON BROWNE

"Doctor My Eyes" (April 1972, Asylum)
"Here Come Those Tears Again" (February 1977, Asylum)
"Running on Empty" (March 1978, Asylum)
"The Load-Out"/"Stay" (medley) (July 1978, Asylum)
"That Girl Could Sing" (October 1980, Asylum)
"Somebody's Baby" (August 1982, Asylum)
"Cut It Away" (October 1983, Asylum)

WITH LINDA RONSTADT

"How Do I Make You?" (February 1980, Asylum)
"Get Closer" (October 1982, Asylum)

WITH STEVIE NICKS

"Edge of Seventeen" (March 1982, Modern)
"After the Glitter Fades" (June 1982, Modern)
"Stand Back" (August 1983, Modern)

WITH BOB SEGER

"Even Now" (1982, Capitol)
"Roll Me Away" (1982, Capitol)

D.J. Fontana

9

". . . He was kind of flamboyant."

IN 1956, AMERICA'S EYES were on Elvis Presley's hips. Elvis's hips drove everyone wild, from Ed Sullivan's TV censors to the screaming girls in his teenaged audience. So intense was the reaction, that on Elvis's third appearance, on January 6, 1957, the cameramen were instructed to focus on Elvis, but only from above the waist. Amidst all the commotion, no one was watching those hips more closely than drummer D. J. Fontana.

D. J. Fontana's influence is felt throughout rock & roll. He was Elvis's original drummer and was with him for fourteen years, playing on "Hound Dog," "Heartbreak Hotel," "Jailhouse Rock," "I Got a Woman," "You're So Square (Baby I Don't Care)," and many other records made back when Elvis had *the* voice and the band to go with it.

D.J.'s style evolved from the influences of the swing era of the forties and his personal experiences with the world of the bump and grind. On songs such as "Hound Dog" and "Jailhouse Rock," that approach fit perfectly with Elvis's rocking blues. "Hound Dog" has one of the greatest grooves and drum fills of any song I've ever heard, and apart from Elvis's vocal, "Jailhouse Rock" is distinguished by the subtle interplay between the members of the rhythm section. It is an example of a straight-ahead rock feel played to D.J.'s swing. He plays one rhythm, and Scotty Moore and Bill Black, on guitar and bass, play the riff.

It's still astounding, but to D.J., he was "just doing what came naturally."

I met D.J. at his home, a tidy suburban house close to the center of Nashville. On the walls of his kitchen hang mementos of the years gone by. There are many pictures of Elvis. They are not stock photos, but candid snapshots, taken at diners, backstage, or in dressing rooms.

D.J.'s memory for detail is acute, and he views the history he helped create with great objectivity. His gift of gab is completely absorbing; he shared many fond memories and told a great many stories. Two of them, not on tape for the interview, bear repeating here.

Once, when the boys were all set to record "You're So Square (Baby I Don't Care)," Elvis had an idea for a riff that he wanted Bill Black to lay down on the bass guitar. Bill couldn't quite get the part right and had gotten a bit frustrated; he set down his bass. Elvis went over, strapped on that bass, and played the hell out of that intro riff. So, though the rock history books have Bill Black listed as the bass player on "You're So Square," it is Elvis making his debut on the bass.

D.J. joined the band after Elvis had left Sun Records for RCA in 1955. Consequently, he didn't play drums on the Sun sessions for "Good Rockin' Tonight," "I Forgot to Remember to Forget," and "Mystery Train." When I asked D.J. who *had* played on those tracks, he confessed that he didn't know either. We speculated that it could have been James Van Eaton, the Memphis drummer who'd recorded with Jerry Lee Lewis. But we couldn't be sure, and I let it go, thinking it would remain one of rock's quirky mysteries.

We talked for hours and I didn't want the day to end. On the way to the airport, D.J. suggested we go talk to Scotty Moore—if we could find him.

We drove around Nashville looking for Scotty's pickup truck. D.J. drove to one of Scotty's businesses—no luck. D.J. had one more place to try.

We found him. There he was, wearing the same grin I'd seen in so many pictures. Winfield Scott Moore—the man who played The Guitar that Changed the World.

Setting the mood, D.J. took Scotty back thirty years to the days when they were doing *their* thing. His natural enthusiasm infected Scotty, and he got into the swing of things: "D.J., remember the time I had that big amp made so's I could hear over the screams?" It was great—I just stood there and took it all in. The thrill of rock & roll is still very much alive in the hearts of these two men.

"Scotty," D.J. asked, "who was it that played drums on that stuff you cut at Sun? Do you remember?"

"Sure," he replied, "that was Johnny Bonero."

Johnny Bonero? I'd never found that name in any history of Elvis

Presley. Scotty told me that Johnny used to play with them and was even in the band for a while but didn't work out. Later, I found out that Johnny Bonero had been in a local Memphis group called the Atomics; nothing more is known. Wherever you are, Johnny Bonero, your place in rock & roll history is assured.

The Elvis Presley phenomenon has been the subject of countless exhaustive studies. Every aspect of his life has been intensely scrutinized and analyzed. Throughout all of my reading, the only information I found concerning D.J. was that he met Elvis while performing on "The Louisiana Hayride," a weekly musical variety show broadcast over radio station KWKH from Shreveport, Louisiana.

Apart from what he told me in conversation, I can tell you this about D. J. Fontana: When he speaks of the old days and the good times spent with Elvis, Scotty, and Bill, his eyes light up. He lived through an incredible time; he has no regrets.

MAX: *For many people, myself included, you started it all—rock & roll drumming, that is. But I'm sure there were predecessors who started it for you.*

D.J.: Back in the forties and early fifties I was into the Big Bands. Sonny Igoe, when he was with the Herman band, was thunder. Then there was Shelly Manne and Don Lamond, who also played with Woody Herman. I used to listen to those guys. Not that I could play like them, but we'd listen to records of Big Bands. We had a Big Band teacher, J. B. Mullins, who was a fantastic musician. He won a national drum contest when he was four years old. This guy would drop his sticks and they would practically play themselves. He was all wrist and fingers. He had a brother that was working in Big Bands, with Claude Thornhill, I believe. His brother was coming from the Meadowbrook Club or Vegas or somewhere, and we'd always listen to him on the radio. This was around 1947. I was fourteen or fifteen.

Had you already been playing drums?

No, not really, just in high school bands, marching bands, ROTC, and stuff like that. My cousin was a drummer and we'd go to his house. He had a set and he'd listen to records and play. That's how I kinda picked up what he was doing. Just by watching him and other people play. And every time there was a Big Band or a concert at the college, we'd all go out there and watch them. Man, those guys played everything, and everything they played was so good. Don Lamond was probably my favorite. He played a lot different from the Buddy Riches and Gene Krupas. He had more taste.

What do you mean by "taste"?

He wasn't a showboater; he played *with* the Herman band. He'd play a tempo and then double-time or triple-time it. That was great. It sparked me to watch him.

Western swing was a little before your time, wasn't it?

Yeah, that was earlier, but I played some of that in a few of the local country bands. I listened to Bob Wills. His band had horns and everything. Bob was probably ahead of his time, with the horns and rhythm section.

After the war, the jump blues bands became popular. Louis Jordan, for one.

Yeah, he had the Tympani Five. I never did see them, but I used to listen to their records. They played a hell of a shuffle—fast and clean.

Do you remember your first set of drums?

Oh yeah. My first set was a Slingerland set. My parents bought it for two hundred dollars. Had a bass drum, one tom-tom, one cymbal. Enough to get by. What a feeling! I thought I was the biggest guy in the world. I thought I was great. Couldn't play a lick.

What was your first gig?

It was a strip club, with comedians and strippers. I think we had five musicians. I was about sixteen years old. I worked there about a year. That was kinda fun. They all had different types of music to play with the crashes and the bumps and the grinds, and you had to catch everything, or they'd get mad at you. A lot of times those dancers would never do the same things twice. You had to really watch them because every night they'd kick in a different spot.

That must have prepared you for working with Elvis.

I guess maybe it did; I guess that's where I learned it. With Elvis too, there was no definite pattern to play. Whatever we felt like playing, he said, "Play it. If we don't like it, we'll do it again." A lot of the things I played came about because he'd jump around and cue with his hands or kick his legs. If he'd want a *BOOM* accent on the bass drum, he'd let you know where he wanted it. Elvis would never do anything in a pattern. He never went out there and said, "I'm gonna do 'Hound Dog' or 'Don't Be Cruel' or 'That's All Right, Mama.'" We didn't know what he'd call out. Every night was a different thing. I just watched him real close, that's all.

Elvis would play the crowd. He could feel them. If there wasn't nothing happening—if they weren't responding to him—he'd just keep twisting them around and do different songs until he found something they liked.

In October 1954, Elvis made his first appearances on "The Louisiana Hayride," the Delta country's most popular radio show. That was a turning point in his career. What was playing there like?

Well, you know, for a long time they wouldn't use drums. When they first started considering drums at all, the announcers said, "We've never used drums, so we'll put them behind the curtain." That didn't make any sense. I couldn't see what the artist was gonna do. So finally, after two or three weeks, they decided they'd put me out front, but with just a snare drum and a stick and brush-type thing at first. No complete set.

D. J. FONTANA

D. J. and Elvis

Was there one basic beat you played?

Basically it was a dotted eighth-note shuffle, kinda bouncy, plus a little backbeat. No fills. If you did a little fill on the cymbal, man, that would upset them. Better to do it simple. You know, Elvis was basically simple. He mentioned a lot of times—when we cut his earlier records—he'd say, "Boys, play it simple because some of these guys in those club bands can't learn this stuff if it gets too complicated." He said, "Let's play it so they can play exactly what we're playing." He said a lot of times, "Let's don't get funny or fancy."

Had you heard of Elvis before he got booked on the "Hayride"?

We had heard the records because they were getting played, say, out of Memphis down to Louisiana, into Texas, East Texas, and Arkansas. So the "Hayride" decided to use him on a couple of shows.

What did you think of the records when you first heard them?

I thought they were great. "That's All Right, Mama" and "Blue Moon of Kentucky" were some of them. Tilman Franks, the booker for the "Hayride," called me down one day and said, "This boy Elvis is comin' in. I want you to listen to this record and see what you think. I think we're making a mistake by getting him."

He thought that?

Everyone at the "Hayride" did. They weren't sure about getting Elvis, so they asked me, "What did you think of this record?" And they played it again and I said, "Man, that's a great record!" You never heard a record like that before, with the echo and slapback and whatever else they were using.

So Frank Page and Horace Logan, the announcer, decided to book Elvis for a couple of weekends to see what happened. The first weekend the reception wasn't anything exceptional.

Did you rehearse with them?

No. Scotty came over and asked me if I wanted to help them out. I said, "I don't mind," since that's what I was there for. I said, "Let's talk about it." So we did. We went back to the dressing room. They started to play it down, so I said, "I'll just find me a hole and stay out of your way. I'll play a backbeat for you." On their own, the sound they had was incredible.

You know, Bill could slap the fire out of a bass. No notes, just wood; and Scotty had this little echo type of thing, and Elvis was playing rhythm hard enough that it would go through his voice mike. He played *real* hard.

What did you think of Elvis when you first heard him?

Not a lot. I thought, "Well, just another kid trying to get started." But even after the first show, I knew he had something, but it was something you couldn't put your finger on.

You said before that the response to the first show wasn't that great.

Well, the folks weren't ready for Elvis. They were used to the customary C&W—"I love you darling"—and all that. And he had a little bit of something different. Elvis jived 'em up a bit. After the second or third show he had the people on his side.

He was a good-looking kid; handsome guy with the sideburns and the light brown hair. And he was kind of flamboyant. He was always wearing white shoes. He didn't just get into that; he wore those clothes almost from the first day. He wore the same clothes onstage as he wore on the street because that's all he had, you know.

What was it like the first time you played with him?

It was different. It wasn't the run-of-the-mill country songs. They had a blues and gospel flavor, a mixture of all of that.

How many times did you play with him before it really started to feel like you'd gotten ahold of it?

About the third time. You see, I was learning the tunes and watching the boys—seeing what they were doing. I got a little bit freer then. I said to myself, "I'll just play this if I want to. If it don't work, they'll tell me."

What was the time span between his engagements on the "Hayride"?

They had hired him for three weeks. If I'm not mistaken, they were pretty darn close together. Right after that he was getting hot over in Kilgore, Lufkin, Longview—little towns out in East Texas. They were gonna go over there for three or four days. So they came back and said, "Would you like to go over to East Texas with us for three or four days?" "Well," I said, "I ain't doin' anything here." So we went over there for four days. It really worked out. Elvis was hiring some other local people. We had Sonny Tremble play steel guitar. And sometimes we'd hire a piano player, Floyd Cramer, who was a Shreveport boy.

Were you still working on the "Hayride"?

Off and on. Of course, when Elvis went out, I went with him. Floyd worked some little ol' concerts with us. Well, they weren't concerts, they were joints—backs of trailers, little bitty places.

We worked a place one time in Shreveport called Lake Cliff. I think it's still there. I'd worked out there Fridays and Saturdays with a country band called Hoot-and-Curley, and they played stone country music. Hoot had worked some of the first records with Slim Whitman. That steel guitar sound you heard in those earlier days—well, Hoot had come up with that idea. This band had worked there for I don't know how many years. The guy who owned the club decided he was gonna put Elvis in there one night. It was either Friday or Saturday night. I don't think the local people really knew they were gonna make a band change. Well, we were there, and about ten o'clock or ten-thirty there wasn't a soul left in the place. Not a soul except the three or four people that Elvis brought with him. We run them off. They didn't understand what Elvis was doin'.

How did all your musician friends react to you joining this guy they called the Hillbilly Cat?

Well, it's like anything else. They just thought it's a good job, you're working, what the heck. Although, at that time they couldn't pay me any money. They were working, but just barely enough to drive to Memphis and all those little towns and pay me my wage. We got maybe a hundred bucks a night for everybody. They had to pay for the transportation and the rooms. So I doubt whether Scotty or Bill or Elvis made a dime. They were paying me a hundred dollars a week. I was the highest-paid player in the band.

Did they consider themselves a band at that point?

Well, yeah, I guess they did. After we had been with the "Hayride" a couple of times and had done those other show dates, they said, "If we get any more dates, would you mind working with us all the time?" Well, the "Hayride" only paid fifteen dollars a night, so I took their offer. I jumped on it.

If they had told you they couldn't pay you as much as the "Hayride," do you think you would still have joined?

Yeah, because the feeling was good. And they were all nice guys, so I'd say, "What the heck, we'll try it." I didn't think twice.

What kind of places did you play at first?

Little bitty schoolhouses, auditoriums, armories, just anything they could book.

What was life on the road like back then? How did you travel?

Just out of the car. Scotty had the first car. I think he was the only one of us who had a car. Then later, Elvis got a Cadillac. After he made a few bucks he had a rack built on the top. Of course, we had the "slap" bass, so we put that on top, and at the back end we put the clothes. We had stuff inside too. That's how crowded it was. Once we started to get bigger, I'd say we were playing six or seven days a week and driving five, six hundred miles a night. Elvis would like to drive at nine, ten o'clock in the morning.

Did the four of you ever talk about making it big?

No, not really. After the records got hotter, we really got busy. And we were working, like I said, six or seven days a week, and every chance we'd get to sleep, we'd sleep. Whoever wasn't driving was taking a snooze. We just never got the time to talk a lot. We were just trying to make a buck, basically.

How long were your shows?

At first maybe an hour on the stage 'cause there were other acts on the show. But after a while, when the Colonel [Elvis's manager, Tom Parker] took over, we were doin' thirty minutes. Get out, don't *ever* come back.

No encores?

No. Very seldom did we come back. Sometimes maybe we'd come back and do the end part of "Hound Dog."

Was it Elvis's decision not to come back?

No, he would have come back. But the Colonel always told us, "Give them just enough to get excited and then get out. Leave 'em hungry. 'Cause the next time we book here we'll get more money. Then they'll come back to see you. Just give 'em enough to get a taste."

Do you think Elvis ever felt frustrated by not playing to his limit?

No, I think at the time when he started doing his show he would give them the best that he could for that thirty minutes. He'd do every damn thing he could in the world to get them people on his side. So, by the end, he was really tired. We'd do one show a night 'cause we were booking out what I called a "Sun Package." On *one* show we'd have Johnny Cash, Roy Orbison, Carl Perkins, and Jerry Lee Lewis. We'd work high schools—fifty cents to get in. Everyone had their own band and had their act *together*. It all worked, and man, it was exciting!

After you'd been with Elvis on the road for about a year, he left Sun Records for RCA; consequently, he moved from recording in Memphis to recording in Nashville.

Yeah, it was at an old church.

The first sessions you made with Elvis were when you cut "I Got a Woman," "Heartbreak Hotel," and "Money, Honey." Many now consider that period Elvis's golden age. What is your recollection of those dates?

Well, we'd go in and do what Elvis wanted to do; I played my drums as little as I knew what to play. And we got the hell out of there as fast as we could. That's basically it.

What was the studio setup like?

It wasn't very good.

Roger Hawkins said that in his early days there were no headphones. Did they have any headphones at RCA?

No.

Could you ever hear Elvis singing?

Well, yeah, but it was more that you could *feel* him. Elvis always wanted everybody in a pile, close together. He didn't want everybody spread out all over the place. So therefore we could hear him a little bit.

Was Elvis pretty much in control at these sessions?

Yeah, basically. We had so-called producers, though.

So-called?

Well, Elvis did what he wanted to do. Steve Sholes [Elvis's first producer at RCA] is a nice fella. But he didn't really say a lot. In fact, about twelve, twelve-thirty, he'd take a nap. He'd sit in the control room and say, "When you all get through, wake me up." Steve was interested, because he brought Elvis to Victor, but he was getting up in age and just couldn't stay up all night long. I don't blame the guy.

Would you go all night?

Sure. Sometimes to five or six in the morning. One time on the Coast, I don't remember what the hell the songs were, but we didn't get *one* song from nine in the morning until about eight or nine that night when we left. Just didn't feel right. Nobody was playing nothing right. Elvis just said, "Boys, let's go home. Let's try it again tomorrow." We'd be tryin' too damn hard. So he'd just call the session. The hell with it—go home.

Was Elvis low-key in his approach as a bandleader?

Most of the time, yeah, he never screamed and hollered like they say he did.

What were Elvis's criteria for picking one take over another?

Back then it was mono, so you got what you got. There wasn't no fixing the tracks. But with Elvis, it didn't matter if somebody hit a wrong note or a strange chord. If it felt good, leave it alone. If *his* performance was good and the tempo felt good to him, he didn't give a damn who made a mistake. Leave it alone. That's the record, the hell with it.

And Elvis always had the final say.

Oh yeah, RCA squawked with him a lot, but he'd say the hell with them. "This is the record we want and this is the way we're gonna do it." He had the power back then.

Would the Colonel have a say in the music?

No, no, no. The Colonel knows nothing about music.

Would he come to the studio?

No, he'd never come and say we're gonna do this and that. No. What Elvis wanted us to do was what we did. The Colonel was not there. He very seldom came in that studio. Oh, he'd pass through, shoot the breeze with somebody for a second, and then he'd be gone. He was always on the phone. He's always trying to make some deals.

You know, there is a great thing that happened on the record "I Got a Woman." The bit I'm referring to is when he got to the end of the song, cut the band, and went into a bluesy, Vegas-type ending. Was that spontaneous?

Yup. I remember that song.

"... We were booking out what I called a 'Sun Package.' On one show we'd have Johnny Cash, Roy Orbison, Carl Perkins, and Jerry Lee Lewis. We'd work high schools —fifty cents to get in. Everyone had their own band and had their act together. It all worked, and man, it was exciting!"

You come in on the backbeat rather than on the downbeat.

Well, it was because we didn't know what he was gonna do. Sometimes, if he just wanted to cut the band, he'd just do like *that*. And you got out. And if he wanted to do something else, you just try to guess what he was gonna do next. Like I said before, we just had to watch him every minute—his hands, legs, hips; we had to do this even in the studio. We didn't know what the hell he was gonna do. We did the same blues thing on "Hound Dog." He went right back into it. "You ain't nothin' but a—"

He did that on "The Milton Berle Show."

Right.

You didn't know he was gonna do that?

Hell, no. We were lucky on that one.

After the 1956-57 Sullivan shows, Elvis became a national sensation. How did all this attention affect you?

We didn't really know how big he was because we were always in the cars. We'd play Chicago one night and have to be in Philadelphia the next day. We didn't know about the local press saying he was a sensation, because we were already gone. Another show, another day.

Nobody had a chance to read any papers. The only time we heard anything was if there was a problem. Like the city of Jacksonville, Florida, didn't want us to come to town; you know, vulgar gyrations and all that. So they sat the vice squad down in the front row. Parent-Teacher Association, the mayor, the whole bunch. The Colonel said there is a bunch of people up front who are gonna film the whole show, so Elvis wasn't supposed to move; if he moved they was gonna have us all arrested and close the show. Well, he saw all those people down there, and he got around them. He said, "Well, we got a lot of nice people down here in the front rows." He introduced them *all*, just about. "Let's see, that's the vice squad over there, and that's the camera crew over there, and the mayor, PTA, and everybody else." He said, "I'm not supposed to move. And I'm not gonna move." But he'd move his fingers. They couldn't say anything about his fingers. We were laughing like crazy because we knew what he was doing. He was doing it just to show that he could do it.

Sometimes bands get into little in-jokes while they're playing.

Oh, we used to do that all the time. We'd sit back there, and Elvis would be on the mike and he'd bounce back to us and say, "You see that little lady down there in the front row? She's a darling." And then he'd say, "You guys look the next time." He'd kinda go over there to her so we'd know who he was talking about. Then he'd come back and say, "Hey, there's another one over there." He'd be talking all the time back to us. During a solo he'd say to Scotty, "Scotty, when you get through playing, that one in the front. Isn't she pretty?" We were watching everybody watching us.

I have a technical drum question for you, and it relates to a session you did in July of 1956. You'd just finished "The Steve Allen Show" and were booked for a recording date at RCA in New York the next day.

Elvis cut "Hound Dog," "Don't Be Cruel," and "Anyway You Want Me." The tunes were recorded back to back and the snare sound on "Hound Dog" is—

Okay, I'll tell you where I got that. I stole that.

I'm not sure that's the answer I was shooting for, but I'll bite. What do you mean you stole it?

Fair and square, I stole that drum part. We went to Vegas in '57 for the first time. We were doing the New Frontier Hotel. We were on the program with the Freddie Martin Orchestra. We got out there with three out-of-tune guitars and, boy, we sounded like hell. We bombed in Vegas that first time. We were booked for two weeks; I think we worked a week. You see, it was a different type crowd for us. It wasn't teenagers, it was a dinner crowd. They were trying to eat their twenty-dollar steaks, and here we are making a lot of noise with drums. We bombed, is what we did.

So you say you stole that drum part—

Okay, well, that week we were there, back then they had these lounge acts, and some of them were great. There was this club in town—I don't remember the name—that had this act out of Chicago, Freddy Bell and the Bellboys. Every night for a week, after we'd get through with our show, we'd run over there and watch them. Sooner or later during the midnight show, they'd play that "Hound Dog" and tear the people up. The drummer, everybody. So we left Vegas, went back to New York, and cut that record just as quick as we could.

So you hadn't recorded it yet?

No.

Were you playing it differently before you heard their arrangement?

In *those* days, I don't think we were even playing "Hound Dog." But we went to New York and cut it after we heard *them* play it. Elvis liked their arrangement. He said, "Remember those nights when we went out to watch them guys?" We said, "Yeah." "Y'all remember how they did it?" That's how he wanted to do it.

D.J., that was a fascinating answer to a question I hadn't even thought of. If Freddy Bell and his band inspired you all to play like that, hats off to him—wherever he is. What I was going to ask was, when you were recording in New York in the RCA Studios with Elvis, was there any consideration given to getting a drum sound?

Oh, no. Just set up and play. One mike over here and that's all we had. Not like today, with drum mikes everywhere.

What is interesting about your sound on "Hound Dog," "Don't Be Cruel," and "Anyway You Want Me" was that though they were recorded at the same time, the snare sounds different on all three. Like, on "Don't Be Cruel," the sound is like a box.

Well, that sound is the back of Elvis's guitar. Elvis was popping on the back of the guitar, and I had his guitar case laying across my lap. I played it with the mallets, or sometimes I'd pump it with my hands.

Why did you use the case instead of a drum?

"We didn't really know how big he was because we were always in the cars. We'd play Chicago one night and have to be in Philadelphia the next day. We didn't know about the local press saying he was a sensation because we were already gone. Another show, another day."

I don't know. Just something we thought of. We said, "Hey, let's try it." And Elvis was always playing on the back of the guitar anyhow. There are a lot of records you'll hear where he's playing the damn back of the guitar with his hands. It's in there 'cause we're only using one mike, and it's picking everything up.

Here I'm thinking you put up another snare drum or tuned differently for each song.

No, I had only one snare drum. That's all I could afford.

Levon Helm told me he saw you play in Marianna, Arkansas, and that your drums sounded like a jazz drum set. He said they were high, ringy, and a lot different than the sound the Memphis drummers had been getting.

Probably by then I would have had my Gretsch set from Blockstein. He was a jazz drummer from Houston who owned a music store, and that was *his* set. That's the set in the *Jailhouse Rock* photo. The front head was unborn calfskin with the hair still on it and all. That would really deaden the bass drum. Then, on the beater side of the bass drum, I put a clear timpani head. But later I used goatskin heads. I had one small tom. I put goatskin heads on that tom and goatskin heads on the floor tom, and that made it have a brighter sound.

You were the hottest act in show business from 1956 to 1960. Elvis had fifteen Number One records during that period. And also the movies, the first of which were critically acclaimed, Love Me Tender *and* Loving You. *What is your recollection of those days?*

Loving You had some good songs, like "Teddy Bear" and the title track. What do I remember? Well, that *Loving You* was a lot of fun. Me and Scotty and Bill had never done anything like that. It was different, so we had a lot of fun. Then we did four or five more and decided this ain't for us. You know, get up in the morning at five o'clock, go through the gate at seven, make up on the lot or the set or wherever you're supposed to be at eight. Sit around until noon, dinner break, go back, maybe film thirty seconds and you're through. But you got to be there *all* day long. Not for me.

When you began recording in Hollywood, were there any conflicts between the Southern way of recording and the Hollywood approach?

Well, we didn't have any problems as far as them trying to tell Elvis what they wanted to do. But they had choreographers that were there. We had to have X amount of time for the dance routines, the singing routines. It got technical then; it wasn't just playing music.

Did it draw him away from the band?

A little bit. Elvis was never happy with some of that stuff. But it was back to the same thing; the Colonel made the deal and Elvis would do it.

The first time, on *Loving You*, we were in there playing around, doing one of those country songs, and the conductor comes up and says, "Boys, would you all not play so much, because I've got to score all this stuff later." Scotty's guitar was mostly what he was talking about, because Scotty was just playing whatever the hell he wanted to. The man was trying to clear that up because he had to write all the parts for the score. But Elvis said, "Don't worry about it. Just play what you want to play. Let him worry about scoring it. That's his job." He wasn't trying to be funny or smart. Elvis wanted what he wanted and he wasn't going to let that guy worry him.

It was that first picture, though, that gave us the most problems. We didn't know what the hell we were doing out there—a bunch of guys from Tennessee—and we didn't know the technical aspects of movies. Whatever they wanted to do, we'd do it. But Elvis wasn't gonna let them change us. He told us, "Don't worry about nothin'. We'll play like we've been playin' for years." After Elvis told us not to worry, well, we didn't worry.

Jailhouse Rock came after Loving You, and your drumming on that title track is really exciting. When you hit with those opening snare shots—

Now that's an example of something that had to be done. The choreographer said, "We need a musical thing to go with the dancing." They wanted to be able to visualize a jailbird breaking rocks. So I tried to think of someone on a chain gang smashing rocks. I came up with those shots. Me and Scotty started playing it and it worked. Just a freak of luck.

You know, there is something else you did on that song, going into the solo. I don't know if you remember this, but you lay into a roll, and when you come out of it, you drop a beat. It's one of those moments that give the track a little extra personality.

You know, I've listened to that record, and I don't know what the heck I do there. When I played it, I know it felt like the bottom dropped out. Something happened, but I don't know what.

Did anyone in the studio comment on it at the time?

I don't think anyone knew the difference. I thought then that it didn't make any difference—and I'm not sure yet if it does. Whatever we did was right off the top of our heads. Just doing what we had to do at the time.

The next movie you did, King Creole, *had two songs that were perfectly suited to your style—"Trouble" and "King Creole."*

Well, I enjoyed those because they had some Dixieland in them. Put me back in the strip joints. You know, a few years back I did that movie *Nashville*. They needed somebody to back a stripper, so they said, "Call D.J."

But getting back to Hollywood, after a while it got to a point where it was no fun anymore doing those movie things. The movies were terrible; we all knew that.

Did Elvis know that the three of you guys were unhappy doing this kind of stuff?

No, we just told him we didn't want to do pictures anymore. We'd still go out and do all the sound tracks, but we just didn't want to be in the movies, on screen, anymore. We weren't actors and weren't comfortable doing it.

"In those days, I don't think we were even playing 'Hound Dog.' But we went to New York and cut it after we heard them *play it.*"

How did Elvis react to that?

He didn't mind. He said, "Hell, I don't blame you. These pictures are bad anyhow." He didn't question it too much. As long as we played the sound tracks with him, he was happy. Elvis didn't want no strangers around him. With us, he could be himself.

The music was getting further away from what you did in Nashville. Did Elvis ever say to the movie people, "Hey fellas, this isn't where we're coming from. Let's get back"?

Nah, unless a song was absolutely atrocious. He'd do the damn thing, though sometimes I'd seen Elvis stop and say, "We can't do this." And if the writers were around, he would say, "Take this back. Rewrite it; do something with it." Then if it was suitable, the next day maybe we'd do it. But he would seldom do that. That was his problem: Elvis should have said something, but he wouldn't. Also, the Colonel would never let him cut more than the amount of stuff they needed. Just go in, do three or four songs, that was it. That's why there's no stuff in the can now. After all those years, they should have thousands of songs.

Elvis would just go ahead with the program and get the picture done. You see, the Colonel's theory was *don't make any waves;* don't let me have to make a deal with these people, because they're gonna want to come back and make a deal with me. And the Colonel didn't give deals, he took deals. If there was any favors to owe, *you* owe the Colonel.

Did you guys in the band have much to do with the Colonel?

We really didn't deal with him at all because we were on Elvis's payroll, not the Colonel's. Elvis said, "If there's a problem, come see me—I'll work it out."

We've always heard about Elvis's mother's influence. How did she fit in with his whole career situation?

Well, you know, Elvis loved his mother a lot—used to call her three or four times a day when we were on the road. You know that movie with Shelley Winters as his mama? Well, I don't know how she researched the role, but Elvis's mother was *exactly* like the lady in the film. Elvis was always worried about the bad things people were saying about him, the hip shaking and stuff, you know, that he was vulgar. His mama would say, "Don't worry about it. You're not vulgar to me." That meant a lot to Elvis. She could be pretty critical if she thought he was doing something wrong. And you bet she'd tell him too. And he'd listen to her.

Was there a power struggle between Elvis's mother and the Colonel?

If Elvis's mother said something was wrong—it was wrong. The Colonel had no control of that. If the Colonel said it was right and his mama said it was wrong—it was wrong, take it or leave it. Nobody ever said *anything* against that lady.

Of course, in 1958, at the height of his popularity, Elvis went into the army and your career was—

Shot to hell, plain and simple.

How did you carry on?

Well, I lived in Shreveport and my dad still had his grocery store, so I helped out. Then I went out with Gene Vincent and the Blue Caps.

That's something I never knew. What was it like working with Gene Vincent?

Well, they were really nice guys, but a little kooky. I was a little bit older than them. When I got to Dallas, I said, "Gene, don't ever call me again, please!" Those guys would do anything—and not just on that tour. They told me they done all kinds of other things—paint rooms, tear up stuff, set fire alarms off, shoot fire extinguishers up and down the halls.

Did you cut up like that on Elvis's tours?

No, the press thought we were rambunctious, but we weren't. We were a little bit older—not much—but we had a lot of respect for other people's stuff. And Elvis was who *he* was, so we didn't want to reflect bad stuff on him. We'd treat everybody decent. We wore bow ties and suits. We were gentlemen.

Were you with any other groups?

No, Gene Vincent was the only one. They called me from Fargo, North Dakota, one time. And I said, "Where in the hell is Fargo, North Dakota?" I asked, "When do you want me there, next week?" They said, "No, tomorrow night." I got some reservations to go up there and I worked about thirty days. Went all up through there. Up to Canada and back. Those guys drove me crazy. Nice guys, really nice guys. But I was afraid I was gonna get locked up somewhere and not be able to get back home.

From "The Dorsey Brothers Show"—1956

When Elvis came back in 1960, he re-formed the group and resumed recording. This time, however, he augmented the group, and you and Buddy Harmon began double-drumming. In fact, you were one of the first double-drumming teams in rock & roll. How did you work out what you'd play?

Well, you know, Buddy's a darn good drummer. All we'd do is say to each other, "Okay, Buddy, I'll play rhythm on this one and you fill," or "D.J., you fill and I'll play a backbeat." We'd stay out of each other's way. If he'd play on his ride cymbal, I'd stay over here on the hi-hat. We just kinda mixed it up.

Why do you think Elvis brought other musicians in?

The sound had to get bigger. Piano, bass, drums, vocal groups. I guess the sixties trend had changed things by then.

Well, the Beatles and the so-called British Invasion created the same kind of excitement as you all had years earlier. Throughout the early sixties Elvis had been making records primarily in support of his movies. You were working in Nashville. How did the English groups affect your scene?

The Beatles killed us. They just hit the world by storm. That guy managing them kind of reminded me of the Colonel. I remember before they even had a record out, you'd read *Billboard* and all the trade papers and see "The Beatles Are Coming!" We said, "Who the hell are the Beatles? What is it?" You know, what are they?

Did Elvis ever view the Beatles as his competition?

He never commented on it. He really liked everybody. I used to go to his house, and by the pool he had a big jukebox. But he didn't have even one record of his own on it. I said, "What's the matter? Don't you like your records?"

"I hear them all the time," he said. "But these people I don't hear all the time."

Did this whole new wave of music have any effect on Elvis's approach?

No, I don't think so. What the hell, *he* was Elvis.

It's generally believed that your relationship with Elvis ended when he got out of the service and stopped doing personal appearances. Is that true?

I was with Elvis from '54 until after his comeback special in 1968. We did all those movie sound tracks—at least three a year—so we were busy enough.

Were you still in Shreveport at this time?

Yeah. See, I was working some with Elvis and still going out to Arkansas and East Texas with some of the "Hayride" artists. Then I'd come back and do a few club dates. Of course, I still worked in my dad's store. I moved from Shreveport up here to Nashville around '66. I started to work quite a bit then. Guys like Bob Moore, the bass player, and Floyd Cramer helped me out a little bit—put me on their sessions. They didn't need me, 'cause Buddy Harmon was doing all their stuff. I said, "Well Buddy's playing—you don't need me." They said, "Play a tambourine or pick up any damn thing—just play it." Floyd put me on a lot of jobs that I didn't have to be on. Some of his real "class" albums. I was on several of those things and never played a lick.

During the mid-sixties period when you were cutting tracks for the movies, did you have much contact with Elvis?

Not a lot. We didn't shoot the breeze on the phone, if that's what you mean. Elvis never called anybody. I'd hear people say, "Oh, Elvis called me last night." They were full of crap. It wasn't that he didn't want to, he just never had to. He'd tell Red West or somebody to "get so-and-so for me." That was the end of it. Oh, he did call me a couple of times, say, back in '58. We'd finished *Jailhouse Rock*, and Scotty and Bill were gonna quit the band. The three of us discussed it, and I told Scotty and Bill, "You guys have the right to quit. You started the thing." But I told them, "You guys hired me for X amount of dollars a week, and Elvis has always paid me. Whatever it is, good or bad, he paid me."

I really had no quarrel to leave. They said, "Okay, fine." So they left and Elvis heard about it, you see. They sent him a letter or something. Well, Elvis called me, and my wife said he was stuttering. He said, "Barbara?" She said, "Elvis?" Because it was strange for him to call. He said, "Yeah, this is Elvis. Is D.J. home?" And she said, "No, but I'll find him." I was down at the "Hayride" talking to a couple of bookers. I'd told her where I was going. I said, "If anybody calls, I'll be down there, talking to Tilman Franks." She comes down and says, "Elvis just called." I said, "My God. What the hell does he want?" So I went back home, called him, and he said, "Well, I'm glad you didn't quit." He said, "You're the only one who stayed with me." I said, "Elvis, you always paid me. You always did what you said you were gonna do. I'm happy." So Scotty and Bill quit. After that he hired them on a daily basis. You know, I think they hurt his feelings. But I don't blame Scotty and Bill for leaving—they should have been millionaires. In the earlier days, before he recorded with *anyone*, Elvis said, "I want you guys to have a piece of my record." And Scotty said, "No, we're not supposed to do that. You're the artist. That's your money." Because he wasn't recording with anybody then, it didn't make any difference. Elvis tried to cut them a deal, but Scotty said, "No, you do your record deal, and we'll work some clubs and split that up. Elvis was getting fifty percent and they were getting twenty-five percent apiece. That was for the club dates. And fifty percent of a hundred bucks—how much is that? But after he started to be a monster, all this was forgotten.

D.J., I'd like to talk about the last time you and Scotty performed with Elvis. It was the 1968 television special, Elvis's first public appearance in seven years. What do you remember about that night?

Well, I think that was probably one of the best shows he ever did. He looked so good. In fact, I stayed over a couple of days. After we got through with our little segment, I went into Elvis's dressing room and

"The Beatles killed us. They just hit the world by storm. That guy managing them kind of reminded me of the Colonel."

said, "Well, I think I'll go home in the morning." He said, "What are you going home for?" I said, "Well, I don't know. I'll just go on back home. Ain't nothing to do here." He said, "Why don't you just stay around a couple of days? Would you do that?" He just wanted someone there that he felt comfortable around.

The show had a big orchestra with Hal Blaine on drums. They were doing some tune and weren't playing it exactly like the record. Elvis said to me, "D.J., would you mind going over there and showing that conductor, whoever he is, how to play it?" It had something to do with quarter-note triplets. I went over to Hal, because I knew him. I wasn't about to say *nothing* to that conductor. I didn't know that guy from Jesus, so I said, "Hal, Elvis really doesn't like the way you guys are doing it. Can you say something to the conductor?" So Hal said, "I'll say something to him." He told the conductor and the conductor changed it. Elvis just wanted someone there to kind of tell the guy because he wouldn't say anything to him.

How did they put the show together?

We did two hour-and-a-half shows. Originally, they had a set of drums on that stage, but the stage wasn't any bigger than this room here, and visually the drums didn't look good. They wanted the feeling of us relaxed, just sitting in the room, playing and talking. No script, just whatever came up. Elvis agreed the drums didn't look right, so he told them to "just move the drums and we'll get D.J. to play on the back of the guitar case." So there I was playing on top of the guitar case again. I had it laying across my lap. A stick and a brush. But everyone on that damn bandstand was stompin' their feet so loud we had to kind of quiet their feet down because there was feet in every mike, and all you could hear was foot-stompin'.

Did you think at that point you might ever get back to playing with him on tour?

Well, he wanted to go on the road, I think. And we had a lot of chances. We could have gone to London, Australia, a lot of the foreign markets. But it never did materialize. I think it was management again.

In the early days you never went to Europe, right?

We never went to Europe, period.

Why was that?

I got some good ideas, but I don't talk about them. It's back to management. But I'll tell you this—Elvis wanted to go to Europe.

Earlier we touched on the effect the Beatles had on the Nashville music community. I know you worked with Ringo on his Beaucoups of Blues *album in 1970. How did that come about?*

It was set up. He was gonna come in and do a country album with Pete Drake, the pedal steel player, producing. I was working with Pete a lot in those days, and he said, "Hey, we're gonna do Ringo Starr," and I said, "Oh, *sure* you are." Somebody was always gonna do George Harrison or one of the other Beatles. You know how you just pass it off. Well, it damn sure happened, and I'll tell you, Ringo was the nicest man in the world. We did basically all country tunes. And he did whatever the producer told him. A guy with his power, he could have said, "Yeah? Get the hell out of here!" But he didn't. He said, "What do you guys want me to do?" We had some pretty well-known players on that date, so we made him a little nervous, I'm sure. And he made *us* nervous. We had Charlie Daniels, myself, Buddy Harmon. It was just a whole list of people—Jerry Kennedy, Charlie McCoy. Those English people have heard about these people all their lives. But it worked out; it worked out fine and it didn't take very long—maybe two or three days.

Did you ever get into a conversation with Ringo about him playing in the Beatles and you playing with Elvis?

I asked him about the Beatles stuff one time. He said, "I don't really understand the way you guys play over here." And I didn't know what he meant exactly. He said, "You guys do a lot of fills. I never did do a lot of fills." And I know why. I'll tell you a story about Ringo's drumming. We were jamming in the studio one night, and Ringo said, "Do you mind if I play?" I said, "Are you kidding? Play!" I was playing the maracas or something behind him, just listening to him. I swear he never varied the tempo. He played that backbeat and never got off of it. Man, you couldn't have moved him with a crane. It was amazing. He played a hell of a backbeat man, and *that's* where it's at.

After the '68 special, was there ever any talk about a reunion of the original band?

Well, Elvis's management tried to get me and Scotty to go to Vegas. But it was hard to leave Nashville. You know, I'd been trying since '66 to get my feet wet in recording, and to leave town for more than even two weeks was like death to a sessionman. I told that to the Colonel's people; whether or not it got back to Elvis, I didn't know at the time. I was afraid the true story of why I couldn't go with him wouldn't get back to him. So one day I heard he was over at RCA and figured I'd go over and tell him myself. So I went over and said to Elvis, "I want to tell you what happened about that Vegas thing." He said, "I heard the reason." He told me what he heard and I said, "You *did* hear the truth, then—I didn't want you to hear ten different stories." I told him I had kids to raise and was trying to get into recording—I explained it to him again. He said not to worry about it. "If I was in your shoes, I'd do the same thing. If *I* could stay home, I would," he said. He was really nice about it.

When was the last time you saw Elvis?

Well, I think it was early on in the seventies, a few years after the baby, Lisa Marie, was born. Me and my wife would go down and see him every now and again. We'd sit around and talk. All he ever wanted to do was talk about the fifties—the early days. Man, he had an ungodly memory. He remembered everything we ever did. He'd talk about old gigs, places we'd been—stuff I'd forgotten but he remembered.

> "Ringo played that backbeat and never got off of it. Man, you couldn't have moved him with a crane."

One day, it was just me and Barbara sitting around with him. We'd been talking a good while, and he said, "You know, you all are lucky. I get so tired of being Elvis—I don't know what to do. I just wish I could do something else." But, of course, he couldn't do anything else, except sleep all day and roam at night. If he went out somebody might see him; he'd create a riot. You know, I think if he'd been able to relax a bit, maybe leave the house by the back door in a pair of Levis and a cowboy hat—I think maybe he'd still be around.

D.J., does it ever seem like those early days never happened?

Nah, because I've heard it every year for the last thirty. I got lucky. I could have still been working "The Louisiana Hayride," but I was at the right place at the right time—and they needed somebody. That's the way I feel about it. But I'll tell you this much. It's gonna be a long while before something like *that* happens again.

SELECTED DISCOGRAPHY

Singles

WITH ELVIS PRESLEY

"Blue Suede Shoes" (April 1956, RCA)
"I Got a Woman" (1956, RCA)
"Heartbreak Hotel" (May 1956, RCA)
"My Baby Left Me" (June 1956, RCA)
"Hound Dog" (August 1956, RCA)
"Don't Be Cruel" (September 1956, RCA)
"Anyway You Want Me (That's How I Will Be)" (November 1956, RCA)
"Ready Teddy" (1956, RCA)
"Rip It Up" (1956, RCA)
"All Shook Up" (April 1957, RCA)
"(Let Me Be Your) Teddy Bear" (July 1957, RCA)
"Jailhouse Rock" (October 1957, RCA)
"You're So Square (Baby I Don't Care)" (1957, RCA)
"Trouble" (1958, RCA)
"King Creole" (1958, RCA)
"Wear My Ring around Your Neck" (May 1958, RCA)
"(You're the) Devil in Disguise" (August 1963, RCA)
"Return to Sender" (November 1965, RCA)

Dave Clark

10

"The first time 'Do You Love Me' got into the charts at number 48, I was so excited—I can't tell you. That moment, to me, was more important than getting to Number One."

EVERYONE SHOULD have as good a year as Ed Sullivan did in 1964. In March, following the success of the Beatles on three of his shows, Sullivan booked a band from Tottenham, a working-class district in the north of London. The Dave Clark Five landed on America's shores and were met by nearly the same sort of excitement that greeted the Beatles a month earlier.

Popular as they were, the Dave Clark Five's appeal was more difficult to define than the Beatles'. They had their gimmicks: high-heeled boots stomping out the rhythm to their hit "Bits and Pieces," white pants and shirts with strange-looking collars. In addition, they were the only group in the original British Invasion with a sax player. But the main thing that set them apart was that guy out front behind the drums, Dave Clark. Who'd ever heard of a drummer fronting a rock & roll band? But there he was. Smiling, perched high above his drum set, Dave Clark pounded away on his snare drum with a relentless big beat. Barely out of his teens, he also managed the group, was its chief songwriter, and produced the records. In fact, "Glad All Over," the band's first big hit, displaced the Beatles from the Number One slot on the British charts. The year 1964 exploded with new rock & roll talent, and with the beat of his drums, Dave Clark was right in there leading the charge.

THE BIG BEAT

In the spring of that year teenage America lost its mind. I can testify to that. I was in the audience for a Dave Clark Five concert at the Mosque Theater in downtown Newark, New Jersey. It was the first rock & roll show I'd ever seen, and after it, I was never the same. What a scene! The lights dimmed as the band ran down the center aisle and up a ramp to the stage. Dave rolled into "Do You Love Me?" and the place went absolutely crazy—three thousand kids all trying to squeeze into the first row. The DC5 played all their hits and sounded fantastic. I was thirteen years old, and that beat and that energy really got to me.

Twenty years later some people might not remember just how big the DC5 were. They were the first British rock & roll band to hit the road in America. They toured extensively before the Stones and before the Beatles' first big summer tour. In those days sides were taken. You were either a Beatles, Stones, or a DC5 fan. I had a problem. I went nuts over all three.

Dave was also a clever businessman. He knew there were people in the record industry who might take advantage of a young kid who perhaps would do anything and give up anything to get on a record. He'd had experience in films and knew those types. He also knew the only way he would remain happy was if he maintained control over his music. What he did then was an unusually bold move for any newcomer to attempt and very hip for a twenty-year-old to pull off. He negotiated his own record deal. During our conversation Dave explained how he got what he wanted in greater detail.

Dave, along with Ringo, Charlie Watts, and other rock & roll drummers in the late fifties and early sixties, was criticized for his drumming. So-called serious musicians and critics put down these rockers for their lack of "technical" virtuosity, overlooking the fact that musicians bring out emotions in their listeners in many different ways. Dave did what he had to do for the musical situation he created.

People ask Dave how he made all those hit records. When we spoke, he told me about his recording formula. His records, "Anyway You Want It" or "Can't You See That She's Mine," have a raw and infectious drive that is the mark of great dance music. Though straightforward Dave's style was clever. Check the little cymbal accent that picks up the choruses in "Anyway You Want It." That's a little bit of the excitement I'm talking about.

When I first contacted Dave's London office in the fall of 1982, his secretary informed me he wasn't in. Could he ring me back, she asked. Not two hours later I received his return call: "Hello, Max, this is Dave Clark. How can I help you?"

I traveled to London in the summer of 1983 and a meeting was arranged. Sitting in Dave's spacious London penthouse, we found ourselves reminiscing about the sixties, when a skinny kid's head was turned around by this man who played the red drum set.

Dave disbanded the Dave Clark Five in 1970, but the group's records are still around. They stand as classics of pure and powerful pop entertainment. Dave has never wanted to re-form his band for nostalgia's sake: "We quit at the top," he said.

MAX: Why do you think the early sixties was such a great period for British rock & roll?

DAVE: We were the first generation that wasn't drafted. The thing about getting drafted when you were eighteen was that that's the most important time of your life for freedom of expression. For so many, that period was cut short, and you were told what to do, where to go, who to be. Then you got out of the service, got married, and worked a job in a factory. That was it. Had not the government stopped the draft, there would have been no DC5, no Beatles, no Stones. That the English groups expressed themselves surprised a lot of Americans. We said what we felt. In those days, to be a rock & roll star, you had to be perfect. The hair had to be perfect, the dress had to be perfect, everything you said had to be perfect. The thing that worked for the English was we were being ourselves. Before that, the music industry would "package" its stars. The first time we went to America the record company treated us like a product. It frightened the shit out of me. I thought, "The hell, I want to go back home." I never wanted to come to America. When the DC5 started, we used to play the American air bases in England. We played four hours a night. It was hell because the American servicemen were always getting pissed [drunk]. It was the only side of America I'd ever seen, and I didn't care for it.

It wasn't until our first record went to Number Five in the charts, and the Beatles had a Number One and they went over and did "The Ed Sullivan Show" that we were invited to go over and do the show. And at first I said no. See, I produced the group's records and we didn't have a manager or an agent. I said we wouldn't go professional until we got *two* records in the Top Five. Well, our first record, "Glad All Over," went to Number One in England, which was like a dream. Everyone said you must go professional, you must have an agent and all that. I said no, that we'd wait and see how the next record sold.

The second record we did went to Number One too, so we had our two Number One records. Then I got this call from the States: Would we do "The Ed Sullivan Show" now? Well, to be honest, I didn't know who Ed Sullivan was, because we never got the show here in England, you see. And I said no, we didn't want to go. Then I got a call from Sullivan's son-in-law and he said, "We'll pay you ten thousand dollars and air fare for ten people." I said to myself, God, I was earning three pounds [fifteen dollars] a day, working in film, so we went. We arrived in the States unknown.

The format of the Sullivan show was that you'd do a dress rehearsal on the Saturday before the show in front of a live audience, which I didn't know about. It might be listed in the TV guide that you were appearing on the show that week. But if Sullivan didn't like you, he'd pay you off and cancel you, whether you were a big star or not.

Now, if he liked you, he'd put you higher on the bill. We opened the show at the Saturday afternoon dress rehearsal bottom of the bill. But Sullivan liked us. We went over so well he put us on Sunday second from the top and let us play two songs. And then we went over so well on the actual live show that he pulled the top of the bill off before its last number and gave us one more song to do, which made it a total of three. Then at the very end of the show Sullivan told the audience we were going to be back next week.

And you didn't know that he was going to announce that?

No! This story has never been told, incidentally. The following week was our first week as professionals. We were going to play the Liverpool Empire, and it was sold out because we were a big name in England at the time. So I told the Sullivan people I couldn't do the show next week, and I'll always remember the American agent saying, "But you must do it! Mr. Sullivan is God!" I said to him that we were very flattered, but we simply couldn't do it. I can recall Sullivan asking me to come up to his office; he was a very nice man, a straight, regular guy. I just said to him, "I'm sorry, I can't. I appreciate the embarrassing position you're in, but if you'd asked, I would have told you." "But I've told millions of Americans that you and your band are going to be on the show next week. You have to do it," he pleaded. So then he said, "What can I do?" "Well, we're playing our first professional engagement in England. We've been sold out for a week," I said. "I'll buy the show out," replied Sullivan. And I said, "Well, I don't really like New York." "Tell me where you want to go." On the way in from the airport I'd seen this great big poster: Montego Bay: Island Paradise. So very coolly I said, "Well, we'd like to go to Montego Bay." So he flew us all to Montego Bay, Jamaica. We came back to Kennedy Airport five days later and there were thirty thousand people at the airport. We topped the bill that week.

The power of the man and his show were unbelievable. Within the course of seven days we were household names and ended up having five records in the charts at once. It was wonderful. Afterward he asked us to promise that every time we came to America in the future we'd do his show first. I think we did eighteen or twenty Sullivan shows. Looking back, we weren't being slick with him, but totally honest, and I think he appreciated it.

Right from the beginning of your career you were totally involved in the production and recording of the DC5.

Yes, and the reason I did was because nobody else had any interest in us. I used to do stunt work in films, and for one job I was paid three hundred pounds for three nights work crashing a car for the English rock singer Adam Faith. I used that money to make the first record.

Did you know anything about making records at that point?

No, but I always believed that you should always surround yourself with the best people, the best engineer in the case of recording a song. I knew what I wanted and we simply went in and did it.

The first record sounded great, and I went to EMI with it. I'd always wanted to be on Columbia Records, which, by the way, is not the American Columbia Records but rather the Columbia that was owned by EMI Records in Britain. I went into their office and found out what the highest royalty rate was. And I thought, well, I'll ask double. I figured it was a good position from which to compromise. I think because I was only nineteen at the time and the record was fresh and raw, they figured, you know, *maybe* a one-hit wonder. And they agreed to the royalty rate I asked for! I got double the royalty rate anyone else was getting at the time, including the Beatles!

I also did what they call a favored nations deal: If any of their artists got a higher royalty than me, mine would go up. Also, at the end of the three-year contract period, all the masters reverted back to me. So in the end, with the early tracks like "Glad All Over," I got an astronomical amount, royalty-wise.

Are you saying you leased the masters to the company?

Right, because if they didn't promote them the right way, I could take the songs off the label. It was as simple as that. I did it because so many acts are lost not because they're not good but simply due to lack of attention. I've seen a lot of careers go down the drain because of that. It was really for creative control over my own career. I always looked on the long term; I looked ahead. It so happened it was the right decision.

Were you playing drums before you started the group?

No. My wish and love was to be an actor. But I came from a working-class family, so I couldn't afford to go to drama school. We formed the group purely by accident. I used to play soccer, and some of us were invited to play a Dutch team one Easter. We didn't have enough money to pay for the fare to get there. So we formed the group and raised about three hundred pounds, which paid for the fares to Holland. We went over to Holland and won the match. When we came home we had some business cards printed and gave a few of them to a friend's mother who was a maid in Buckingham Palace. This all sounds like some sort of press handout, doesn't it? Anyway, we asked her if she would just slip some cards around the Palace. One day a letter came with the Palace seal on it asking us if we would play the staff ball. It seemed like a joke to me, so I ignored it. Three days later there's a knock at my family's door and it's a footman who asks if the band had made any decision on whether or not it would play the staff ball. I was shocked. Naturally I said yes. We had to go down and get screened by the police and get official passes. We didn't have any money, so we went to the Palace on the subway, got out around the corner from it, and just had enough money to get a cab to go through the gates.

"I think the magic of the Dave Clark Five was that it worked as a unit."

Playing the Palace—we thought we'd be stars overnight, but it didn't happen. We began playing all the dives and dance halls and the American air bases, so we really put our time in. We played places where they'd throw beer cans at you if you weren't any good. But through that type of experience we found out what kind of music people liked. The important thing was to avoid becoming self-indulgent. And I think that's what I tried to put into the DC5 records. There was no message. A lot of people have criticized me for maybe being too commercial. I didn't pretend to be what I wasn't. The records were made purely for entertainment.

I was also not the world's greatest drummer. I mean, I could never be a Buddy Rich in a million years. I always felt the simpler you are, the more of whatever you do stands out. It's what you don't put in a record that makes the record sound good.

In 1964, you and Ringo were two of the most visible drummers in the world. And you both took a lot of heat for the simplicity of your drumming.

I took more heat than Ringo because it was the first time ever that a drummer had been in the front onstage. The audience liked it. But a lot of people in the music industry, such as other groups, singers, and the music press, thought it was wrong. It was mainly other groups that didn't like me out front because they felt the singer should be out there and that's all. The fact that I was out there wasn't intentional or planned. It just happened. Mike Smith had an incredible voice, but he never wanted to perform out front. That's why he hasn't gone on, which is sad. But he's happy doing what he wants to do. He's got a company that's involved in film and jingles work and he's done very well.

You and Mike did most of the songwriting for the DC5. What was your approach?

Normally I knew the direction we wanted to go for the next single. And I would usually come up with a hook, as I did with "Glad All Over" and "Bits and Pieces." Then Mike would put things together and in the studio we'd switch different things around and make the song work. With "Catch Us If You Can," I came up with the hook, but Mike couldn't make it work, so I gave the song to Lenny [Davidson] and he made it work.

I think the magic of the DC5 was that it worked as a unit. We also weren't a manufactured band, so when success came we enjoyed it. We always said that if we ever went out on the road, we'd have to go out on the top of the bill; if we couldn't, we'd just carry on and work our daytime jobs and simply enjoy it.

What became of the other members of the band?

Dennis Payton is in real estate. Lenny Davidson's got three antique shops and has become a bit of a hermit. Rick Huxley has got a partnership in the electronics business and is also doing very well.

Who were the musicians in England that influenced you?

Well, I always remember seeing a Big Band over here in England called the Eric Delaney Band when I was very young. This guy got up

DAVE CLARK

The Dave Clark Five, circa 1964. From left to right: Mike Smith, Lenny Davidson, Dennis Payton, Rick Huxley, Dave Clark

in front and had timpani with the pedals on them and he did this thing—it was very jazzy—but I said, "God, he looks good!" And it was very, very simple. That's the one little bit of inspiration that I always recall.

I always believed in showmanship, but you're very restricted as a drummer. You just sit there. But architecturally, the drummer is the most integral part of any group. Then there's the bass, and it builds up from there. If you haven't got that backbone, you're dead.

The DC5's records reflect that approach.

You see, I wasn't a trained musician. I held my drumsticks, for instance, the wrong way: matched grip. And I was a very heavy player, so when I played, I'd hit those drums hard and heavy.

Your singles were very well crafted. How did you approach recording them?

We only had a four-track tape recorder in those days. We'd work on a little two-track recorder at home and work out the songs so I knew exactly what I was going to do before I went into the studio. If anything else happened in the studio that was spontaneous or magical, we'd just drop our original framework or idea and go with the new one. Once you know what you're going to do you go for a take; past three takes and you go over the top. You're better off to break and go out and have lunch or a beer or whatever. I think it's important to get it in the first three takes. For example, with "Bits and Pieces," we put our tracks down first, and I wanted to put stomping on it. So we put our four tracks down, then we overdubbed and put on something else and then something else and then the last thing was our harmonies or final track of vocals, not our lead vocal. "Bits and Pieces" was supposed to have eight foot stomps in each break, but in one of the breaks there were only seven and a half. I kept it that way because it had energy; it would have been wrong to go back and rerecord it. And then somebody said, "How'd you get that? There's two drummers on there." Well, there weren't two drummers. It was just seven and a half foot stomps and it was a mistake! Sometimes you make mistakes, and out of them, good things happen.

I always liked the beginning of "Bits and Pieces," where that first snare drum roll comes in just a split second late.

That was a mistake! I was slightly behind, if you want me to be honest. But it worked. This was the reason Mike Smith and I worked so well together. Mike had studied classical piano since he'd been about four years old, so musically he knew what was right. But me, I couldn't read a note of music. If it sounded right to my ear, I would do it. Mike might say, "You can't do that because it's not in the book." Well, I wouldn't give a damn about the book as long as it sounded right.

Like on the song "Over and Over"—we finished the track and I played it and realized it was too slow. In those days you didn't have a vari-speed. So what you'd do is put Scotch tape around the capstan—rig it around half a dozen times, put the master on it, and the tape would speed up. You'd keep adding on the Scotch tape until you got it at the speed you wanted. And if you listen to "Over and Over"—the end of the harmonica solo—it's got a vibrato on it and it wavers slightly. You might think it's a special effect of sorts, but actually it's because of a flaw in the way the Scotch tape was put on the capstan—a five-cent roll of technology.

Who inspired you most?

Little Richard, Elvis Presley, Fats Domino, all those great rockers. Also, I'm a great admirer of Phil Spector. I think he was so ahead of his time. I mean, what he did with those early records by the Crystals and the Ronettes. Those were classic records.

You always picked great tunes to cover. I heard your version of "Do You Love Me?" before I heard the Contours' original version.

Well, it's funny. I first heard the Contours do the song in a dance hall in England, and that inspired me to do the song. I think "Do You Love Me?" was also one of our best records. The first time it got into the charts at number forty-eight, I was so excited I can't tell you. I'll always remember shouting out of the car, "We're number forty-eight—forty-eight with a bullet!" Nobody knew who we were. But that moment, to me, was more important than getting to Number One.

Nobody before had attempted the kind of snare drum rolls you put on your records. And you always ended your songs with some kind of little drum thing.

Mainly it was because I wanted people to know I was there. (Laughs.)

To me, you never seemed to overplay.

Once again, I think that was because I wasn't the world's greatest drummer. I'm not trying to be modest in any way. I was never taught to play the drums. And yet I read things about people who supposedly taught me. Somebody will say, "I taught Dave Clark how to play drums." I don't even know the person! I never took a lesson. I think maybe if I did take some lessons the drumming would have been more complicated.

I was asked a question when I had my first Number One record if I thought I was a good drummer. I said, "No, there are thousands better than me and thousands worse. I just play for enjoyment." So the headlines read: DAVE CLARK SAYS HE'S A LOUSY DRUMMER! Sometimes the press wants blood.

I read once where a drummer by the name of Clem Cattini had played on some of your records.

I know Clem. I met him years later. He's a drummer who used to play with a group called the Tornadoes in the sixties. Since then I've used him a couple of times on a couple of records I produced. I'm talking about the late seventies. Up until then, I'd never met Clem.

But that rumor is typical. When you're successful, if people can find a way to knock you down, they will. Everybody loves success and they want to build you up. As soon as you get that Number One spot, then the next thing they want to do is pull you down. It got to the point with us that we were doing American tours and people were saying that we were miming to tapes played behind the stage. What annoyed me about those rumors was that the DC5 had made its name as a live band—before we made any records. At my home ground, a place called the Royal Tottenham, we were packing in six thousand people a night, four nights a week. We even got a gold cup for pulling in the biggest amount of business at the chain of dance halls we worked. With over two hundred bands playing in them, we pulled in the most business in the summer of 1963. And that was without any record, because we had yet to go into the studio. We were a live band. And you've got to work your ass off to play to the same audience three hours a night, four nights a week. You had to change your repertoire and your songs to keep the thing interesting enough to draw the people in. Those rumors hurt me at the time because we'd paid our dues.

One of the few ballads the DC5 did in the early years was "Because." How did that come about?

In England we had hits with very uptempo songs like "Do You Love Me?," "Glad All Over," and "Bits and Pieces." "Because" was the first song I'd actually written on my own. And although I produced the records and leased them out, the record company said, "Look, you've had big hits with uptempo songs. It would be silly to put out a ballad." Well, at the time we had a number two album with "Can't You See That She's Mine" on it, and they wanted us to bring out that song instead. I told them I thought that would stop us from getting a Number One because the album was number two. They said it would make no difference. And I thought, I've been lucky so far. Maybe

> "What annoyed me about those rumors was that the DC5 had made its name as a live band—before we made any records. At my homeground, a place called the Royal Tottenham, we were packing in six thousand people a night, four nights a week. . . . You've got to work your ass off to play to the same audience three hours a night, four nights a week."

they're right. I had written the song myself. Maybe I was too biased. But I did love that song. So I went along with it and "Because" became the B side of "Can't You See That She's Mine" in England. Well, that song went to number two or number three, and by that time the album was Number One. And I think if "Can't You See That She's Mine" hadn't been on the album, it would have gone to Number One.

I really wanted to bring out "Because" in the States. We had about five records out there at the time, and the record company refused to release it. I felt we needed a change. I wanted to do the ballad, then come back with some uptempos. After some transatlantic phone calls I finally said, "Look, either you release 'Because' as a single or I won't deliver any more masters. It's as simple as that." So I got a cable from the president of Epic Records, Len Levy. He wrote, "We are going to release 'Because,' but it will ruin your career. You still have time to change your mind." Well, it was our biggest-selling single.

You produced the group, wrote its songs, managed it. It was a lot to keep together for a twenty-year-old. How were you able to do it all?

Somebody had to make the decisions, otherwise we would have had five different decisions and gone nowhere. A group, like a football team, needs a captain to succeed. To do anything good, you've got to be prepared to fall flat on your face. That's very important. And I was ready to do that.

I always felt that I was as good as my next record. I knew the bubble could burst tomorrow. And I think you've got to have that, because it keeps you down-to-earth. People in our business are constantly judging the public's taste, and that could change tomorrow. The secret with making records is that you peak and then you've got to know when to gradually slow down without people knowing it. Cut down the releases and the amount of touring so that you can reach a level and sustain it.

Why did you disband the DC5 in 1970?

I always wanted to be an actor, you see. And we got involved in our first film, *Catch Us If You Can* [in America, *Having a Wild Weekend*].

By working on the film I found out that I wasn't a very good actor. The band and I rushed into it, and it was the first thing I didn't have creative control of. All the producers were interested in was a cheap exploitation movie.

I realized when I saw the film that I still had a lot to learn. And I thought that when things slowed down, I'd go back and learn the craft properly. I grew a beard and took a couple of auditions for the Royal Academy of Dramatic Art and the Central School of Speech and Film, which Sir Laurence Olivier ran. They auditioned about three thousand people and took thirty: fifteen guys and fifteen girls. I was lucky enough to be selected. We were to work from eight in the morning to ten at night, six days a week for three years, and that was it. So I went there and was making the group's records on Sunday or in the middle of the night. I thought, this *is* the time to stop, really.

Also I was tired of being locked away. The enjoyment of touring had gone, and it seemed time to stop, otherwise the performance would have become mechanical. I was under no illusions. I played shows in the States that had anywhere from ten thousand people in the audience to one that had a quarter of a million people. You can go in there with all that energy and excitement and everything going for you, and for some reason, you get onstage and it doesn't work. The audience is loving you and the harder you try, the worse it gets. You come offstage and people run up and say, "You were fantastic! Great! What a show!" But *you* know when you've performed well. Sometimes it happens and it's wonderful, it's magic. Other times it doesn't happen. And I think that, even if the crowd is screaming their heads off and going wild, you've got to be honest with yourself. I enjoyed every moment with the DC5, but I think we stopped at the right time.

SELECTED DISCOGRAPHY

Singles

WITH THE DAVE CLARK FIVE

"Glad All Over" (April 1964, Epic)
"Bits and Pieces" (May 1964, Epic)
"Do You Love Me?" (May 1964, Epic)
"Can't You See That She's Mine" (July 1964, Epic)
"Because" (September 1964, Epic)
"Everybody Knows" (October 1964, Epic)
"Anyway You Want It" (December 1964, Epic)
"Reelin' and Rockin' " (May 1965, Epic)
"I Like It Like That" (July 1965, Epic)
"Catch Us If You Can" (September 1965, Epic)
"Over and Over" (December 1965, Epic)
"At the Scene" (March 1966, Epic)
"You Got What It Takes" (May 1967, Epic)

Kenney Jones

11

"You can't be a musician unless you're emotional."

The Small Faces, circa 1967. From left to right: Kenney Jones, Steve Marriott, Ronnie Lane, Ian McLagen

IN 1965 ENGLAND, particularly London, was in the grip of a cultural upheaval. Large numbers of English youths, bored with the pedestrian lifestyle offered them, sought to deliver themselves from the tedium around them. Impeccably dressed in the Carnaby Street style of houndstooth jackets and polka-dot shirts, and fueled by handfuls of pep pills, these dandied rebels—the Mods—hung out in the coffee houses that filled London's Soho district. At the Scene, the 2i's Club, the Cavern, and the Marquee, the Mods danced away the dullness of the day by filling their nights with music and excitement.

Modism was advanced largely to the beat of American soul and rhythm & blues records. A Mod's taste in music ran to the coolest of records—James Brown's "Night Train," "What'd I Say" by Ray Charles, and the quintessence of recorded cool, "Green Onions" by Booker T. and the MGs.

Out of this popular movement came two British bands—the Who and the Small Faces—that perfectly complemented their Mod audiences' preoccupation with fashion, soul, and rhythm & blues. The former, of course, went on to become one of rock's most influential and enduring groups. The Small Faces, however, after three stormy yet extremely creative years, disbanded in 1968.

Kenney Jones was a founding member of the Small Faces. With Ronnie Lane on bass, Steve Marriott on guitar, and Ian McLagen on keyboards, they took their name from the Mod expression for the hippest cat around—a "face."

The Small Faces gained their early musical experience as part of the exploding London club scene, where Jones and his mates won a large following due to their success at Soho's Cavern. The band became known for its energetic stage show, its power-pop guitar chording, and Kenney Jones' propulsive drumming. Their first single, "What'cha Gonna Do about It," was released in August 1965 and rose to number fourteen on the British charts. At the age of eighteen, Kenney Jones was a pop star.

The band's first album, *The Small Faces*, released in May 1966, earned Jones and the others a solid place among the growing legion of successful British bands. These four scrappy kids from London's rough East End proved that they could combine the excitement of their live performance with their newly acquired mastery of the recording studio. When "All or Nothing," their fifth single on Decca, rang out from the Number One position that same month, the Small Faces were at their peak.

Kenney's approach embraced many styles. He moved easily from the restraint required of a soul-blues player to the wild abandon of the most pyschedelicized exhibitionist. He quickly learned the art of interpreting Steve Marriott's forays into the dignity of the soul groove and the proclamations of the teenage power-pop hero.

In 1967 the Small Faces sought a new recording deal and found what they wanted in Andrew Loog Oldham's Immediate Records. In order to devote more time and energy to recording, the band limited its touring schedule and eventually abandoned it altogether for the freedom they felt the studio afforded them.

They recorded three albums for Immediate; by the time their third album was released and the live dates were resumed, the spirit had left the group. Financial problems and the failure of the band's next single, "Universal," made it apparent that the Small Faces' end was near. By the end of 1968 Steve Marriott, the group's main songwriter and lead singer, quit the band, and the original Small Faces broke up.

They eventually became simply the Faces after Kenney Jones, Ronnie Lane, and Ian McLagen invited Rod Stewart and Ron Wood to join them. This unit went on to achieve even greater success, especially in America. The Faces were together from 1970 to 1975. Their music is best described in two words—raw and rollicking. Kenney's drumming with the Faces on hits like "(I Know) I'm Losing You" and "Stay with Me," and on Stewart's own "Maggie May," are perfect examples of barrelhouse rock & roll drumming.

After the Faces, Kenney Jones immersed himself in session work. He recorded with Joan Armatrading, the Rolling Stones, and even the Who on occasion. He enjoyed his new stature as a respected session drummer, but when Pete Townshend, Roger Daltrey, and John Entwistle asked him to join the Who in 1979, Kenney Jones accepted the offer and took on the difficult task of stepping in for the late great Keith Moon.

During one of our preinterview transatlantic conversations, Kenney mentioned that he was now realizing a dream of his—to own his very own studio. Since he was not touring, I imagined he was spending a lot of his time there playing his drums. And, in fact, he was doing just that when I met him at his house.

MAX: You're off the road now and you've built your studio. It must give you a chance to stretch out a little.

KENNEY: Yeah, the studio started out as a place to store drums and to set up about five drum kits. I designed the room; it's an old barn. When it started to become a studio and actually look like a studio, I said, "Oh God, what have I built in my back garden?" It was frightening because I don't really like being in the studio in the best of times. So I thought I'd put some windows in so when I was playing I would be able to look outside and see green and horses, and that would make me feel more at home, like I'm not missing out on anything outside. At first I figured I'd put in an eight-track, but then I talked with Pete Townshend and he said, "No, you don't want to go for that. You want to get a twenty-four track." So now I got the works.

The reason I wanted a studio and a great live room to play in is because over the years you get used to monitors and the sheer volume behind you. And when you turn them off, you really miss them. But the room is so loud and ambient that you don't need those big monitors.

Is the studio a substitute for touring and playing live?

No, I don't think it can be a substitute for touring, but it's certainly a vehicle to get me to play. For me to go on tour, it's very, very easy. The last tour with the Who was the easiest thing I've ever done because I gave up drinking three months before the tour—and got incredibly fit before we went out.

Lately, I've been wanting to go back on the road again. You can't keep working out every single day and try to keep yourself one hundred percent fit just for drumming. That becomes boring. Having something to work for—a goal—that's very important.

When you're off the road, do you do session work?

In England the session thing has really gone out the window. The drum machine has really taken over; what I tend to do is stick to playing with friends. And if anything comes out of it, that's great. The only difference is you don't get paid for it. Drummers who depend on session work to make a living have suffered greatly.

What did you think of the Linn drum when it first appeared?

In the Small Faces, Steve Marriott and Ronnie Lane had a drum machine, and they'd ask me my opinion of it. "Too clinical," I'd say. "Don't really like it." They would tease me with it—they'd say they were going to let the drum machine take over my job. But I sat down one day and remembered how I started playing drums and why I started and what my instrument means to me. And I was very proud to realize my instrument is an acoustic instrument.

Pete Townshend was one of the first people to use the synthesizer/sequencer on songs like "Baba O'Riley" and "Won't Get Fooled Again," which was sort of like playing to a drum machine. You've had to adapt to that onstage.

It was difficult to get used to when I first joined the band. And learning all their songs was really a nightmare. I only had five days to learn ten years of material. And my memory was really terrible. All I could remember were Faces songs. And everyone thought I knew all the songs. I said, "I don't know your songs. I'm not *that* much of a fan. I don't go home and play your records all day" (laughs).

How did you learn the songs in such a short time?

We started at twelve o'clock and finished at six. Just an afternoon thing for five days. My first gig with the Who was promoting the film *Quadrophenia*. We did a live show in the south of France. So I was doubly paranoid, you know, with all the glory attached to Keith. I tried to keep it simple. But I thought there was no way I could do it, because all the Who songs are quite complex, with weird accents and counts. Yet with the nods and the winks from Peter and John, it was great. I don't actually read music, so I thought I'd make some notes. I had these great big circles and *X*s and accents. It became a joke at the end, because everyone would sneak up and have a look at my notes and fall about laughing.

The middle part of "Won't Get Fooled Again" comes to mind as a tricky bit of counting.

Yeah, that took me a while to get used to. It's all that synthesizer stuff. When I put the cans [headphones] on for the first time, all I heard was the synth track, nothing else. It was like my eyeballs were crossing over; I couldn't get the beat.

There's that middle section right before Roger's scream, the synth is pulsing and then there's that wild fill from the drums.

Well, that is wild. It comes out in a weird place.

Not on the beat.

It's like half a beat.

Is that the same every night?

Yeah, it's got to be the same. I got so used to that track—I don't know how—but it comes out right. You see, there's a selection of four notes on the synthesizer. The first one you have to ignore even though you actually want to play it. You think that's the cue. But you wait. You say it can't be that one, it must be the next one. It's not the next one, it's the one after. And then you start getting paranoid about it and say maybe the first was the second one and maybe this one was the last one. You start confusing yourself. When you approach it, you have to discipline yourself and say, "Right, I'm listening now for the first four, then the next four, and the third four and then *bam*, I'm off."

The beauty of those songs is that I can actually do some rehearsing before the band even gets there. I play to the tapes with the headphones on. It's like a click track. The reason I practiced to them a lot was because we went to France to play that first gig, and on the way back we did two gigs in Paris where Roger introduced "Who Are You." That's another one of those strange songs, you know. For one strange second, I went out and just couldn't get back in. It was terrible. Afterward, we all finished rolling about laughing, and Roger says, "We're renaming that 'Where *Were* You.'" I'm not letting that happen again.

Was there any time after you were asked to join the band that you thought twice about it?

Yeah. I felt a bit awkward because knowing Keith Moon as a friend, there's no way you can replace Keith. And there was no way I would ever want to change my thing. I wondered if everyone was going to try to change me. I *slowly* accepted the fact that I was going to be in the band. I said to myself, "If anyone tries to change me, I'm off. That's it." But no one did. They just sort of let me do my own interpretations of the songs. Of course, there are certain bits that have to be played just the way Keith played them.

In an interview, John and Pete said that because of Keith's flamboyant style, they were never exactly sure where he was in a song.

Keith always knew where *he* was. The only saving grace was that Pete and John knew that Keith was actually aware of where the beat was. They described him as having a built-in metronome. All they had to do was keep up with him.

One would imagine that coming into the Who after Keith's sudden death was a difficult transition in terms of the loss to the band and the start of a new beginning.

A lot of people on the outside felt that, but being on the inside, it wasn't that bad. Having known the Who since I was in the Small Faces, we got to know each other as friends, drinking partners, fellow musicians, and God knows what else. We were the only two Mod bands around in the early days. It was only learning the songs and how everybody else was going to react to me that was hard. Everybody in the band backed me. It was, "If they don't like me, fine." I've lived through hell, what with bands forming and having great success and then being silly enough to fold. I thought, "Well, what have I got to lose on this one?" Actually, I didn't really want to get back into that kind of band situation because I was having a great time being with my family. I was off the road, and all I was doing was riding horses and doing sessions. I was earning enough money to make ends meet. I was very happy. And when I actually decided to join the band after meeting with Pete, I got a little bit concerned; you

"There's no way you can replace Keith."

know, "What's going to happen now? Am I going to get my hopes up to be let down again?" I didn't really want to go through that again, knowing full well that once you do put yourself in that position, the day will come when it ends. It's very emotional. It's got to be emotional. You can't be a musician unless you're emotional.

But I've kind of accepted that now. And as far as I'm concerned, when the Who don't work, I don't think about it. I think, well, it's folded—until we work again. It keeps it more sane. Everything that happens is a bonus.

It's been said that you brought a stability to the Who. How do you respond to that?

I've watched the others really enjoy my input. I've also seen them a bit lonely and left out in the cold in terms of humor from an outrageous drummer like Keith, who would go completely nuts onstage.

What was the London music scene like in the sixties?

It was very exciting. Because of the fashion that's tied to the music these days, what's happening now is like a modern-day version of the sixties. But there's much more of an artistic influence in terms of songs and video.

In the sixties we too wanted to make it and be rich and famous, but it was afterward that we said that. I mean, I actually didn't go out and buy a set of drums to become rich and famous. I'd watch different TV programs and get excited. "I'd like to be like that someday," I'd think. But now you get kids who go out and buy a guitar or drums *because* they figure that's the way to become rich and famous. In the sixties, we didn't even make money when we *became* rich and famous!

Is the Who's recording technique much different from the Faces'?

Well, you see, the Who just go in and make an album with some songs that are mostly leftovers from solo projects. And that's frustrating. You listen to a Townshend solo album or an Entwistle solo album and you hear all these great songs. You wonder, "Why didn't the Who do them?" And that's the tragedy of it. If anyone asks why the Who isn't selling as many records as it was before, it's because they're not getting the material.

Do you often feel detached from the other members of the Who?

I think that I've still got great loyalty to the Small Faces, it being the first band I was in that ever made it. So I'm kind of loyal in that area, even though I grew up with the Who as friends. I did feel part of the band when I joined it, and I do today. After all, we've known each other a long time.

Did it take you a while to accept the Who's offer to join the band?

When I got the phone call, I thought, "Well, what do you do in this situation?" One of the things that made up my mind was when they said the record contract had run out, and they were going to negotiate a new one. I thought, "Yeah! Lots of money!" Actually, I didn't really think that, but it did help to make up my mind.

Pete said that they could have actually taken a young drummer off

Kenney getting the nod from Pete Townshend

the street and thrown him into that hot seat. And he'd be pretty excited and all. And after a while it would go to his head and the pressures of Moonie and all that would start to get to him. So they actually gave it a great deal of thought. I'd played with the Who before on many different occasions and on many different projects; sometimes when Moonie was out of it, I'd get a call. I did the *Tommy* sound track, for instance. So Pete was actually quite right when he said that, because I lived through the bad times. If it didn't work out with the Who, I was strong enough to take it.

I'm grateful the Who didn't embarrass me by saying, "Well, we'll give you a small percentage and a wage," because they knew my feelings on that. I've never been on a wage or taken a percentage in a band. I've always been a full member, and I react best that way. And they knew that. As old mates they would never insult me like that. Besides, I think they wanted me to feel at home. For instance, if you got a young kid in the hot seat and you tell him, "You're on a wage," he wouldn't give a shit if he was earning nothing. He'd say, "Great! The glory of it!" But he would never feel part of the band.

Another thing, when we would have meetings, I would actually speak my mind. It was something they were used to. Moonie had an opinion too. They still needed that input.

It must have been interesting for them—having to deal with a new person who has his own ideas and his own experiences.

Funny enough, it all came quite naturally, much to my surprise. It was just like another group meeting. And because I've known everyone over the years, it was almost similar to the Faces. It's all part of the big "family" of English musicians from the sixties. I mean, I've played with the Stones, the Stones played with the Small Faces, the Faces played with the Stones and the Who. Everyone has played with everyone else.

What was playing with the Stones like?

Well, I played on "It's Only Rock 'n' Roll." In fact, that session was where the expression came from as well. Ron Wood called me up. We lived at Richmond Park; I lived on one gate and Woody lived on the other and Ian McLagen lived on the other. Woody had a studio in his basement, and he always lived through the night. And he'd always call me up. Like, if Clapton was playing, Woody would call me up and say, "We haven't got a drummer. Do you fancy coming over and playing?" Well, I'd say, "Oh shit, it's four o'clock in the bloody morning, Woody." In the end he'd make me feel guilty, so I'd go over and play and have a great time.

It was the same thing with Jagger. Jagger came out one night, and Woody called me up and we just played. We were just pissing about really, just a bunch of old riffs. And then Jagger said to me, "Why don't you play it this way?" And I said, "No, I want to play it this way." So he said, "It's only rock & roll." And I said, "But I like it." Suddenly he started going, "It's only rock & roll, but I like it." We did it in five minutes flat.

Later, I actually felt really bad about it. Once I knew the Stones were going to put it on their album and release it as a single, I said, "Shit, what about Charlie? He's my friend. I don't want him to think I invaded his territory." So I spoke to Charlie and said, "Listen, I feel quite bad." He said, "Don't worry. It sounds like me anyway."

During the late fifties and early sixties, there seemed to be a great difference between the northern England and southern England music scenes. Can you tell me about that?

It was like rock & roll picked up more in places like Liverpool. Whereas you came down to London and it was more blues and jazz influences. The Stones were more blues and jazz; they weren't really rock & roll. Suddenly they developed into a rock & roll band. In the sixties in England there were the Mods and the Rockers. The Beatles were Rockers. They'd wear leather and that sort of thing, slick back their hair, and play very fast Buddy Holly stuff. I would say that's where the rock & roll influence came from, and it only slowly came down to London.

In the beginning the Who had a much more R&B sound, as did the Small Faces.

Two of my influences were James Brown and Booker T. and the MGs. And then I found out that Al Jackson had played on all the Otis Redding stuff, so he became a strong influence. I learned a great deal from him—how to play behind the beat, to relax, and just to make something out of nothing. His authority was just great—right at the end of a song, just one little fill. It was nice to see a drummer know his place and be a drummer. After listening to him on record, I couldn't wait to see what he looked like and how he played. I saw the Stax Revue show in 1967. He was absolutely great. He had unbelievable stage presence. At the end of every song, he'd hit it and stand up on the very last note.

I heard a great story years ago that the way Booker T. and the MGs knew that a song was good enough and had the right groove was that they'd give it the "car-park" test. They'd do the song, and then the engineer would play it back to the guy who parked cars. If it made his foot tap, that was the take. In the sixties I didn't listen to too many English drummers, because they always tended to play ahead of the beat. And it used to annoy me something terrible. So I'd always listen to American drummers like Jackson.

The first time I was in America, I went to New Orleans to a place where they were jamming away. I couldn't believe it. All the musicians would do a solo. And there's this big black drummer, about sixty, just sort of keeping the beat. About twenty people have already taken solos and I'm wondering what the drummer is going to do. So I'm waiting for this whacking great drum solo, and they introduce him and motion for him to take his solo. What does he do? He sings! He kept playing, but he sang and had the most incredible voice. I thought it was great, because as a drummer, you have to do something they don't expect.

You brought that funky, behind-the-beat kind of feeling to the last two Who albums. "Eminence Front," for instance.

There were bits of that album that reminded me of recording with the Small Faces. That album isn't going to set the world on fire, but I thought it actually put the Who on the right road, especially after that load of junk, *Face Dances*. On that record, I liked the songs, but I just thought the chemistry of the band and producer wasn't right. The sound was too laid back: like rubber. It simply wasn't right. The Who should be something to the effect of "put them in the middle of the city and let them go wild."

Do you think the Who are getting back to that?

Well, *It's Hard* did because we were using Glyn Johns, for a start; he did *Who's Next* and produced lots of early English stuff as well—the Stones, the Faces. Once again, it was amazing what we came out with, because we only had two songs. The rest were a bunch of riffs. And because we approached it more like a workshop thing, it brought us all back together, which I think is what I found similar to the Small Faces. In the Small Faces we always worked together and just jammed a bit and saw if it worked. Then we discussed what we had and all put our own input into one song. And that's what the Who were doing.

What's the best way for someone to approach producing the Who?

I don't really know. I think Glyn Johns is the right type of producer, if not *the* right producer. I think we tend to fall into a trap when we go in the studio. It's like, here's the demo, let's play it. The Who should actually play and fool around and jam a bit, loosen up. And the Who don't do that. What we do is, the three of us just put the track down

"Al Jackson... became a strong influence. I learned a great deal from him—how to play behind the beat, to relax, and just to make something out of nothing."

and add bits to it. Many times I'll say later on, "I wish I knew that synthesizer was going to go on the track; I would have done something different drum-wise."

With the Small Faces we all were always in the studio, and we always played together on the track. If anything was added, it was maybe another guitar. But the performance was captured.

So if you had your preference, it would be for performance rather than precision.

Yeah. I think if you actually sit down and try and be precise and technical and all that, what challenge is that? You know damn well you can do it with modern technology. You can do the track bit by bit. The performance is the thing that's going to capture the feeling and the emotion.

SELECTED DISCOGRAPHY

Singles

WITH THE SMALL FACES

"Itchykoo Park" (January 1968, Immediate)
"Tin Soldier" (April 1968, Immediate)

WITH THE FACES

"Stay with Me" (1972, Warner Bros.)

WITH ROD STEWART

"Maggie May" (October 1971, Mercury)
"(I Know) I'm Losing You" (December 1971, Mercury)

WITH THE ROLLING STONES

"It's Only Rock 'n' Roll (but I Like It)" (September 1974, Rolling Stones Records)

Albums

WITH THE SMALL FACES

Small Faces (1966, Decca)

WITH THE FACES

First Step (1970, Warner Bros.)
A Nod Is as Good as a Wink to a Blind Horse (1972, Warner Bros.)
Ooh La La (1973, Warner Bros.)

WITH ROD STEWART

Gasoline Alley (1970, Mercury)
Every Picture Tells a Story (1971, Mercury)

WITH THE WHO

Face Dances (1981, Warner Bros.)
It's Hard (1982, Warner Bros.)

Charlie Watts

12

"I would love to have been born in an era when jazz was the thing.... When jazz musicians were the stars and it was a struggle to get in the door."

IN A WORLD of many musical styles—in which the definition of rock is ever changing—it is comforting to know that Charlie Watts lives and plays the drums.

Charlie Watts of the Rolling Stones. The qualifier is really superfluous: Charlie's drumming is so important to the sound and feel of the Rolling Stones that it is impossible to think of one without the other. Since 1963, Charlie has drummed for a band that has personified the spirit of rock & roll. As a member of the Stones, Charlie has participated in a musical institution that has not only exceeded his own expectations, but has created a unique and powerful legacy as well.

Charlie's drumming is admirably consistent, powerful, and spontaneous. His style has become a genre in the field of rock & roll. As Robyn Flans observed in *Modern Drummer* magazine: "Pick up a copy of the *Village Voice* and look in the back, where bands advertise for musicians. Invariably there will be a couple of ads that say something like: 'Charlie Watts–style drummer wanted for rock band.'"

Charlie is unique. His backbeat chops like an ax, yet he has a jazzman's sensibility. Charlie's drumming style is the result of several generations' influences—combining an affection for pre–World War II jazz and postwar rhythm & blues with a dash of Third World syncopations. Perhaps his musical orientation gave him a super-defined sense of playing on the edge. His style is amazing, for he can hold the beat tight yet at the same time appear on the verge of losing it. But—he stays with it.

As musicians and personalities, the Rolling Stones have always been entertaining. Still, nothing was ever more important than their music. The songs have survived the test of time, and Charlie's contributions stand as examples of solid, expressive drumming. Consider the barrelhouse funk of "Honky Tonk Women," the galloping tom-toms of "Paint It, Black," the classic drive of "Satisfaction," his New Orleans-style drumming in "Rocks Off," the toughness of "Street Fighting Man" and "Gimme Shelter," on up to the more contemporary "Miss You" and "Start Me Up." Lifted by Charlie's drumming, Keith Richards's guitar playing and Mick Jagger's vocals, the Rolling Stones have consistently shown an ability to rock *or* roll in a variety of styles and have it all wash as Stones music.

I first met Charlie during the Stones' 1981 American tour. We talked a while when he and the band were in New York City, and we made tentative plans to meet again.

On September 8, 1983, I received a phone call from Charlie's London office informing me that he would be in London from September fourteenth through the twenty-first: Would I be available to come to England then? What a question! I flew to England to talk with Charlie.

He was in London to perform in two concerts for the benefit of England's Action Research into Multiple Sclerosis. At the suggestion of Ronnie Lane, the ex-Small Faces bassist stricken with this disease, Eric Clapton had organized this supersession. With Eric Clapton, Jeff Beck, Jimmy Page, and sessionman Andy Fairweather-Low on guitars, Steve Winwood on vocals and keyboards, Bill Wyman on bass, and Charlie, Kenney Jones, and Ray Cooper on percussion, it promised to be an incredible show.

Charlie invited me to the rehearsal the day before the concert, and even *that* was a remarkable event. Out from under the pressure of center stage, each musician seemed to enjoy a relaxation that drew out some very special performances. Seeing Eric, Jimmy, and Jeff together, on the same stage during that first concert was expecially thrilling. Each a former member of the legendary sixties group, the Yardbirds, their passionate, soaring version of Eric's "Layla" was more than an encore—it was history in the making.

The next day, as we sat in his sunny parlor overlooking the Thames, Charlie served tea. As he had to be on stage three hours later, we had to be brief. With the television on in the background, Charlie leaned over to me and softly said, "I never do interviews. Can't stand them—bloody waste of time. . . ."

MAX: *In that case, I'd like to jump right into this, Charlie, and ask you this: If there were any other time in history in which you could have lived and played your drums, when would that have been?*

CHARLIE: Well, when I think of it, I would love to have been born in an era when jazz was the thing. I wish I could have been around when it was a struggle to get in the door, when *jazz* musicians were the stars. It must have been incredible. Not like today, when they can hardly fill a club. I mean, I would love to have seen Gene Krupa in 1941 when he had "Let Me Off Uptown" with Roy Eldridge on trumpet. God, that must have been something else. For two years every song was great. Though it was probably no different than it is today, with what they call rock & roll. You know, nowadays it's the singers and the guitar players. It must have been incredible to have had the trumpet player the star.

With the Rocket '88 band, you had the experience of playing with horns—

Well, there's one thing that happened the other day during the rehearsals for this benefit. I had a gig with [Stones aide and piano player] Ian Stewart's band. He has four horns and a guitar player. It's not like playing with the Stones, where you're following the guitar player and, obviously, the singer. Here you're following the horns, and when horn players play slow, they can play *so* slow—it's all air. Unlike the guitar. It's unbelievable, really.

Did you find yourself having to change your playing to fit a horn band?

Yeah, sort of. I try to play with them. That's the art of a good drummer. Not that *I'm* a good drummer. A *good* drummer can play with anyone.

One element that helps make a drummer good is an ability to play in a variety of styles. With the Stones, you've certainly had to adapt to many different feels and styles.

The Stones are a good band to play with if you like that sort of thing. I mean, one minute you're trying to be D. J. Fontana, then you're Earl Palmer.

What was it like when you first hit the States?

Well, when the Stones actually got to tour America, I got to go to New York, and that was *it*. I never really wanted any more. In those days, the only way to get to New York was in a band on a cruise ship. I was lucky to get there right before Birdland closed. We first went to New York in nineteen sixty-whatever-it-was, and I think it closed about two years later. I saw Charles Mingus there with a thirteen-piece band. I also saw a marvelous Sonny Rollins period, where the band would stop and Sonny would just go on for hours. *That* was America. After that, I met Hal Blaine, but that was a whole other scene. He was a lovely man. He had the first remote-controlled garage door opener I'd ever seen.

I remember reading in a fan magazine in 1965 where you said your goal was to look like a black American jazz drummer.

I always wanted to be a black New Yorker. You know, the sharpest one on the street.

Did you have any one particular drummer in mind for a model?

No. It must have been a mixture of everyone, really. I suppose Tony Williams would have been one. His action looks so good; whether the notes are better than anyone else's, I don't know. I did see Gene Krupa at the Metropole, however. I never really liked his style. Everything he did was exaggerated. His cymbal would be level with his arms and his head would be level with his cymbal. It was very funny, I mean, instead of just throwing it away, every move was a big deal. But he *was* one of the best. Actually, I'd prefer to look at Buddy Rich rather than Gene Krupa. Buddy looks like he's giving it all away. I mean, how does he do it? When they talk about god-given talents, well, there you are. For fifty years Buddy Rich has staggered the drum world. He's played with every great musician, from Ravi Shankar to Charlie Parker.

You mention Charlie Parker; I know he's one of your great inspirations. You wrote a book about him, right?

Yeah. It was the story of a little bird. It was a kid's book. I just strung all the pieces together—the dates and things like that. It was just a bird instead of Charlie Parker. I was about twenty when I did it. The guy who published it used to do magazines called *Beatles Monthly* and *Rolling Stones Monthly* and *Beat Monthly*. It was when John Lennon brought out his book, *In My Own Write*. Well, this chap saw my book and said, "Ah, there's a few bob in this!" But of course John Lennon had a far greater appeal than me and Charlie Parker.

What is it about Charlie Parker that appealed to you then?

He sort of epitomized an era of my life. If I could have played an instrument, that's what it would have been. Even now, although I may only play him once a month, maybe six times a month, or not once in six months, every time I get to a good record of his, I still get that good feeling. Parker was just unbelievable—and dead at thirty-five.

Charlie, how did you actually get started on drums?

Well, I had a banjo first. I tried to learn that, but I couldn't quite get the dots on the frets right. It drove me up a wall. So I took the thing apart. Luckily, it wasn't a really good banjo. I made a stand for it out of wood and played on the round skin part. It was like a drum, anyway. I played it with brushes. I got my first kit when I was about fourteen. Had a lot of fun with that. But I really taught myself by listening to other people and watching.

What were your early gigs like?

Well, I played jazz on weekends when I was working in the art studio. But I've done other things as well, you know, Jewish weddings, and that sort of thing. I never knew what the hell was going on. I'm not Jewish, you see. What you really need on those jobs is a good piano player. If the piano player's daft, you've got no chance. I don't care if you're Max Roach—you'll only last a half-hour.

You really got your start in the burgeoning London blues scene during the early sixties. Can you tell me about that?

I used to play in a coffee bar two days a week, and it was there at the Marquee that I met Alexis Korner, who was really responsible for the start of R&B music in England. I remember I told him to turn his amp down! Ginger Baker used to sit in as well.

Ginger was such a powerful drummer with Cream. What did he sound like in the early days?

Ginger was an incredible jazz drummer; always in the best bands. He had a homemade kit; the first perspex [plastic] set I'd even seen. This was in 1960. He'd put his own fittings on, which were probably Ajax. And he used to have calfskin heads. They felt a quarter of an inch thick. He also had this really big ride cymbal with lots of rivets that he kept tightly buttoned down; it would not move an inch. One night when he was playing with Graham Bond, the organ player, I borrowed his kit. Ginger had been playing with Alexis, but that band folded. Anyway, this one night the Stones split the bill with Graham's band at a church in Harrow, and Ginger loaned me his set. But I couldn't play it, nothing would happen. I broke three pairs of sticks in one set! He had them set up so the angle was all wrong for me. It was total work. But Ginger could play them because his chops were so great. His wrists were amazing too.

How did you come to meet Mick and Keith in the first place?

Through Alexis, really. I'd been playing with Alexis before I met them. See, Alexis and Cyril Davies were the only ones really playing blues in London at that time. Cyril was a great harmonica player; he made a couple of very good records—"Country Line Special" was one. He and Alexis got together while Alexis was playing with Chris Barber, who had one of the biggest trad bands.

Can you define the term "trad"?

Trad is white revivalist traditional jazz. It was sort of like our Dixieland music. Very popular in the fifties. Anyway, Alexis would play the interval between sets and got the idea to form his own group. He teamed up with Squirrel, which was Cyril's nickname. Then Alexis asked me to join. I was away working in Denmark, but he waited for me to come back. After I'd joined up, we got the opportunity through Chris Barber, who owned the Marquee, to do the off-nights. This was the old Marquee on Oxford Street, not the one now on Wardour. We played there on Thursday nights. After two weeks, Alexis held the record for people in attendance. Lots of musicians who were interested in that sort of music used to come. You'd get people playing bottleneck guitar, but if it wasn't a saxophone, I wasn't interested.

To get back to your original question, one night Mick and Keith came to one of our sessions. Mick did a few gigs with the band. It was quite hard to get singers; actually, it still is. We did a few things

"I always wanted to be a black New Yorker. You know, the sharpest one on the street."

without really knowing one another. Mick never really liked the music we were doing. So they decided to get a band together on their own—or it might have been before I met them. Mick was at school then; I'm not sure whether Keith was at school or college. He might have been just roaming around. Brian Jones I met through Alexis as well. Brian loved the blues; he loved Elmore James. That scene became the only chance you had to play that music. It was a chance to talk about those records. Alexis was very knowledgeable. A lot of guys who played the Marquee went away and made their own bands up. At least, the next time I saw them they had their own bands.

You mean Mick and Keith?

Yeah, them and Paul Jones, who was with Manfred Mann. I'd seen Manfred Mann in clubs, not as a R&B band, but as a jazz band. You know, I used to play with Alexis and didn't really know what to play. He taught me to listen to blues records.

Whose records did you listen to?

Well, Jimmy Reed for one. I think Earl Phillips, who used to play with Jimmy Reed is a marvelous player. His drumming is the subtlest playing of that particular style. I mean, if you listen to Jimmy Reed, Phillips has everything, really. He has terrific dynamics and quite a bit of technique. Yet, he's not sitting there doing paradiddles all over the place. He does some marvelous triplet things. And his cymbal work is beautiful. Another guy was Francis Clay, who plays on *Muddy Waters—Live at Newport*. He is incredible. He plays Chicago style; the pickups are marvelous. He had this cymbal that curled up like a Texas hat. He played it around and around.

What you're doing looks like an old-fashioned dinner triangle—like "come and get it!"

It was a beautiful concept. Clay is a brilliant drummer. By anybody else, I suppose, it would be sloppy, but because it's him, it's right on. He's whacking all over the place—sort of mad playing. Oh, it's perfect, but I used to play more Muddy Waters than Jimmy Reed when I was with Alexis. In those days, Muddy Waters's tunes were like standards.

Did you leave Alexis at that point to join the Stones?

When I left Alexis, Ginger took over, and I went around with a few different bands. I was sort of between jobs, as they say. I used to play with three bands at once. You'd play with people you knew because they knew that you knew what song they were talking about. But Keith and Mick were looking for a drummer and asked me if I'd do it. So I said yeah. I had nothing better to do. Getting with them was just luck, really. I didn't expect it to go on; bands usually don't. So I kicked in with them. I was young, and you never see the end of the year, do you? I guess they became rather important, didn't they?

I've heard that the Beatles helped the Stones a bit in the beginning. Is that true?

I tell you what they *might* have done. I think John, because he knew

The Rolling Stones at Wembley, circa 1964

Mick and Keith, or Mick and Keith knew him; I personally didn't know them that well. Obviously, Ringo I knew because drummers tend to gravitate toward each other (laughs). John let them have "I Wanna Be Your Man." I think that was where the help came in. We used to see them about when they first moved to London. And we played with them at the Royal Albert Hall. That was the first time we played with them; the second time was at Wembley Stadium. It was incredible, man. Both times were for a *New Musical Express* poll. We went on first at Wembley because they had invented a "new" category called R&B for us, and the Beatles closed the show. We were so popular in London; we were like the "in" thing, really. We won the Wembley. I remember that you couldn't hear anything—it was just screaming girls. We went through that as well. I actually stood at the side and watched them. You couldn't really hear; the amps were so small and there were no mikes on Ringo's drums. Everyone was screaming.

Coming from a jazz purist background, how did you react to the audience screaming over your band?

I never understood it, actually, but I loved the adulation when we were on stage. After that I hated it. The days when you couldn't walk down the road without people running after you—literally. *That* was the most awful period of my life. I mean, it didn't happen to me that much, fortunately. I always kept away from that. I really couldn't stand it. It's quite incredible to go on stage and have that happen to you. Jellybeans getting thrown is really amazing. But that's part of youth, isn't it?

Having spent half your life performing with the same band, can you point to any changes that have had a significant impact on the Stones?

I think one of the biggest changes this band has faced was in terms of performing. We did this one particular tour of America during the mid-sixties. We returned three years later, and during those three years—because of groups like Led Zeppelin—everything changed. Suddenly it was that period where shows were incredibly long and there would be no audience reaction until after the number; then everyone went mad. It was really a concert. We'd always done shows for twenty minutes; now we had to play for two hours. We used to play a lot of times—when we were with other stars, if you like—on shows that were like revues. You only had twenty minutes because there were eight or nine other acts on the bill. Here we were coming from playing two to three hours nonstop in the clubs, to playing for twenty minutes a night. Then the kids would start shouting. We had a period where I never played more than ten minutes a night. It was every single night, but only for ten minutes—twenty minutes maximum. We never finished a show for about a year because someone would get hurt in the front row and we'd have to stop, or it would be chaos and people would run all over the stage. I can tell you—it didn't help my drumming much, but, you know, it was just part of being with the Rolling Stones.

Over the last twenty years, the Stones have recorded a vast amount of material. When you work that closely with people over such a long period of time, work patterns become quite established. When Mick or Keith present a song, how do you develop your ideas?

I try to help them get what they want. I mean, you do it a few times and you realize all your messing about ain't getting you nowhere, so you play it straight. Then, if they want something else, they'll tell you. It's very easy working with them, actually.

Do you find yourself referring to other recordings you've made?

Oh yeah, sure. You try not to when you're playing, but there are things I do automatically that are just part of me. You know, maybe a certain fill or a hi-hat thing. It all comes from playing with the same people, doesn't it? You just get used to them.

I've always found it interesting to hear what fellow members of your band—or any band, for that matter—think about the role another member of the band plays. Keith, for example, always refers to your unique feel—that you are the heart of the Stones.

Lovely! I've heard him say that about the feel. But I get the feel off of him, really. You know, when we play in those ridiculous places—stadiums and that lot—all I really hear is him. When I talk to Kenney Jones, he tells me about the Who's amps. Now *that's* equipment. Kenney has a monitor bigger than him for those gigs. I never worked like that. All I hear is Keith's amp, which is not that big. And I really listen to him all the time. If I wasn't able to hear Keith, I would get completely lost. It all comes from him.

Your drum sound seems to stay remarkably consistent from track to track and album to album, particularly your snare. How do you achieve that tuning?

For me, it's really how it feels more than how it sounds, somehow. I play the military-style grip, and the hard thing about that, when you're playing rock & roll, is to get the volume. The nicest sound is not to hit a rim shot like Krupa used to—you know, the high, ringy one that you hit with the narrow part of the stick—but to take the fat part of the stick and hit across the drum onto the rim. You'll get a thick sound, especially if the top head ain't too tight. Also, I don't play very loudly; the sound doesn't really come from the volume. It's getting the thing to hit right all the time. That's when I feel comfortable; when it's on and you don't even think about it.

One aspect of your playing and recording with the Stones was that you went from playing a boom-ba-boom bass drum pattern to a straight-four beat. Did you just fall into that or was it a conscious thing?

Yeah, that *was* conscious. I think the reason for that was, well, the old beat became unhip, didn't it? Unhip—I'm a bit too old for that. But the straight-four thing worked really well. It's funny you should mention that. I found playing that straight-four way very hard for me to do. I used to play the one and the three. To go straight through—I found that very hard to do. Keith and Mick would say, "Keep it going at the same volume," and you'd think, "Yeah, that's easy," and you'd start tapping your foot. But I found when I was going like that, the two and the four would be softer because of my left hand playing the backbeat.

It seemed Mick and Keith started writing songs that lent themselves to that feel, like "Miss You."

That was a very popular song, and it became sort of the "in" thing. I mean, there's a load of "Miss You"s, aren't there?

I'd like to try something, which is for me to throw out some song titles and have you—

—sing them (laughter).

Sure, if you like, but first tell me what comes to mind when I say "Satisfaction."

Oh, blimey! Jack Nitzsche, I suppose. He was standing in the corner of RCA's studio in Hollywood playing the tambourine. Phil Spector was there as well.

"Street Fighting Man."

God, it's Mick and Keith, really, that one.

One of my favorite songs is "Rocks Off."

Keith—that's all Keith.

How about "Beast of Burden"?

That's Keith too, really. That one came easy. It sounds odd but we just did it.

"We never finished a show for about a year because someone would get hurt in the front row and we'd have to stop, or it would be chaos and people would run all over the stage. I can tell you—it didn't help my drumming much, but, you know, it was just part of being with the Rolling Stones."

One or two takes?

Yes, it was as easy as that. It sounded so good; it's fun to play on stage. It's a lovely track.

"Paint It, Black."

That just fell, that tom-tom part. I mean that's a good example of what I mean when Keith plays a song—it was just the right thing to do. If I could have played a tabla, I might have put it on that track. Actually we ruined a marvelous pair of tablas trying to be Indians. You're not supposed to use sticks on them!

One of your funkiest tracks is "Honky Tonk Women."

I can see Jimmy Miller, the producer, playing the cowbell. One take, I think it was.

"Tumbling Dice."

Me and Jimmy Miller played it. Jimmy played drums on "You Can't Always Get What You Want." Did you know that? Jimmy Miller was *the* person in the studio who helped me an awful lot; he showed me how to do it. By that I mean he didn't stand over you, but he showed me certain things that would work and things that wouldn't, like fills and things. He didn't actually sit down and show them to me, but he used to love playing drums, so he'd play. Sometimes I couldn't play what he wanted, so he'd do it.

How did he help you?

He could hear songs better than I could. There's a whole period where Jimmy helped me out a lot without saying or doing anything. The result was that I began to realize I should work harder on my drumming, so I started to practice. Not on the drums, mind you, I practiced on my legs to keep my chops together. I can't stand practicing on the drums.

Keith said that if he doesn't see you or play with you for six months, suddenly you come back five times better.

Dunno 'bout that.

He actually said that.

Did he really? He is an incredible guy. Marvelous.

Would you say all you guys are close?

Yeah, I think we are, but we never see one another. You know how it is. At times you see them every bloody day, and then, when you're doing nothing, you might never see or hear from 'em. I suppose I speak to Mick more than any of the others because we talk about album covers or cricket or things like that. But sometimes I don't see Mick for weeks. There's a reason for that. I'll tell you—our band never would have stayed together. The Beatles seemed to be together all the time. I wonder if that had a bit to do with their breaking up.

I've been very fortunate in being able to get together with so many of the drummers I admire, but of course there are going to be some missing chapters. You knew both Keith Moon and John Bonham. Could you talk about them?

I was talking to Kenney Jones and I asked him what it was like going on the road with the Who and taking over Keith's seat. Of all the drum chairs to assume, to me that certainly would have been one of the most difficult. Keith's style was *so* flamboyant, I could not have gotten into that for a start. When we were working on *Some Girls* in Paris, Keith came over. It was an hilarious three days. He played with me in the studio, sort of stood behind me with all his tom-toms. I'd hired a couple of drums to make like I knew what was going on—you know, make the kit bigger. I never used them. But there was Moonie, a maniac really, always very charming, yet completely mad. I went out with him one day—the whole day—and it was the most hilarious thing. I always thought there was a limit, but he'd go on and on. You know, when the champagne's finished, let's go on to the brandy. There aren't many personalities around that were bigger than him. As far as his drumming, he was an innovator; he played with such style. He said Krupa was his big influence; well, you can see Krupa in him. It's a coincidence, really, that Keith and Ginger and myself are from the same area of Wembley. But I'll tell you what Keith Moon is—Keith Moon is what legends are made of.

Did you know John Bonham very well?

No. I met John a couple of times, that was all. He was an incredible player too, a wonderful player. His foot was the thing, for me, anyway. His foot was so strong. "Kashmir" and those lovely songs. I know Jimmy [Page] misses him. You can tell that even at the rehearsal yesterday. Me and Kenney—or, really, Ray Cooper and Kenney—were playing with him: we just knew that if Bonham had been there, he would have done what had to be done. You know, you need a drum about *that* big and be able to hit it *so* hard. Bonham—you won't get another one of him.

We've talked before about our mutual respect for Al Jackson. What would you say was his greatest talent?

Al Jackson was the best drummer of a slow tempo I've ever heard. It is very difficult to play that slowly. Also, I don't know anyone who could play as strongly as him. I've seen him play, and he could do everything.

The Stones' music goes on and on. As a band, you've faced many musical trends and created a large niche for yourselves in each. What do you think the Rolling Stones' greatest influence has been?

Well, I think what the band has done is helped put rhythm & blues in the place it should be.

Simple enough. Charlie, I have one more question; it's about something you mentioned before, that the art of a good drummer is the ability to play with anyone. But you also said that you don't think you are a good drummer. Why?

Well, I don't think what I do is particularly difficult. What is good, though, is that people look at me and say, "Well, I can do that." I like

"I'll tell you what Keith Moon is—Keith Moon is what legends are made of."

that. The drumming *I* do ain't hard, but drumming is hard when you take it a step beyond me, which is where you should be if you really want to be good. I ain't that good, and it's taken me twenty years—though I think the band I'm in is pretty sensational.

SELECTED DISCOGRAPHY

Singles

WITH THE ROLLING STONES

"Not Fade Away" (July 1964, London)
"It's All Over Now" (September 1964, London)
"Time Is on My Side" (December 1964, London)
"The Last Time" (May 1965, London)
"Satisfaction" (July 1965, London)
"Get Off of My Cloud" (November 1965, London)
"19th Nervous Breakdown" (March 1966, London)
"Paint It, Black" (June 1966, London)
"Mother's Little Helper" (August 1966, London)
"Have You Seen Your Mother, Baby, Standing in the Shadow?" (October 1966, London)
"Ruby Tuesday" (February 1967, London)
"Let's Spend the Night Together" (February 1967, London)
"Dandelion" (October 1967, London)
"We Love You" (October 1967, London)
"She's a Rainbow" (January 1968, London)
"Jumpin' Jack Flash" (July 1968, London)
"Street Fighting Man" (September 1968, London)
"Honky Tonk Women" (1969, London)
"Brown Sugar" (May 1971, Rolling Stones Records)
"Wild Horses" (1971, Rolling Stones Records)
"Tumbling Dice" (May 1972, Rolling Stones Records)
"Angie" (October 1973, Rolling Stones Records)
"Miss You" (July 1978, Rolling Stones Records)
"Start Me Up" (August 1981, Rolling Stones Records)

Albums

WITH THE ROLLING STONES

The Rolling Stones (1964, London)
Got Live If You Want It! (1967, London)
Let It Bleed (1969, London)
Get Yer Ya-Ya's Out! (1970, London)
Sticky Fingers (1971, Rolling Stones Records)
Exile on Main Street (1972, Rolling Stones Records)
Some Girls (1978, Rolling Stones Records)
Tattoo You (1981, Rolling Stones Records)

Jim Keltner

13

"I used to think, 'Why me, man?' There were so many incredible drummers around then. . . . I always felt that it was something that John and Yoko liked about me as a person, as well as a drummer."

JON LANDAU once wrote, "The best rock guitarists emerge as solo artists, while the best rock drummers remain in the studio." I know he had Jim Keltner in mind when he made that observation.

Since the late sixties, Jim has been one of America's top supersession drummers. Though Jim is an internationally acclaimed heavy-hitter, his approach and attitude bear no resemblance to what Roger Hawkins calls the "hip studio cat vibe." When Jim plays he is committed and has rocked with some of the best—John Lennon and Yoko Ono, Bob Dylan, Ringo Starr, George Harrison, Phil Spector, Delaney and Bonnie, Joe Cocker, and Leon Russell are a few.

Throughout the seventies, Jim occupied the best seat in the house for some of rock's most historical events. He was a member of Joe Cocker's Mad Dogs and Englishmen group in 1970, and he double-drummed with Ringo in the benefit concerts for Bangladesh, at Madison Square Garden in August 1971. Returning to the Garden the following year, Jim performed at the One to One charity concert, backing John Lennon in one of his rare post-Beatles public appearances. And George Harrison enlisted Jim's aid when he hit the road in 1974.

Having recorded with Bob Dylan in the early seventies ("Knockin' on Heaven's Door") and again on his 1981 *Shot of Love* album, Jim worked Dylan's American and European tours during 1981. I saw Cocker's 1970 Fillmore East show and Dylan's 1981 Jersey concert and can testify to this: Jim Keltner didn't simply bask in the reflected glory of these superstars—he helped them shine.

One of the things that makes it easy to admire Jim's work is that there is a lot to listen to. But it is difficult to pick one or two records that best represent his style. To complicate things further, that style is likely to change with whatever the day's work might bring. Yet Jim's approach always remains unique.

Like the only kid on the block who can construct a model airplane using all the parts and without letting the cement overrun the edges, Jim is a perfectionist, attuned to detail. Bob Glaub, bassist with Jackson Browne and Stevie Nicks, whose first professional record date had Jim on drums, put it this way: "Even before he sits down to play, like on the run-through of a tune, Jim will just sit there listening for the moves. He has great ears and a great imagination—always coming up with the perfect fill. And he always goes for the unexpected."

I remember talking to producer Chuck Plotkin, who had worked with Jim on Dylan's *Shot of Love*. Chuck ranks Jim as one of his favorite drummers. He gave me this illustration of Jim's imagination: "Keltner can make music on anything. I remember one night he came into the studio, turned over a garbage can, and kicked it for a bass drum. Then he chugged a soda, used the empty can as a snare, and played the damn thing with two pencils. The amazing thing was that he was able to balance it all and make it musical. It sounded great. Jim Keltner has a magic touch."

I first came to know Jim's work through John Lennon's records. That work and those years comprise some of Jim's fondest memories. As he explained during our conversation, John and Yoko, moved by his imagination and ease of expression, chose him to work on several of their projects. Soon after, Jim found himself working with George Harrison and Ringo Starr. For Jim, this was almost too good to be true. Inspiring the man who inspired him, Jim became Ringo's favorite drummer!

After driving through a torrential Southern California rainstorm, I arrived at Jim and Cynthia's Griffith Park home. The Keltners made me feel right at home. With mementos spread out all around us, Jim suddenly left the room, to return a minute later with a small, frayed black book. "This is a diary of every date I've ever played—recordings, club dates, dances—it's all here." As a personal history, from the earliest free demo work to triple-scale sessions with the world's most demanding artists and producers, Jim's ledger is a cherished document. As we turned the pages, I discovered its great story.

JIM: One of the most thrilling moments of my life was when John and Yoko called me to record with them. I was on a cloud. Those were the days when the Beatle thing was very, very fresh. It was important and still very much in front of your face. If you were a musician, your life was affected. When they called, I was just beside myself, because they said, "We want you to come to New York. We don't know what we're gonna do, but whatever it is, we want you to be part of it." I'll never forget that—it was wonderful. Just being in the same room with them really blew me away. And they said that again: "We're thinking about doing a lot of things. We're thinking of touring some, we're thinking about making some records and some films. We're going to do a lot of things, and we want you to be a part of it." And I said, "Whoa! What can I say? I'll think it over." (Laughs.) It was an incredible time. That began a whole series of things for me that was just wonderful. *Mind Games* was recorded in August of 1973 and was the first time I really felt the magic of John Lennon and the world he lived in at that time.

MAX: You had worked with them before, though.

Yeah, I played on *Imagine*, but only because I happened to be in England at the time. I was at a session of John's and they were having trouble with the rhythm section on one tune. I felt I could play the shit out of it, and I must have had the look on my face. But I didn't say anything. I'm not one of those guys who goes around saying, "Hey man, I can do that," acing my brother out of a gig. But they saw it in me, and somebody said, "You wanna play on this?" I said, "Yeah, but not right now, please." It wasn't cool. So they called me the next day. I went in and cut it, and then we cut "Jealous Guy," which is still one of my favorite songs. Actually, I had established a relationship with Yoko before John. I'd played on her album *Fly* the week before. I knew a lot of the jazz musicians she knew from New York. So we had a lot to talk about. And I've always loved the avant-garde. Yoko turned John on to me.

What were the recording sessions with John like?

They were just unbelievable. John was so fast. He just played the song, and if he liked what you were doing, he'd say so, and if he didn't, he'd ask you to change it. Generally his songs played themselves because they were written by a man who knows how to write songs. He was one of the best in the whole world. His songs were structured, but they could be weird too. A lot of John's songs have a flow from end to end, but if you check them out real close, they have some funny little structures in them. But he was never aware of a 7/4 bar or a 5/4 bar or a 6/4 bar. Everything was just real natural.

It must have been tremendously exciting, having grown up with the Beatles, to be playing with John and then later with George and Ringo.

There's no way I can describe it to you. It's fun talking to somebody who has appreciation of the awe. It's a corny thing, but I love talking

> "*Mind Games* was recorded in August of 1973 and was the first time I really felt the magic of John Lennon and the world he lived in at that time."

about it. But I don't like talking about it to people who think it's kind of corny. I just wish I had the proper words to describe what my feelings were in those days. It was a magical time. I felt like I was floating around all the time. I used to think, "Why me, man?" There were so many incredible drummers around then, and I always felt that it was something that John and Yoko liked about me as a person, as well as a drummer.

Were you at all affected by the political controversy surrounding John and Yoko at that time?

Well, you've probably seen on TV the recent disclosure that the FBI in fact did tap John's phone. My wife, Cynthia, and I were watching the news report on that, and we looked at each other when that came on and said, "Do you remember the time? . . ." All those clips they showed on TV with John and Yoko and Jerry Rubin, Rennie Davis, and all those other guys: Bobby Seale and the Black Panthers, and the Chicago Seven. All the political things, and "The Mike Douglas Show." I wasn't on camera for that, but I was right there with them. That was part of that whole scene when John and Yoko wanted me to do everything they did. We traveled from New York to Philadelphia and back—John, Yoko, Tom the driver, me, and Jerry Rubin.

I remember that Jerry Rubin was intense about everything. For "The Mike Douglas Show" he was really wired and came across that way on camera. We drove back to New York that afternoon and Jerry was really, really bugged, saying, "Oh man, I blew that!" And John said, "Look, the only thing you've got to remember; you must remember this: Don't ever take speed before you go on TV." Oh man, I thought I was gonna die. It was *so* funny, but I felt bad. The poor guy had stumbled around so much, and in contrast, John—if you ever saw John on TV—he was just so masterful. He'd field any question. He had a brilliant mind. So he was able to pull off almost anything. I guess that's why Nixon and those people were afraid of him. They thought he had so much power that he would organize these big things and disrupt the Republican Convention and things like that. And you know, a funny thing with that story about tapping John's phone: We were constantly in touch back and forth on the phone. And every time I would be talking with John there would be a little click. So now it comes out. It could be that somewhere in government files our conversations are on tape.

Jim, can you recall one of your happiest moments in the studio with John Lennon?

You know, I *can* think of one of the most magical; it was a song called "You Don't Know What You Got until You Lose It" from *Walls and Bridges*. It was the first time I was able to get radical with the sound. I wanted to get a drum sound that was open and ringy from the snare and the tom-tom. They let me get away with it. I loved that. That's got to be one of my happiest moments in the studio. I loved the way I played. I loved the way it sounded. I loved the song. I loved the words: "You don't know what you got until you lose it." It was perfect for him at the time because he was insane over the breakup with Yoko. He wanted to get back with her so bad. He loved her so much.

JIM KELTNER

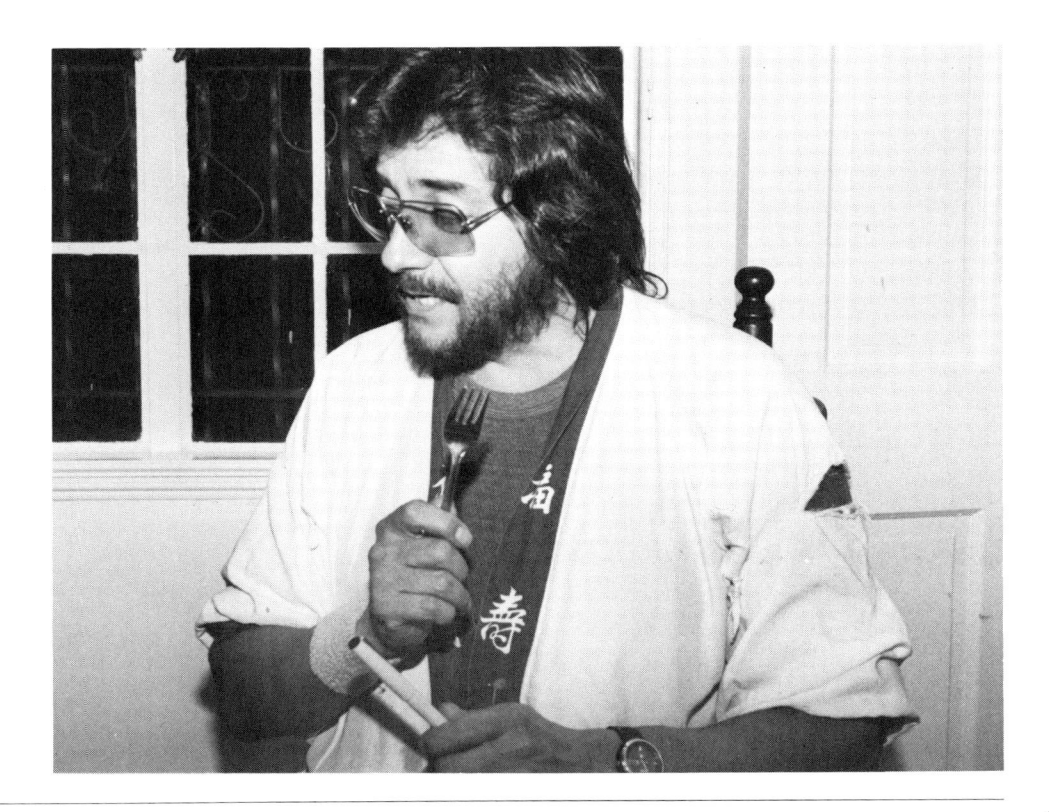

You've also worked with Phil Spector. What was that like?

Phil is awfully difficult for an artist to deal with because he is so strong. I was there at the beginning of one project, George's *Living in the Material World*. It usually started off real good with Phil and the artist, and then a lot of tension arose due to the different conceptions of what they wanted to go down. In the end, I do know this: Phil worked with George on *All Things Must Pass*, and that's generally regarded as George's best work since he left the Beatles. And the next best one was *Living in the Material World*, which Phil was also there for. And he was there for *Imagine*, which is one of John's best works. So, disregarding his own body of work that brought him to fame, the records Phil Spector made with the Beatles individually were incredible. In the end you've got to judge the work. That tells the story for me.

When you worked with Phil for the first time, was he as wild as some people say?

No. I didn't see any of that until much later. I saw a taste of it during *Living in the Material World*, though. He was pretty wild. For example, during the making of the *Rock 'n' Roll* album [John Lennon's], he pulled out a gun. I mean, you never knew what he was going to do. The night would start off really innocent and fun; he'd come in with a fairy wand and light it up. Sometimes he'd have on a white butcher's outfit with blood on it, and he'd go around directing people. One night he came in with little name tags and put one on each guy. It was great fun, and a lot of good music was played. But one time, like I said, he pulled out a gun and shot the floor, and the bullet ricocheted into the ceiling and scared the crap out of every-

"Jim Keltner can make music on anything."—Chuck Plotkin, 1983

body. One of the engineers walked out and went home. Then people started to fear what could happen if it *really* got out of hand. In defense of Phil, I've gotta say that one of the last times I saw him was when he was producing the Ramones. I've never seen him as straight. He was funnier than any other time I've ever been around him. He was totally straight as an arrow because Joey Ramone told him that if he wanted to finish the project, he'd have to straighten up. *They* gave Spector an ultimatum! And he straightened up. That's how much he respected them. I've had a great deal more respect for Phil since then. Phil, man—I always loved working with Phil Spector.

You got your big break, so to speak, with Gary Lewis and the Playboys in the sixties. How did that come about?

In September of '65 I got that gig by teaching Gary drums. I was working in a music store, and he came in one day and wanted to take lessons.

I got the road gig originally, because Hal Blaine was the drummer in the studio. I started on salary with Gary making two hundred fifty bucks a week.

I recorded the song "Just My Style," which was Gary's fifth hit. His first was "This Diamond Ring." Hal played on that. I also played on the album that was called *She's Just My Style*. I was with Gary for seven months.

You never did make it to "The Ed Sullivan Show" with the band, did you?

No, that was Jimmy Karstein. They fired me the night we got to New York because I was getting a little too big for my britches. I was starting to believe that the shit was real.

What did you do after you left the Playboys?

I came home and immediately started collecting unemployment and doing a nightmarish gig: an accordion duo. I felt like Gene Krupa must have felt in the days after he was busted for pot and couldn't get a job and was working strip joints. I was miserable. One night on a break I went for a ride in my car because I had no one to hang out with, and I smoked some grass and I got lost. I couldn't find the way back to the club—I was so high—and I got back about thirty minutes late for the set. Everyone was very, very irritated, and I was fired on the spot. Nineteen sixty-six was a weird year for me.

When did things start to pick up with recording?

In 1967 and 1968. I was doing demos at that time. In March '67 I was playing some jazz too, with John Handy, who is a sax player out of San Francisco. So I was doing that, collecting unemployment and playing with a little Afro-blues group around L.A. I was kind of oblivious to the rock scene in '67, to be honest with you. By 1967 the Beatles were incredible. Everybody was waiting for each record to come out. It was a big event all the time. *That's* what I liked about rock & roll. I think I was making a switch at that time from playing jazz to playing rock & roll.

In those days there were demos and a tremendous amount of studio work. It was great training. By 1971 I was working all the time. One day Barbra Streisand, the next day Randy Newman, the next day Ben Sidran, the next day Jimmy Haskell, Richard Perry, Johnny Rivers, Sergio Mendes, Ry Cooder, then Eric Clapton, then John Lennon, then B. B. King, then Harry Nilsson, then on to London for another session with B. B. King, then George Harrison, and Leon Russell in Tulsa, Oklahoma. On and on like that. And this was when I was just getting really started. It was all like a rush.

Was it intimidating to be called by Barbra Streisand, and turn around and do, say, Leon Russell?

That was the value of doing those demo sessions; that experience was really important for me. I did a lot of demos for Bob Summers and Sidewalk Productions. The money was slim, which was good for him, and I got plenty of experience, which was great for me. I didn't play great on everything, though. I stumbled and screwed up on a lot of things. But he would say okay, and then he would explain where I'd gone wrong: "Try this and do that." And I didn't know anything about tuning drums. I knew about Hal Blaine and I listened to his records, but I couldn't understand how he got such great sounds. I saw his set a few times and went nuts checking it out real close. And each time I got a little closer to getting a real good sound, a good Hal Blaine sound.

How would you describe the Hal Blaine sound?

Well, it was a snare that sounded snappy and didn't ring and had a good pop to it. In those days that was real important, a pop from the snare drum. And the bass drum—there's no way to describe that beautiful sound. Like the song "Taste of Honey"—just perfection. The man had perfection and time and feeling and sound. And I just studied the shit out of it. On those demo sessions I learned the discipline of going in, sitting down, and looking at a simple chart, maybe a chord chart, and playing a feeling on this song or that song, playing a shuffle one time, a heavy rock thing another time. Psychedelic stuff, the *Sgt. Pepper's* thing, was in at that time, and I was trying to get those big Ringo sounds, and it was impossible because we didn't record on the same kind of equipment. I had thought that Ringo had a secret to the way he tuned his drums or something. And in fact he didn't.

Did you ever ask him how he got that sound?

No, I found out later on without having to ask him. John told me a lot of things, and George told me a lot of things about the way they recorded. They used English eight-track recorders, all tubes stuff, and they didn't muffle the drums; they let them ring out. They started taping down the drums after *Rubber Soul. Revolver*, I think it was. They started getting that more crunchy sound. I loved Ringo's sound and wanted to bring that approach into my studio playing. It was wonderful, but I couldn't get away with it. Hal Blaine didn't do that, so nobody did it. You played the way Hal Blaine played or you didn't get called. Every time I sat next to Hal I was so damn thrilled, the command he had, the funk with which he played, man. I remember one time he played a Bo Diddley beat on a Big Band thing, and it was

"Every time I sat next to Hal I was so damn thrilled, the command he had, the funk with which he played, man. I remember one time he played a Bo Diddley beat on a Big Band thing, and it was so good. And to this day I can't play what he played; I don't know how he did it."

THE BIG BEAT

Jim with Ringo at the Concert for Bangladesh, 1971

so good. And to this day I can't play what he played; I don't know how he did it. I've asked him a few times to play it, but he doesn't know what I'm talking about.

What was your first big record date?

It's unusual for me to pin anything down in my career, but that I do know. It was in 1968, a Jimmy Webb date. It was live, and I was substituting for Hal Blaine. That was when I knew I was cool. The whole picture was perfect. It was a kind of difficult thing too, in that the chart wasn't all that hard, but one of the guys wanted to make it a little more interesting, so they said, "Let's do the same thing, only transpose it into 5/4." I went, "Oh shit, how do you do that? I just made it through 4/4. What are they trying to do?" I was always panicky inside like that. But I prayed a lot and I got through. Later, I listened back to that sucker, and it worked, and everybody was patting me on the back and saying, "Hey, real good job." Well, I was walking tall. I got home and I was telling everybody on the phone, "Yeah, I'm doing record dates now." I felt great. And then, what made me feel even more incredible was when I would go scanning the radio and hear that tune a few times, and I knew that was *it*. I remember hearing "Just My Style" on the radio, and being thrilled.

Jim, your relationship with Ringo is one of your most successful. Can you tell me how you met and why you think drumming together clicked?

I first met Ringo when I had done something for George, who then invited me to the session one night for "It Don't Come Easy." So I played maracas on that song with Ringo. I met him and told him how great I thought he was, and he said, "Come downstairs and play some maracas." That was my introduction to Ringo. The first time we played together was the Bangladesh concert. It was perfect. I didn't have to play real time because Ringo was there. That was the other thing: It started me realizing that the only way to do it is to set up right down next to each other, as close as you can get. If you ever saw the movie of the concert, I'm just watching his left hand. Every time his left hand came down, my left hand came down. The right hand on the hi-hat—he's playing *ching, ching, ching, ching, ching.* It wasn't good for me to play the same thing he was playing, because it was unnecessary. I would have been doubling up on something that didn't need to be doubled up on. So that's when I started going, *ching, ching, pat. Ching, ching, pat.* Taking the two and the four off so that the backbeat would be the most important thing. And if you hear the record, or anything that we played together—all the Ringo stuff: "You're Sixteen," "Oh My My"—the backbeat is real nice and fat because we're playing together, right on it. I'm looking right at his hand. Every time his hand goes down, I'm right there with him. That gave him a feeling of confidence. We're a good combination.

SELECTED DISCOGRAPHY

Singles

WITH GARY LEWIS AND THE PLAYBOYS

"She's Just My Style" (January 1966, Liberty)

WITH GEORGE HARRISON

"Bangla Desh" (July 1971, Apple)

WITH RINGO STARR

"Photograph" (September 1973, Apple)
"You're Sixteen" (December 1973, Apple)
"Oh My My" (March 1974, Apple)

WITH JOHN LENNON

"Mind Games" (October 1973, Apple)
"Whatever Gets You Through the Night" (September 1974, Apple)
"No. 9 Dream" (December 1974, Apple)

WITH RANDY NEWMAN

"Short People" (January 1978, Warner Bros.)

Tracks from Albums

WITH JOE COCKER

"Honky Tonk Women" from *Mad Dogs & Englishmen* (1971, A&M)
"Delta Lady" from *Mad Dogs & Englishmen* (1971, A&M)

WITH RITA COOLIDGE

"Ain't That Peculiar" from *Rita Coolidge* (1971, A&M)

WITH JOHN LENNON

"Bony Maronie" from *Rock 'n' Roll* (1975, Apple)

WITH RY COODER

"Speedo" from *Borderline* (1980, Warner Bros.)
"Why Don't You Try Me" from *Borderline* (1980, Warner Bros.)
"Across the Borderline" from *The Border* (soundtrack) (1982, MCA)

Ringo Starr

14

"And by some freaky accident . . . we made it to the top. If we hadn't, I would still be playing drums in some little nightclub somewhere because that's what was me. My soul is that of a drummer."

WE WERE IN MANCHESTER, England, in the spring of 1981, booked to play the Apollo, an old movie house. The marquee out front read: TONIGHT—LIVE ON STAGE—BRUCE SPRINGSTEEN. You don't see many LIVE ON STAGE signs anymore; I loved it. The Apollo was a classic, straight out of the fifties: pink sparkle walls and well-worn black seats. It was a small house, maybe fifteen hundred seats. You could see the crowd and it felt good.

We'd been doing "Twist and Shout" as an encore all along on the tour, and pounding out the number that night, my imagination ran wild. After the show I wandered around backstage and thought of the rock 'n roll history made there. I bet the Beatles played here, I thought to myself. Yeah, they probably did; most likely they played "Twist and Shout" too. I looked at my drum platform, set center stage. On it stood my four-piece Ludwig drum kit. I imagined another little set of Ludwig drums on that same spot, perhaps fifteen years earlier—Ringo's drums.

More than any other drummer, Ringo Starr changed my life. The impact and memory of that band on Ed Sullivan's show in 1964 will never leave me. I can still see Ringo, in the back, moving that beat with his whole body, his right hand swinging off his sock cymbal while his left hand pounds his snare. He was fantastic. But I think what got to me the most was his smile. I *knew* he was having the time of his life.

I wanted some of that. A few years earlier, D. J. Fontana had introduced me to the power of the Big Beat. Ringo convinced me just how powerful that rhythm could be.

Ringo's beat was heard around the world and he drew the spotlight toward rock & roll drumming. From his matched grip style to his pioneering use of staggered tom-tom fills, his influence in rock drumming was as important and widespread as Gene Krupa's had been in jazz.

The records Ringo made with the Beatles and on his own proudly stand the test of time. The performances speak for themselves, though some of my personal favorites are: "Tomorrow Never Knows," "Magical Mystery Tour," "She Loves You," "Sgt. Pepper's Lonely Hearts Club Band," "Rain," "A Day in the Life," "Twist and Shout," "Carry That Weight," "Rock and Roll Music" (what a relentless groove!), and "Long Tall Sally." Of his solo work I particularly enjoy "Photograph," "Back Off Boogaloo," and "It Don't Come Easy."

I cherish the music the Beatles made and I miss them as a band and as a musical force. I remember once hearing someone refer to Beatles music as the soundtrack for the sixties. For a lot of what I like to remember, their music *was* that. In my darker moments I listen to Beatles music, and those jangling guitars and Ringo's riveting beat make me recall what the Beatles did. They made me feel good.

Ringo's eyes tell a story. They are a deep and vibrant shade of blue. Whether he speaks of the time spent playing and growing up with "his band," or the joys of drumming, those eyes radiate the happiness you know he felt.

But Richard Starkey's sense of humor has *always* enabled Ringo Starr to carry on. He is a funny man, and his timing for a joke is as sharp as his drumming. Our meeting took place on the porch of his country home in England. We found having a mutual admiration for Jim Keltner was a good place to start the conversation.

RINGO: I love double-drumming with Jim because he's the most versatile drummer I know, and from the first day we met we became great pals. It was just a natural, mutual love for each other. We'd share the weight. I just love playing with Jim. I'd play the rock & roll and he'd fill all the gaps. We worked *together*. We weren't trying to prove anything to each other. I respected him and he respected me. You have to respect the artist you're playing with. Jim knows that, for instance, when there's a singer, there's no need for you to be soloing and drum boogying all over the place. But if he stops, you just get in and fill all the spaces. Half the time it's better if you don't fill them at all, though sometimes you can do fills that completely reverse the mood of the song. If you know your job, you know when the song needs to be raised a bit and when it needs to be brought down.

MAX: How would you bring the mood of a song down, say, going from the middle eight (the bridge), to the third verse?

It depends on the song. If you're playing on the ride cymbal you could do it by going back to the hi-hat. Or, you can do a fill that will bring the color of the song onto a lower attitude.

The middle eight in "I Want to Hold Your Hand" going into the third verse ("And when I touch you . . .") is a good example of this. It's a specific technique: You play the hi-hat open, and then you close it, and that really brings the mood down to a certain place. And then you open it up again for a lift. Simple, but effective. In the early sixties you took a lot of heat for playing so simply.

Well, the focus was always on John and Paul; they were the songwriters. As for the drummer, there could have been a gorilla up there. Drummers aren't really treated like human beings. We're a bit like second-rate citizens. I was doing my best and I was doing some good shit. But I felt as if I was being passed over. I wanted to be considered a member of the band like everyone else. In reviews of the records and stories about the music we were playing, very few writers happened to note whether I was playing good or bad. I wouldn't have minded if they said I was crap, as long as they mentioned my name in those days. But when I met Jim Keltner he was a great ego booster for me because he'd go to all these sessions and they'd say to him, "play like Ringo." I thought maybe I had done something right. It gave me more confidence in myself.

Did Paul or John move you to play a certain way?

A drummer always works as if everyone else in the band thinks he's also a drummer. I was always pushed by the other three because they wanted so much from the drummer and drums. John would play tracks for me, songs he liked, and say, "Play it *this* way." I'd listen to the song and say, "But John, there's two drummers on that. I can't play the part of *two* drummers." So, I'd just try to play what he wanted. Though, in the end, it's still me. I mean, I'm your basic offbeat drummer with funny fills. The fills were funny because I'm really left-handed playing a right-handed kit. But I write with my right hand because my grandmother thought if you were left-handed you were possessed by the devil. I can't roll around the drums because of that. I have to start with my left hand. If I come off the snare onto the tom-tom, I can't go on to the other tom, to the floor tom. That's why we used to call them funny fills. (Ringo demonstrates.)

What's your favorite piece of work you did as the drummer for the Beatles?

My favorite piece of me is what I did on "Rain." I think I just played amazing. I was into the snare and hi-hat. I think it was the first time I used this trick of starting a break by hitting the hi-hat first instead of going directly to a drum off the hi-hat. But I couldn't do that anymore because that came out of something that could only happen back then.

It can't be any preset arrangement with me. I can't do it twice the same—ever. I mean, I could do a straight shuffle or something, but fills are never the same, take to take. I couldn't do it that way again the following week, let alone twenty years later. I was into another space in my head in the way I was playing then. I couldn't ever double-track a fill. When I'd do a fill I always felt I went into a blackout. I didn't know what I'd do. How are some drummers able to figure out the fills? I've never been able to do that.

I've heard you say that Sgt. Pepper's *was just like cutting tracks, not making music.*

With *Sgt. Pepper*, I felt more like a session man because we were interested in making an *album* with strings and brass and *parts*. Everyone says that record is a classic, but it's not my favorite album. By the way, I'll bet you didn't know that Mal Evans, our roadie, came up with the "Sgt. Pepper" title. He didn't get the credit, though. Anyway, the White Album [*The Beatles*] is a much better album for me in that period because I felt we were becoming a group again. With the group recording at one time, it was great. You'll struggle like mad over that bloody track and it won't work, it doesn't work, there's nothing you can do to make it go. So you have a cup of tea and you come back and you've got it—it fits. I love recording. You know, with John, Paul, and George I think it was telepathy in the studio. I would *know* when John was going to do something.

It's interesting that you refer to the time of the White Album as the time when the Beatles were once again becoming a real band. The media perceived it just the opposite way. John coming in with his songs and Paul with his.

That's just the songs you're talking about. The band would play together, though. John and Paul weren't writing together, but we'd all support the songs as a band. It didn't matter who wrote them. You know, I left the group during the recording of that album because I felt I was playing like shit. And those three were really getting on. I had this feeling that nobody loved me; I felt horrible. So I said to myself, "What am I doing here? Those three are getting along so well, and I'm not even playing well." So I went over and knocked on John's door one day and said, "I'm leaving the band. I'm not playing well and you three are *so* close." And he says, "I thought it was *you* three!" And then I went to Paul's. Knock-knock. And he says, "I thought it was *you* three!" after I tell him I'm leaving the band. That was madness, so I went away on a holiday to sort things out. I don't know, maybe I was just paranoid. You know that to play in a band you have to trust each other. That's when Paul played drums on "Back in the USSR."

Shortly afterward I got a telegram from the boys. They said I was the greatest rock drummer on earth, and it just lifted me spirits. I came back and George had the studio full of flowers. We were all back together again. We finished the album and it was great. That's why I've always felt we were more of a band at that time. We weren't like session players trying to get the bloody arrangement down pat. We were a band.

You once said that when you first got in the Beatles you felt a little detached from the others.

That's the drummer's lament. On stage, you're in the back. You're always looking at the back of your mates' heads. It's a drummer's back-of-the-bus complex, I guess. All drummers experience it. But at the time it hits you, you think it's only you. You just feel sometimes that you're the dog of the group. That's our cross. But you know what else we know? That the band would be shit without us. You have to know that you are as important as they are. I mean, apart from drumming, can you imagine when I started writing songs and I had to present them to the two finest songwriters on earth? My songs were just silly little songs, and they were writing some amazing songs. I mean it took me months to present my things. I had "Octopus's Garden in the Shade." And they had things like (sings seriously) "Eleanor Rigby...." But they were my pals, and they all dove in it with me. They'd say, "Well, we'll change this a bit and that a bit." George was always great, because I'd write a song and give it to him because I could play only three chords. And he'd show me that it would take actually seven chords to play the song, because you have passing chords and things like that. I love the way guitarists just say, "Well, we'll put a G sharp in here."

What mattered most to the outcome of a Beatles session?

The priority was always the song. The song is what remains. It's not how you've done it. I honestly believe in the song more than the music. It's the song people whistle. You don't whistle my drum part. And John and Paul wrote some amazing songs.

How much of a role did George Martin play in the studio?

You know, in the studio you do a song a few times and you put it down on tape. We used to do a song and say, "George, did you get it?" We had to teach George: "You tape *everything*, George! It's only fucking tape!" But in those days it was, "Okay, you guys rehearse for two hours before we roll the tape." When I first went into the studio with the Beatles, George brought in another drummer; I wasn't what he wanted. He wanted a studio musician. He brought in Andy White and it crushed me, I'll tell you. I mean, the first time I was going to be on a piece of plastic and there's another kit in the room.

When you were coming up, who did you listen to?

Well, Elvis changed my head around. He was the first teenager in my life. Johnnie Ray, Frankie Laine, and Bill Haley were my early heroes, around '54. But they were always a bit like me dad. Elvis was the first *lad* who came out. The kid. He totally blew me away. I loved him so. And D. J. Fontana—D.J. was the first rock & roll drummer who people knew. They knew he played on Elvis's records. He preceded me as a *known* drummer, a drummer within a group.

But in Liverpool I saw the George Lewis Traditional Jazz Band in the fifties, and all these little old guys made up the band. The drummer had a snare, a cymbal, and a bass drum. It was great because every time he came to tom-tom stuff, he would just duck

*"You'll struggle like mad over that bloody track and it won't work, it doesn't work, there's nothing you can do to make it go. So you have a cup of tea and you come back and you've got it—it fits.
I love recording."*

down and do it on the bass drum! It blew me away. What showmanship!

There was a change in the Beatles' rhythm approach around 1967. The first time I noticed it was on "Lady Madonna." You went from a straight 4/4 rocker thing to half time.

I have very few tricks I can do. One is using the tom instead of the hi-hat. The other is that you play at half the tempo. And most of my fills are, more or less, half the tempo. I do it just to change the feel. I mean, they're not really tricks, and now they're laughable when I think of them. The idea that I'm playing on three when John, Paul, and George play on two and four. At the time it was a revelation. "Hey, wow, what have we invented?" You know, you've got twelve tracks on an album, so you try to vary the rhythm.

What kind of music did you listen to growing up in Liverpool?

Liverpool's a port and it's probably the biggest country & western town in England. With all the guys coming off the ships, they'd bring with them all these country & western records. But I was into the blues. I wanted to emigrate to America because of Lightning Hopkins.

How did drums enter the picture?

I became a drummer because by two months I missed being called up into the army. My opinion why music suddenly shot out of England in the sixties is that we were the first generation that didn't get regimented and didn't go into the army. Music was a way out. We all wanted to leave. Everyone wants to fly. Music was my way. Back then every street had a band. You could hear it all over. Everyone was playing, and mostly it sounded real bad, but they were playing. We all picked up guitars and drums and filled our time with music.

That's how I started. I got a kit of drums in January and was in a band in February. And the only reason they took me in was because in those days if you had the instrument, you were in the group. None of us could play except the guitarist. It would be hysterical. I had no sense of timing. And we'd still play. I had a snare and a cymbal because that's all I could carry on the bus; I had no car. We'd play and people would dance, but the beat would get faster and faster like an express train. No one in the band could hold it back because it was so exciting just to play.

What were your aspirations back when you were playing in Liverpool?

When I was playing Liverpool, to play even *outside* Liverpool was a big deal. Forget about the rest of the world.

How did you see rock & roll drumming back then?

Rock & roll to me is pounded out, straightforward. I used to have terrible arguments in Liverpool years ago, before the Beatles. The bands all knew each other and we'd meet in this one club which was open all night. It probably was the same for you; there's a band on every street, and each one wants to be the best in town. No one was famous or anything. We were just musicians who made up the local bands. I used to sit with some of the drummers and chat a bit, and I used to get real uptight because I honestly felt if it's rock, it's rock. Don't get busy.

How do you feel about the new electronic drums?

Well, I understand drum machines. No drummer can hold the beat perfectly throughout the whole song. Listen to the Beatles' records. There's a little bit of speeding up and a little bit of slowing down, but the band is all doing it together. There's nothing wrong with it. It's a natural thing. We're not machines, we're human beings. I'm such a shithead, though. I've always said, "Fuck the machines. I hate machines." And as soon as I came back to England, I bought myself a Linn! (Laughs.) I mean, you do such crazy things to your head. With Paul now, it's a click track all the time, because he wants it perfect. I'm not putting him down for using one, but we never had a click track, the Beatles that is, and we didn't do so bad.

Tell me more about your hi-hat approach and drumming in the studio.

If I didn't have a hi-hat, I'd be lost. It's the center of the kit, actually. I like it tight and I tend to play on the edge. It's a better sound for me.

How about tuning?

I tuned the drums for how I wanted them to sound in front of me. I'd tune them and then go up to the booth and listen while someone played them for me. The problem is, with all our technology, you get a sound you love but it doesn't translate through the wires. You might have a great bass drum sound, but it's not kicking through, perhaps because of the other instruments. So maybe you tighten the head a bit. Of course, you'd always complain to the engineer that the bloody bass drum sounds like a cardboard box.

Did that happen at Abbey Road?

Yeah, and it still happens today.

There's a great drum sound that you have on Abbey Road.

Abbey Road was tom-tom madness. I had gotten this new kit made of wood, and calfskins, and the toms had so much depth. I went nuts on the toms. Talk about changes in my drum style—the kit made me change because I changed my kit.

You also went from one rack tom to two.

That's right. You know, I'm like a caveman, I think drums should be made out of wood and should have skins on them. You can't beat the sound. My kit, though, has a very recognizable sound. When people ask me to play on their records, I think it's more the kit they want than me. They love its sound, and it's a sound that's been around a long time. That kit would have a recognizable sound even if *you* played it. When I toured, I used plastic heads. And I used that minikit. Do you know why?

Why?

Because I'm only five foot seven and I wanted to look tall.

"My opinion why music suddenly shot out of England in the sixties is that we were the first generation that didn't get regimented and didn't go into the army."

Is that really the reason?

I'm a show-off, man!

You and Paul had an amazing drummer-bass player relationship.

The bottom of your track is the bass drum and the bass. But the two don't have to play the same things. It's very important that the bass player is your friend, because playing together is complementing and supporting, not competing.

When you play with Paul these days, do you two automatically lock in?

I think we both relate to when we played together, to all those years. We've had many musical experiences together. I don't know about him, but when we play together I certainly relate to how we used to play. Paul is such a powerful and melodic bass player. He just knows how to play and complement the track.

Was it difficult going from playing with a group that you'd been with for so long to recording with session players?

Oh, yeah. Recording solo projects with session players is never the same as recording with the band. It will never be the same for me to play with anyone else. That's not because the Beatles were greater than anyone else, it's just that it takes all those years to be able to play together. The telepathy and the magic isn't there with session people. It was like there were five people playing in the Beatles—the four of us and the magic. Now when I record, it's not magical anymore. You get off and record some great tracks. But I've never done anything outside of playing with those three men that has got me off as much. That's not to say every time we played it was great, because some days it got real shitty and boring. But overall I was in the best band in the land.

Were you in favor of stopping the touring when it actually did stop?

The decision to stop touring was a unanimous one. We felt that we were getting real shitty as musicians. And what people forget was that we were musicians first and personalities second. First and foremost I am a drummer. After that I'm other things. But as musicians playing live, we couldn't hear ourselves and we weren't playing good. If you look at the film footage of us playing live, I'm always looking at John, Paul, or George to find out where we were. You couldn't hear with the screaming that went on. If I did anything but the offbeat, it was like playing into thin air. I mean, in the end, to keep us all together, I had to just *nail it down*. It hurts when you don't play good. We could've played every night to make money. But I didn't play drums to make money: I played drums because I loved them. And by some freaky accident, let's call it—I mean, no one knew how big we would get—we made it to the top. If we hadn't, I would still be playing drums in some little nightclub somewhere because that's what was me. My soul is that of a drummer. It was luck that I happened to play in the biggest band on earth. We did make some real good music. But playing was all it was. If it hadn't happened, we

RINGO STARR

could just still be playing Liverpool. At one time I was an engineer in a factory and played drums part-time. But it came to where I had to make a decision—I was going to be a drummer. Everything else goes now. *I* play drums. It was a conscious moment in my life when I said the rest of the things are getting in the way. I didn't do it to become rich and famous. I did it because it was the love of my life.

These days do you ever get the urge to go and sit with a local band?

No, because the local band won't play if I get up and jam. They get too nervous. I mean, if I get up and play, they're not themselves. I've been in sessions where the whole room changed because, "Hey, it's one of *them!*" I'm just a player, guys, you know? But I can't help all of that. That goes on. I don't create it, they create it. That's why it would be silly to get up with a local band. I did get up with the band on the *QE2* because they're all sailors from Liverpool. They played every Beatle song as a shuffle. They play all our old Beatle numbers, and, as anyone knows, you forget things. Well, I got up with them and forgot a bloody break in one of the songs, and they all turned around and shouted at me! (Laughs.)

Bernard Purdie, one of the great session players from the sixties, says that he played on twenty-one Beatles tracks.

Well then, what was I doing in the studio? You know, I've heard that rubbish before. Everyone was expecting me to come out and fight it. You don't bother fighting that shit.

Was there ever a point, say in '64 or '65, where the hysteria over the band got so out of control that you were actually frightened?

Well, one of the most bizarre situations we found ourselves in was a thing we did for our fan club in England. They put us in a cage so the

Ringo and his minikit, circa 1964. Note the *white* drums.

fans could get a look at us but wouldn't be able to get at us. I mean, we were like camels in the zoo, sitting in this bloody cage saying, "Hello. Hi." People would get hysterical and want to take a piece of you home.

Apart from the hysteria, the potential the band had for changing the world, so to speak, was incredible.

Did you know that a million kids voted for me to be president of the United States and I wasn't even 35? But we never used the power we had. We were not politicians, we were musicians. Looking back, it's all conjecture now, but if we had used that power, maybe we could have made the world a different place. Maybe if we just said, "Okay, we'll rule." But we were musicians; that was our game. Later on, John got political and created a few storms. You know, I was highly disappointed when flower power didn't work. Peace and love failed. I was very disappointed. But good always winds up winning over evil in the end.

Well, the music always had that kind of influence. One of my favorite quotes was that "the Beatles' music was the soundtrack for the sixties." Do you ever listen to those old records?

Let me tell you where we were coming from. Back then, once we made the record, played the acetate, checked out the cover, and played it once, we never played it again. When we split up, I wouldn't play any Beatles records. But in 1978 I started playing them again, and that's when I got back into Beatles music all over again. Now I listen to it, with nothing else going on, and I can just hear the music, if you know what I mean. Then I started listening to me, my drums, on the records. And I'd say to myself, "Shit, I did real well on that one."

What made you get back to listening to the music?

I just decided—let's put them on and listen, and I thought, "Shit, that one's great!" That's how I rediscovered "Rain." I think it's the best out of all the records I've ever made. "Rain" blows me away. It's out of left field. I know me and I know my playing, and then there's "Rain." I think, if you'd play all those records, you'd not find that type of drumming from me anywhere else. I can see my ups and downs as a drummer, and above all, like a bright light, that one stands out. If I had one track to take to a deserted island, it would be "Rain."

Now that you've rediscovered all these fantastic songs, how do they hit you?

They affect me emotionally. But the nice thing is that I can listen to them as records even though I still remember the things that went down the day we recorded them, the exact date and so on. Some days I'll pull out stacks of Beatle records and play them for my wife Barbara and say, "Listen to this, Barb, or this one." They're great tracks. Like, for example, I think "A Day in the Life" is a great Beatles track. You really had the two distinct personalities of John and Paul come out on that one. And I love the second side of *Abbey Road*, where it's all connected and disconnected. No one wanted to finish those songs, so we put them all together and it worked. I think that piece of that album is some of our finest work.

RINGO STARR

My wife, Becky, and I relate more to Beatles songs than any others we know. When we're down or things are going wrong around us, we'll listen to some of those old tracks, and they make us feel better.

That's because they're all love songs, you know. "Love Me Do," "I Want to Hold Your Hand," "If I Fell." *We* made it on love songs.

You've done so much in your career, Ringo. Do you have any unfulfilled ambitions?

Well, my one ambition was to have been in the audience when the Beatles played. It must have been great.

SELECTED DISCOGRAPHY

Singles

WITH THE BEATLES

"Please Please Me" (February 1963, Vee Jay)
"She Loves You" (September 1963, Swan)
"I Want to Hold Your Hand" (January 1964, Capitol)
"Twist and Shout" (March 1964, Tollie)
"A Hard Day's Night" (July 1964, Capitol)
"I Feel Fine" (December 1964, Capitol)
"She's a Woman" (December 1964, Capitol)
"Eight Days a Week" (February 1965, Capitol)
"Ticket to Ride" (April 1965, Capitol)
"Help" (August 1965, Capitol)
"We Can Work It Out" (December 1965, Capitol)
"Day Tripper" (December 1965, Capitol)
"Rain" (B side of "Paperback Writer") (May 1966, Capitol)
"Penny Lane" (February 1967, Capitol)
"Strawberry Fields Forever" (February 1967, Capitol)
"I Am the Walrus" (November 1967, Capitol)
"Lady Madonna" (March 1968, Capitol)
"Hey Jude" (August 1968, Apple)
"Revolution" (August 1968, Apple)
"Something" (October 1969, Apple)
"Come Together" (October 1969, Apple)
"Let It Be" (March 1970, Apple)

Tracks from Albums

WITH THE BEATLES

"Long Tall Sally" from *The Beatles' Second Album* (1964, Capitol)
"Rock and Roll Music" from *Beatles '65* (1965, Capitol)
"Boys" from *The Early Beatles* (1965, Capitol)
"What You're Doing" from *Beatles VI* (1965, Capitol)
"You're Going to Lose That Girl" from *Help!* (1965, Capitol)
"In My Life" from *Rubber Soul* (1965, Capitol)
"Taxman" from *Revolver* (1966, Capitol)
"Tomorrow Never Knows" from *Revolver* (1966, Capitol)
"Sgt. Pepper's Lonely Hearts Club Band" from *Sgt. Pepper's Lonely Hearts Club Band* (1967, Capitol)
"With a Little Help from My Friends" from *Sgt. Pepper's Lonely Hearts Club Band* (1967, Capitol)
"Helter Skelter" from *The Beatles* (also known as the White Album) (1968, Apple)
"I Want You (She's So Heavy)" from *Abbey Road* (1969, Apple)
"Carry That Weight" from *Abbey Road* (1969, Apple)

Solo Singles

"It Don't Come Easy" (April 1971, Apple)
"Back Off Boogaloo (March 1972, Apple)
"Photograph" (September 1973, Apple)

Index

A&M Records, 85, 177
A&R Studios, 41
A-1 Studios, 67
Abbey Road, 185, 190
Abbey Road Studios, 185
ABC Records, 43, 72, 102
"Across the Borderline," 177
Adams, Justin, 88
Adderley, Cannonball, 35
"After the Glitter Fades," 106
Against the Wind, 59
"Ain't That a Shame," 95
"Ain't That Peculiar," 177
Aja, 72
Alexander, Arthur, 46, 50
"All or Nothing," 144
"All Shook Up," 128
All Things Must Pass, 173
Allen, Lee, 88, 92
Allen, Pistol, 2
Allison, Keith, 9
American Federation of
    Musicians, 88
Analytical Drum Tuning, 105
"Angie," 166
Animals, 5, 69, 70
Anka, Paul, 77
"Anyway You Want Me (That's
    How I Will Be)," 119, 128, 132,
    141
Apollo, The, 179
Appice, Carmine, 2
Apple Records, 102, 177, 189, 190
April Wine, 25
Apted, Michael, 42
"Aquarius," 85
Armatrading, Joan, 144
Artie, 82
Asher, Peter, 102-3
Association, 85
Astronauts, 98
Asylum Records, 106
"At the Scene," 141
Atco Records, 14, 72, 85

Atlantic Records, 21, 22, 23, 24, 46,
    53, 54, 55, 58, 59, 67, 72, 95
Atomics, 111

"Baba O'Riley," 146
"Baby I Love You," 47, 76
"Back in the USSR," 182
"Back Off Boogaloo," 180, 190
Backstreet Records, 177
Badanjek, Johnny "Bee," 1, 5-14
Baker, Ginger, 2, 159, 160, 165
"Ball the Wall," 91, 95
Band, 27-28, 33-43
Band, The, 28, 33-34, 41, 43
"Bangla Desh," 177
Bangladesh, Concert for, 169, 176
Banker's Club, 18
Barber, Chris, 159
Barbieri, Gato, 62, 72
Barge in East, 21, 22
Barnum, H. B., 81
Barons, 99
Bartholomew, Dave, 87, 88, 90, 91,
    92, 93
Basement Tapes, 39, 41, 43
"Be My Baby," 75, 76, 80, 85
Beach Boys, 76, 82, 85, 95
"Beast of Burden," 163
"Beat Goes On," 85
Beat Monthly, 158
Beatles, 5, 20, 22, 23, 25, 68-70, 83,
    94, 124, 126-27, 131, 132, 133,
    160-61, 164, 171, 173, 179-90
Beatles '65, 189
Beatles, The, 182, 190
Beatles Monthly, 158
Beatles' Second Album, 189
Beatles VI, 189
Beaucoups of Blues, 126
"Because," 139-40, 141
Beck, Jeff, 9, 62, 156
Beckett, Barry, 45, 46, 54, 55, 56,
    58
"Bed of Fire," 24

Bee, Johnny. See Badanjek,
    Johnny "Bee"
Bell, Al, 57
Bell, Freddy, 119
Below, Fred, 2
Benjamin, Benny, 2, 67-68
Bernstein, Sid, 22
Berry, Chuck, 2, 9, 29, 76
Best of Percy Sledge, 45, 59
Best, Pete, 83
Bevis, Fred, 54, 55
Bevis Recording Studio, 46, 54
Billboard, 9
Birdland, 157
"Bits and Pieces," 136, 137-38, 141
Black, Bill, 30, 109, 111, 114, 115,
    120, 125
Black Panthers, 172
Blackburn, Lou, 79
Blackwell, Chris, 56
Blaine, Hal, 1, 56, 75-85, 88, 93, 95,
    126, 157, 173, 174 175-76
Bloomfield, Mike, 8
"Blue Hawaii," 84
Blue Hawaii, 84
"Blue Moon of Kentucky," 113
"Blue Suede Shoes," 128
"Blueberry Hill," 87
Blues Project, 8
Bond, Graham, 159
Bonero, Johnny, 110-11
Bonham, John, 2, 165
Bono, Sonny, 79
"Bony Maronie," 177
Booker T. and the MGs, 48, 52,
    143, 150, 151
Border, 177
Boudreaux, John, 2
"Boxer," 82
"Boys," 190
Boz Scaggs, 59
Breakout, 11, 14
"Bridge over Troubled Water," 62
Brigati, David, 20

Brigati, Eddie, 20, 21, 22, 23
Briggs, David, 46, 49
Brother Julius, 83
Brown, James, 8, 10, 12, 62, 66, 70, 72, 143, 150
"Brown Sugar," 166
Brown, Thurlow, 32
Browne, Jackson, 97, 104, 105, 106, 170
Bulldog, 25
Butterfield, Paul, 8
Byrds, 75, 82, 85, 101

"California Dreamin'," 75, 85
Campbell, Glen, 76
"Can't You See That She's Mine," 132, 140, 141
Capitol Records, 14, 43, 54, 59, 85, 106, 189, 190
Carlyles, 29
Carrigan, Jerry, 46, 49
Carroll, Jon, 28
"Carry That Weight," 180, 190
Cash, Johnny, 116
"Catch Us If You Can," 136, 141
Catch Us If You Can, 140
Cate Brothers, 38
Caton, Roy, 79
Cattini, Clem, 139
Cavaliere, Felix, 20, 21, 22, 23
Cavern, The, 143, 144
"CC Ryder," 14
"Chain of Fools," 47
Charles, Ray, 11–12, 62, 70–71, 143
"Chest Fever," 28
Chester, Gary, 2
Chicago Seven, 172
Choo Choo Club, 20, 21
Christie, Lou, 9
Clapton, Eric, 150, 156, 175
Clark, Dave, 131–41
Clark, Dick, 9
Clark, Gene, 101
Clay, Francis, 160
Cliff, Jimmy, 56
Cline, Patsy, 29
Clive Bessicks Orchestra, 64
Clowns, 29
Coal Miner's Daughter, 41
Cocker, Joe, 169–70, 177
Cogbill, Tommy, 53
"Cold Sweat—Part I," 62, 66, 72
Cole, Cozy, 48
Coleman, Bobby, 19
Columbia Records, 23, 42, 58, 85, 135
"Come on Up," 24
"Come Together," 190
Contours, 138

Cooder, Ry, 175, 177
Cooke, Sam, 81, 91
Coolidge, Rita, 177
Cooper, Alice, 13, 14
Cooper, Les, 61, 72
Cooper, Ray, 156, 165
Cornish, Gene, 20, 21, 25
"Country Line Special," 159
Covay, Don, 68, 72
Cramer, Floyd, 114, 124–25
Cream, 2, 12, 101, 159
"Creeque Alley," 85
Crewe, Bob, 6, 7–8, 10
Crystals, 76, 85, 138
Curtis, King, 18, 53, 62, 65–66, 70–71, 72
Curtis, Peck, 30
"Cut It Away," 106

"Da Doo Ron Ron," 76, 85
Daltrey, Roger, 145, 146, 147
"Dance, Dance, Dance," 76, 85
"Dandelion," 166
Danelli, Dino, 17–25
Daniels, Charlie, 127
Danko, Rick, 27, 28, 33, 37, 41, 42
"Dark End of the Street," 45, 51
Darrow, Chris, 102
Dave Clark Five, 131–41
Davidson, Lenny, 136, 137
Davies, Cyril, 159
Davis, Rennie, 172
Davis, Willie, 22
"Day Dreaming," 72
"Day in the Life," 180, 188
"Day Tripper," 190
"Deacon Blues," 72
Decca Records, 144, 152
Dee, Joey, 20, 22
Delaney and Bonnie, 169
Delory, Al, 76, 79, 80
"Delta Lady," 177
Derringer, Rick, 13
Detroit, 12–13
"Detroit City," 92
Detroit Wheels. *See* Mitch Ryder and the Detroit Wheels
"Devil with a Blue Dress On," 5, 6, 8, 9, 14
Dew Drop, 93
Diddley, Bo, 175
Dino's Casino, 18–19
Disciples of Soul. *See* Little Steven and the Disciples of Soul
Dizzy Gillespie at Montreux, 72
"Do You Love Me?," 132, 138, 139, 141
Dr. John, 6, 13–14
"Doctor My Eyes," 106

Dodds, "Baby," 87
Domino, Fats, 87, 88, 90, 91, 92, 93, 95, 138
"Don't Be Cruel," 112, 119, 128
"Don't Do It," 35, 40
"Dorsey Brothers Show," 123
Doucette, Salvador, 88
Douglas, Steve, 76, 79, 82
Dowd, Tom, 53
Drake, Pete, 126
Drifters, 8
"Drum Boogie," 18
"Drumsville," 48
Dunhill Records, 85, 102
Dupree, Cornell, 66
Dylan, Bob, 8–9, 28, 38, 39, 40, 43, 169–70

Early Beatles, 189
"Ed Sullivan Show," 1, 36, 109, 118, 131, 133–34, 174, 179
"Edge of Seventeen," 106
"Eight Days a Week," 190
Eighth Wonder, 8
Eldridge, Roy, 157
"Eleanor Rigby," 183
Electric Flag, 101
Elektra Records, 14
Elliott, Earl, 7
Elvis TV Special, 84
EMI Records, 24, 135
"Eminence Front," 151
Entwistle, John, 145, 146, 147, 148
Epic Records, 14, 140, 141
Epstein, Brian, 22, 69
Eric Delaney Band, 136
Ertegun, Ahmet, 21, 22
Esposito, Joe, 78
Evans, Mal, 182
"Even Now," 106
Everlast Records, 72
Every Picture Tells a Story, 152
"Everybody Knows," 141
Exile on Main Street, 166
Ezrin, Bob, 13, 14

Face Dances, 151, 152
Faces, 144, 146, 148, 149–50, 151, 152. *See also* Small Faces
Fairweather-Low, Andy, 156
Faith, Adam, 134
Fame Recording Studio, 46, 49, 50, 54
"Fat Man," 87, 91
"Fat Man Blues," 92
Fields, Frank, 88
Fifth Dimension, 1, 75, 76, 85
Fillmore East, 170
Fillmore West, 70

INDEX

"Fire and Rain," 97–98, 101, 103, 105, 106
First Step, 152
Flans, Robyn, 155
Fly, 171
Flying Dutchman Records, 72
Fonda, Peter, 101
Fontana, D. J., 1, 2, 30, 40, 109–28, 157, 180, 183
Fotomaker, 25
Four Freshmen, 91
Four Seasons, 9
Fox Theatre, 10
Francis, Panama, 2, 67
Franklin, Aretha, 45, 46–47, 53, 58, 62, 70–71, 72
Franks, Tilman, 113, 125
Freddie Martin Orchestra, 119
Freddy Bell and the Bellboys, 119
"Free Ride," 6, 13, 14
Frizzell, Lefty, 29
"Fun, Fun, Fun," 76, 85

Gaines, Steve, 13
Garden State Arts Center, 34
Garfunkel, Art, 78, 82
Garvin, Tom, 90
Gary Lewis and the Playboys, 174, 177
Gasoline Alley, 152
Gaye, Marvin, 10
Gene Vincent and the Blue Caps, 123
George Lewis Traditional Jazz Band, 183
"Get Closer," 106
"Get Off of My Cloud," 5, 166
Get Yer Ya-Ya's Out!, 166
Gillespie, Dizzy, 62, 72
"Gimme Shelter," 156
"Girl Like You," 24
"Glad All Over," 131, 133, 135, 136, 139, 141
Glaub, Bob, 170
Goldberg, Barry, 8
"Good Golly Miss Molly," 5, 14, 87
"Good Lovin'," 17, 19, 21, 22, 24
"Good Rockin' Tonight," 110
"Good Thing," 85
"Good Vibrations," 76, 85
Goodman, Benny, 19
Got Love If You Want It!, 166
Grass Roots, 85
Green, Al, 54
Green, Marlin, 50
"Green Onions," 143
Griffin, Paul, 66
"Groovin'," 17, 24

Halbert, Charlie, 32
Halee, Roy, 82, 83
Haley, Bill, 183
Hall, Dolores, 63
Hall, Rick, 49–50, 54
Hammond, John, Jr., 8
Hampton, Lionel, 19–20
Hamptons, 21
Handy, John, 174
"Hard Day's Night," 190
"Harder They Come," 56
Harmon, Buddy, 2, 124, 125, 127
Harrison, George, 126, 169, 170, 171, 173, 175, 176, 177, 182, 183, 184, 186
Haskell, Jimmy, 174
Hathaway, Donny, 66
"Have You Seen Your Mother, Baby, Standing in the Shadow?," 166
Having a Wild Weekend. See *Catch Us If You Can*
Hawkins, Roger, 45–59, 61, 116, 169
Hawkins, Ronnie, 20, 27, 31, 32, 33, 34, 43
Hawks, 20, 27, 32
Haynes, Louie, 35
Haywood, Leonard, 64
"Heartbreak Hotel," 109, 116, 128
"Heavy Makes You Happy (Sha-Na-Boom Boom)," 56, 58
Helm, Levon, 2, 20, 27–43, 120
"Help," 190
"Help Me, Rhonda," 85
"Helter Skelter," 190
Hendrix, Jimi, 12
"Here Come Those Tears Again," 106
Herman, Woody, 111, 112
"He's a Rebel," 76, 85
"He's So Fine," 67
"Hey Jude," 190
"High Heel Sneakers," 67
Highway 61, 9
Hi-Lo's, 91
Holland, Milt, 84
Holly, Buddy, 150
Hollywood Be Thy Name, 14
"Honky Tonk Women," 156, 164, 166, 177
Hood, David, 45, 46, 54, 55, 56, 58
Hoot-and-Curley, 115
Hopkins, Lightning, 184
"Hound Dog," 1, 48, 109, 112, 116, 118, 119, 128
"How Can I Be Sure?," 24
"How Do I Make You?," 106
Howe, Bones, 84

Hudson, Garth, 27, 28, 33–34, 37, 41
"Hullabaloo," 20–21
"Hungry," 85
Huxley, Rick, 136, 137

"I Ain't Gonna Eat Out My Heart Anymore," 20–21, 24
"I Am the Walrus," 190
"I Feel Fine," 190
"I Feel the Earth Move," 106
"I Forgot to Remember to Forget," 110
"I Found a Love," 11
"I Get Around"," 76
"I Got a Woman," 109, 116, 117, 128
"I Got You Babe," 85
"I Got You (I Feel Good)," 62, 72
"(I Know) I'm Losing You," 144, 152
"I Like It Like That," 141
"I Never Loved a Man (the Way I Love You)," 47
"I Saw Her Again," 85
"I Wanna Be Your Man," 161
"I Want Candy," 9
"I Want to Hold Your Hand," 20, 181, 189, 190
"I Want You (She's So Heavy)," 190
"If I Can Dream," 84
"If I Fell," 189
Igoe, Sonny, 111
"I'll Take You There," 56, 58
"I'm Walkin'," 87, 95
Imagine, 171, 173
Immediate Records, 144, 152
Imperial Records, 85, 95
"In My Life," 190
In My Own Write (Lennon), 158
Iovine, Jimmy, 61
Island Records, 56
"It Don't Come Easy," 176, 180, 190
"Itchykoo Park," 152
"It's All Over Now," 166
It's Hard, 152
"It's My Life," 5
"It's Now or Never," 78
"It's Only Rock 'n' Roll (but I Like It)," 150, 152
"It's Too Late," 106
"It's Wonderful," 23, 24
"I've Been Lonely Too Long," 17, 24
Ivey, Quinn, 50, 51, 54

J&M Music Shop, 92

J&M Recording Studios, 87
Jackson, Al, 2, 40, 52, 97, 150–51, 165
Jagger, Mick, 6, 150, 156, 159–60, 161, 162, 163, 164
"Jailhouse Rock," 109, 128
Jailhouse Rock, 120, 121, 125
James, Elmore, 160
"Jealous Guy," 171
Jemmott, Jerry, 62, 66
"Jenny Jenny," 14
"Jenny Take a Ride," 5, 7, 9, 14
Jo Mama, 104
Jobete Music, 67, 68
John Wesley Harding, 40
Johns, Glyn, 151
Johnson, Jimmy, 45, 46, 50, 53, 54, 56, 58
Jones, Brian, 160
Jones, George, 29
Jones, Kenney, 143–52, 156, 161, 162, 164, 165, 177
Jones, Mickey, 38
Jones, Paul, 160
Jones, Will Pop, 32
Jordan, Louis, 92, 112
"Jumpin' Jack Flash," 166
Jungle Bush Beaters, 32
"Just Once in My Life," 95
"Just One Look," 68

Kahn, Tiny, 81
"Kansas City," 66
Karstein, Jimmy, 174
"Kashmir," 165
Kaye, Carole, 76, 80
Keltner, Jim, 2, 75, 169–77, 180, 181
Kennedy, Jerry, 127
Kessel, Barney, 76
"Kicks," 85
"Kid Charlemagne," 72
King, B. B., 9, 175
King Biscuit Boys, 29
"King Biscuit Hour," 29
King, Carole, 97, 103, 105, 106
"King Creole," 121
King Creole, 121, 128
"King Harvest," 28
King Records, 72
Kingpins, 62, 65, 70. See also Curtis, King
"Knockin' on Heaven's Door," 169
"Kodachrome," 57, 58
Korner, Alexis, 159, 160
Kortchmar, Danny (Kooch), 103–4
Krupa, Gene, 18, 19, 81, 87, 111, 157, 158, 163, 165, 174, 180
Kubert, Joe, 7

Kudlets, "Colonel" Harold, 27, 32–33
Kunkel, Russ, 2, 97–106

"Lady Madonna," 184, 190
Lake Cliff, 115
Lamond, Don, 111
"Land of 1,000 Dances," 46, 52, 53, 58
Landau, Jon, 169
Laine, Frankie, 183
Lane, Ronnie, 143, 144, 146, 156
"Last Time," 166
Last Waltz, The, 42, 43
Lattimore, Carl, 22
"Lawdy Miss Clawdy," 87, 92, 95
"Layla," 156
Led Zeppelin, 2, 162
Lee, Peggy, 90
Lennon, John, 158, 160–61, 169, 170, 171–72, 173, 175, 177, 181, 182, 184, 186, 188
"Let It Be," 190
Let It Bleed, 166
"(Let Me Be Your) Teddy Bear," 120, 128
"Let Me Off Uptown," 157
"Let the Sunshine In," 85
"Let's Spend the Night Together," 166
Levon Helm, 43
Levon Helm and the RCO All-Stars, 43
Levy, Len, 140
Lewis, Gary, 174
Lewis, Jerry Lee, 29, 31, 110, 116
Lewis, Smiley, 91
Liberty Records, 177
Linn drum machine, 52, 145–46, 185
Little Green Men, 29
"Little Latin Lupe Lu," 5, 14
Little Richard, 1, 11, 87, 91, 92, 93, 95, 138
Little Steven and the Disciples of Soul, 18, 24
Live at the Fillmore West (King Curtis), 62, 71, 72
Live at the Fillmore West (Aretha Franklin), 62, 72
Live Rockets, 14
Living in the Material World, 173
"Load Out," 106
Logan, Horace, 113
London Records, 166
"Long Tall Sally," 95, 180, 190
Longhair, Professor, 90–91, 95
"Louisiana Hayride," 111, 112–15, 124, 125, 128
"Love Me Do," 189

"Love Me Tender," 1, 120
Love Me Tender, 120
"Loves Me Like a Rock," 57, 58
"Lovin' Feeling," 93
Loving You, 120, 121
Lowe, Junior, 50
Lowe, Sammy, 66
"Lucille," 1, 87, 95
Lynyrd Skynyrd, 13

Mad Dogs and Englishmen, 169
Mad Dogs & Englishmen, 177
"Maggie May," 144, 152
"Magical Mystery Tour," 180
Mamas and the Papas, 75, 85
Manfred, Mann, 160
Manne, Shelly, 111
Manuel, Richard, 27, 28, 33, 40, 41
Marcus, Greil, 28
Marquee, 143, 159
Marriott, Steve, 143, 144, 146
Martin, George, 183
Marvelettes, 10
Matassa, Cosimo, 87, 92
"Matchbox," 48
McCartney, Paul, 181, 182, 184, 185, 186
McCarty, Jim, 6, 9, 10, 12
McCoy, Charlie, 127
McLagen, Ian, 143, 144, 150
McLean, Ernest, 88
Meadowbrook Club, 111
Melcher, Terry, 82, 84
"Memories," 84
"Memphis," 85
"Memphis Soul Stew," 62
Men without Women, 18, 24
Mendes, Sergio, 175
Mercury Records, 152
"Mercy, Mercy," 68, 72
Metropole, 18, 19, 20, 158
"Mickey's Monkey," 11
"Midnight Confessions," 85
"Midnight Hour," 52
Migliori, Jay, 79
"Mike Douglas Show," 172
Miller, Jimmy, 164
"Milton Berle Show," 118
Mind Games, 171, 177
Mingus, Charles, 157
Miracles, 10, 11
"Miss You," 156, 163, 166
Mr. Dynamo, 43
"Mr. Tambourine Man," 75, 82, 85
Mitch Ryder and the Detroit Wheels, 5–12, 13, 14, 17
Modern Drummer, 155
Modern Records, 106
Moman, Chips, 53
"Monday, Monday," 85

INDEX

"Money, Honey," 116
Monkees, 69, 70
Monroe, Bill, 29
Moon, Keith, 2, 145, 146, 147, 148, 149, 165
Moondog Matinee, 43
Moore, Bob, 124
Moore, Scotty, 30, 109, 110–11, 114, 115, 118, 120, 121, 125, 127
Morello, Joe, 48
Morrison, Van, 101
Mosque Theater, 131
"Mother's Little Helper," 166
Motown Records, 5, 7, 10, 11, 12, 62, 67
Muddy Waters—Live at Newport, 160
Mullins, J. B., 111
Murray the K, 11, 21
Muscle Shoals Rhythm Section, 45, 46, 47, 58
Muscle Shoals Sound Studio, 47, 54, 55
Music from Big Pink, 28, 40, 43
"Mustang Sally," 21, 46, 52, 58
"My Baby Left Me," 128
"Mystery Train," 110
Mystery Train (Marcus), 28

Nashville, 121
National Association of Recording Arts and Sciences (NARAS), 11
Nelson, Sandy, 48
"Never Loved a Man," 53
New Frontier Hotel, 119
New Musical Express, 161
New Orleans Piano, 95
New Voice Records, 14
Newman, Randy, 88, 175, 177
Nicks, Stevie, 97, 106, 170
"Night Moves," 59
"Night They Drove Old Dixie Down," 28
"Night Train," 143
Nilsson, Harry, 175
"19th Nervous Breakdown," 166
Nitzsche, Jack, 76, 79, 83, 163
"No," 25
"No. 9 Dream," 177
Nod Is as Good as a Wink to a Blind Horse, 152
"Not Fade Away," 166
Nugent, Ted, 12

"O Sole Mio," 78
O'Brian, Joel, 104
"Octopus's Garden," 183
O'Curran, Charles, 78, 79

Ode Records, 106
"Oh My My," 177
"Oh Well," 14
Oldham, Andrew Loog, 6, 144
Oldham, Spooner, 46, 48, 50, 53
Olivier, Sir Laurence, 140
Olympic Brass Band, 90–91
Once upon a Dream, 23
Ono, Yoko, 169, 170, 171–72
Ooh La La, 152
"Ophelia," 35
Orbison, Roy, 116
Orlons, 9
Osborne, Joe, 76, 80
"Out of Left Field," 51
"Out of Sight," 67, 72
"Over and Over," 138, 141

Pablo Records, 72
Page, Frank, 113
Page, Jimmy, 156, 165
Page, Patti, 78
Paine, Rebel, 33
"Paint It, Black," 156, 164, 166
Palmer, Earl, 1, 2, 48, 87–95, 157
"Papa's Got a Brand New Bag," 62, 66, 72
Parker, Charlie, 158
Parker, Colonel Tom, 116, 117, 118, 120, 122, 124
Parker, Junior, 30
Paul Revere and the Raiders, 9, 85
Paul, Steve, 12
Paulman, Jimmy Ray, 31
Payton, Dennis, 136, 137
Peaceful World, 23
"Penny Lane," 190
"People Got to Be Free," 17, 22–23
Peppermint Lounge, 20
Perkins, Carl, 48, 116
Perry, Richard, 175
Philles Records, 85, 95
Phillips, Earl, 160
"Photograph," 177, 180, 190
Pickett, Wilson, 11, 21, 45, 46, 52, 53, 58
"Please Please Me," 190
Plotkin, Chuck, 170, 173
Pohlman, Ray, 76, 79
"Poor Side of Town," 85
Presley, Elvis, 1, 19, 30, 46, 48, 77–78, 84, 109–11, 112–28, 138, 183
Presley, Lisa Marie, 127
Preston, Billy, 66
Price, Lloyd, 49, 87, 95
Purdie, Bernard "Pretty," 2, 8, 53, 61–72, 187
Putnam, Norbert, 46, 49

Quadrophenia, 146
Quinn-Ivey Studios, 46, 50

"Rag Mama Rag," 28
Raiders, 9, 85
"Rain," 180, 181, 188, 190
Raitt, Bonnie, 88
Ramirez, Bobby, 12–13
Ramone, Joey, 174
Ramones, 174
Randi, Don, 76, 80
Rascals. *See* Young Rascals
Ray, Jimmy, 32, 33
Ray, Johnnie, 183
RCA Records, 81, 84, 110, 116–17, 118, 119, 127, 128, 163
"Ready Teddy," 128
Rebennack, Mac. *See* Dr. John
Redding, Otis, 11, 150
Reed, Jimmy, 160
Reed, Lou, 14
"Reelin' and Rockin'," 141
"Respect," 46, 53, 54, 58, 62
"Respect Yourself," 56, 58
"Return to Sender," 128
"Revolution," 190
Revolver, 175, 190
Rich, Buddy, 30, 48, 81, 84, 111, 158
Rich, Kathy, 84
Rich Kids, 8
Richards, Keith, 6, 156, 159–60, 161, 162, 163, 164
Righteous Brothers, 17, 88, 95
Riley, Billy Lee, 29
"Rip It Up," 87, 128
Rita Coolidge, 177
Ritz, Lyle, 79
"River Deep, Mountain High," 88, 94, 95
Rivers, Johnny, 85, 175
Roach, Max, 159
Robertson, Robbie, 27, 28, 33, 37, 38, 40, 41
"Rock and Roll Music," 180, 190
Rock 'n' Roll, 173, 177
Rock of Ages, 40, 43
"Rock Steady," 62, 72
Rocket '88, 157
Rocket Roll, 14
Rockets, 6, 12, 14
Rockets, 14
"Rocks Off," 156, 163
"Roll Me Away," 106
Rolling Stone, 8
Rolling Stone, 11, 166
Rolling Stones, 5, 6, 8, 68, 70, 83, 101, 132, 144, 150, 152, 155–56, 157, 160–61, 162–65, 166
Rolling Stones, 166

195

Rolling Stones Monthly, 158
Rolling Stones Records, 152, 166
Rollins, Sonny, 157
Ronettes, 75, 76, 85, 138
Ronstadt, Linda, 97, 106
Rosemart Records, 72
Ross, Diana, 88
Roulette Records, 43
Roxy, 101
Royal Albert Hall, 161
Royal Tottenham, 139
RSO Records, 14
Rubber Soul, 175, 189
Rubin, Jerry, 172
"Ruby Tuesday," 166
Ruff, Chuck, 12, 13
"Running on Empty," 106
Russell, Leon, 76, 80, 169, 175
Ryder, Mitch, 1, 6, 7, 8, 10, 11, 12, 14. See also Mitch Ryder and the Detroit Wheels

"Sailing," 59
Sam and Dave, 11
Sands, Tommy, 78
"Satisfaction," 5, 156, 163, 166
"Say a Little Prayer," 53
Scaggs, Boz, 59
Scene, 143
Scott, Sandy, 20
Seale, Bobby, 172
Search and Nearness, 23
"Secret Agent Man," 85
Seger, Bob, 12, 45, 59, 105, 106
"Sgt. Pepper's Lonely Hearts Club Band," 180, 190
Sgt. Pepper's Lonely Hearts Club Band, 175, 182, 190
"Shakin' with Linda," 11
Shankar, Ravi, 158
"She Loves You," 180, 190
"She's a Rainbow," 166
"She's a Woman," 190
"She's Just My Style," 174, 176, 177
She's Just My Style, 174
Sholes, Steve, 117
"Short People," 177
Shot of Love, 169, 170
Shottard, James, 32
Showstoppers, 20
Sidewalk Productions, 175
Sidran, Ben, 175
Sill, Joel, 102
Simon and Garfunkel, 9, 78, 80, 82
Simon, Paul, 45, 57, 58, 78, 82
Sinatra, Frank, 77, 88
Sinatra, Nancy, 78
Singleton, Zutty, 87

"Sitting in Limbo," 56
"634-5789," 52
Sklar, Lee, 103, 104
Sledge, Percy, 50, 51, 52, 58, 59
"Slippin' and Slidin'," 95
Small Faces, 143–44, 146, 147, 148, 150, 151, 152, 156. See also Faces
Small Faces, 144, 152
Smash Records, 72
Smith, Huey "Piano," 29
Smith, Jimmy, 22
Smith, Mike, 136, 137, 138
"Sock It to Me—Baby," 5, 14
"Solidarity," 24
Some Girls, 164, 165
"Somebody's Baby," 106
"Something," 190
Sonny and Cher, 85
Soul City Records, 85
Spacek, Sissy, 42
Speakes, Ronnie, 19
Specialty Records, 95
Spector, Phil, 76, 79–80, 83, 88, 93–94, 138, 163, 169, 173–74
"Speedo," 177
"Spirit in the Dark," 62, 71
Springsteen, Bruce, 77, 179
Stage Fright, 43
"Stand Back," 106
Staple Singers, 56–57, 58
Starr, Ringo, 1, 2, 22, 69, 83, 126–27, 132, 136, 161, 169, 170, 171, 175, 176, 177, 179–90
"Start Me Up," 156, 166
Stax Records, 40, 52, 53, 57, 58, 151
"Stay," 106
"Stay with Me," 144, 152
Steely Dan, 62, 72
"Steve Allen Show," 118
Stewart, Ian, 157
Stewart, Jim, 53
Stewart, John, 102
Stewart, Rod, 45, 59, 144, 152
Sticky Fingers, 166
"Stone Soul Picnic," 85
Stowe, Michael, 99–100
Strangeloves, 9
Stranger in Town, 59
"Strawberry Fields Forever," 190
"Street Fighting Man," 156, 163, 166
Streisand, Barbra, 175
Sullivan, Ed. See "Ed Sullivan Show"
Summers, Bob, 175
Sun Records, 31, 40, 48, 110, 116
Supremes, 10

Surfaris, 98
"Surfin' Safari," 76, 82
"Surfin' U.S.A.," 76, 84
Swan Records, 189
Sweet Baby James, 97
"(Sweet Sweet Baby) Since You've Been Gone," 47, 53, 58
Szelest, Stan, 33

Take a Ride, 14
"Take Five," 48
"Take Time to Know Her," 45, 51
Tapestry, 97
"Taste of Honey," 82, 85, 175
Tattoo You, 166
"Taxman," 190
Taylor, James, 97, 102, 103, 105, 106
Tedesco, Tommy, 76, 84
Tee, Richard, 66
"Teen Beat," 48
Temptations, 10, 88
Tex, Joe, 11
"That Girl Could Sing," 106
"That's All Right, Mama," 112, 113
"Then He Kissed Me," 76
They Only Come Out at Night, 13
Things to Come, 101, 103
"Think," 53
"This Diamond Ring," 174
Thomas, Danny, 9
Thomas, Tony, 9–10
Thompson, Terry, 50
Thornhill, Claude, 111
"Ticket to Ride," 5, 190
Tijuana Brass, 82, 85
Tillotson, Johnny, 9
"Time Is on My Side," 166
Time Peace/The Rascals' Greatest Hits, 24
"Tin Soldier," 152
"Tipitina," 91, 95
Tollie Records, 189
Tommy, 149
"Tomorrow Never Knows," 180, 190
Tony Thomas Group, 9–10
"Topsy," 48
Tornadoes, 139
Toussaint, Allen, 40
Townshend, Pete, 145, 146, 147, 148, 149
Traditional Jazz Band, 183
Traffic, 56, 101
Transfer Station, 19
Tremble, Sonny, 114
"Trouble," 84, 121, 128
Trousdale Music, 102
Troy, Doris, 68

INDEX

Trude Heller's, 5–6, 8
Tubb, Ernest, 29
"Tumbling Dice," 164, 166
"Turn On Your Love Light," 10
Turner, Ike, 95
Turner, Tina, 88, 94, 95
"Tutti-Frutti," 95
Twenty Grand, 11
"Twist and Shout," 179, 180, 190
Twitty, Conway, 29, 32–33
2i's Club, 143
Tyler, "Red," 88, 92
Tympani Five, 112

"Under the Gun," 24
Ungano's, 8
United Artists Records, 14
"Universal," 144
"Until You Come Back to Me—That's What I'm Gonna Do," 72
"Up on Cripple Creek," 28, 35, 36, 41
"Up, Up and Away," 76, 85
"Uptown," 85

Vagrants, 8
Van Eaton, James, 31, 40, 110
Van Zandt, Steve, 18. *See also* Little Steven and the Disciples of Soul
Vanilla Fudge, 2
Vee Jay Records, 189
Village, 10
Vincent, Gene, 123
Vitale, Joe, 105

"Walkin' to New Orleans," 88, 95
"Walking in the Rain," 76, 85
Walls and Bridges, 172
Walsh, Dan, 102
Warner Brothers, 42, 59, 85, 106, 152, 177

Waters, Muddy, 2, 29, 30, 160
Watkins Glen, 37
Watts, Charlie, 22, 83, 132, 150, 155–66
"We Can Work It Out," 190
"We Love You," 166
"Wear My Ring Around Your Neck," 128
Webb, Jimmy, 176
"Wedding Bell Blues," 85
"Weight," 28
Wembley Stadium, 161
Welcome to My Nightmare, 14
West, Leslie, 8
West, Red, 125
Wexler, Jerry, 46, 52–53, 55, 57
"What'cha Gonna Do About It," 144
"What'd I Say," 21, 143
"Whatever Gets You Through the Night," 177
"What You're Doing," 190
"When a Man Loves a Woman," 45, 46, 47, 50, 52
"When the Saints Go Marchin' In," 90
Whisky-A-Go-Go, 101–2
White Album. *See The Beatles*
White, Andy, 183
White Trash, 12–13
Whitman, Slim, 115
Who, 12, 143, 145, 146, 147–51, 152, 164
"Who Are You," 147
"Whole Lotta Shakin'," 31
Who's Next, 151
"Why Don't You Try Me," 177
"Wiggle Wobble," 61, 72
"Wild Horses," 166
Williams, Charles "Hungry," 2, 87, 91
Williams, Earl, 91
Williams, Tony, 103
Williamson, Sonny Boy, 29, 30

Wills, Bob, 112
Wilson, Brian, 11, 76, 82
Wilson, Dennis, 76
"Windy," 85
Wingate, Jack, 37
Winter, Edgar, 6, 12, 13, 14
Winters, Shelley, 122
Winwood, Stevie, 56, 156
"With a Little Help from My Friends," 190
"When a Man Loves a Woman," 58
Wolfgang, 103
Womack, Bobby, 53
Wonder, Stevie, 10
"Won't Get Fooled Again," 146
Wood, Ron, 144, 150
Woodstock Festival, 34, 37
"Wouldn't It Be Nice," 85
Wrecking Crew, 76, 79
Wyman, Bill, 6, 156

Yakus, Shelly, 61
Yardbirds, 9, 101, 156
Yesterdays, 72
"You Better Move On," 46, 50
"You Better Run," 17, 22, 24
"You Can't Always Get What You Want," 164
"You Don't Know What You Got Until You Lose It," 172
"You Got What It Takes," 141
Young Rascals, 8, 17, 19, 20–23, 25
Young Rascals, 24
"You're Going to Lose That Girl," 190
"You're Sixteen," 177
"You're So Square (Baby I Don't Care)," 109, 110, 128
"(You're the) Devil in Disguise," 128
"You've Lost That Lovin' Feeling," 88, 95